The Court-Martial of
Jackie Robinson

BOOKS
BY MICHAEL LEE LANNING

The Only War We Had: A Platoon Leader's Journal of Vietnam

Vietnam 1969–1970: A Company Commander's Journal

Inside the LRRPs: Rangers in Vietnam

Inside Force Recon: Recon Marines in Vietnam (with Ray W. Stubbe)

The Battles of Peace

Inside the VC and NVA: The Real Story of North Vietnam's Armed Forces (with Dan Cragg)

Vietnam at the Movies

Senseless Secrets: The Failures of U.S. Military Intelligence from George Washington to the Present

The Military 100: A Ranking of the Most Influential Military Leaders of All Time

The African-American Soldier: From Crispus Attucks to Colin Powell

Inside the Crosshairs: Snipers in Vietnam

Defenders of Liberty: African-Americans in the Revolutionary War

Blood Warriors: American Military Elites

The Battle 100: The Stories behind History's Most Influential Battles

Mercenaries: Soldiers of Fortune, from Ancient Greece to Today's Private Military Companies

The Civil War 100: The Stories behind the Most Influential Battles, People, and Events in the War between the States

The Revolutionary War 100: The Stories behind the Most Influential Battles, People, and Events of the American Revolution

At War with Cancer (with Linda Moore-Lanning)

Tours of Duty: Vietnam War Stories

Tony Buzbee: Defining Moments

Texas Aggies in Vietnam: War Stories

Double T Double Cross Double Take: The Firing of Coach Mike Leach

The Veterans Cemeteries of Texas

Dear Allyanna: An Old Soldier's Last Letter to His Granddaughter

The Court-Martial of Jackie Robinson

The Baseball Legend's Battle for Civil Rights during World War II

Michael Lee Lanning

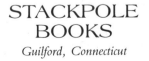

STACKPOLE
BOOKS
Guilford, Connecticut

STACKPOLE
   BOOKS
Published by Stackpole Books
An imprint of The Rowman & Littlefield Publishing Group, Inc.
4501 Forbes Blvd., Ste. 200
Lanham, MD 20706
www.rowman.com

Distributed by NATIONAL BOOK NETWORK
800-462-6420

British Library Cataloguing in Publication Information available

Library of Congress Cataloging-in-Publication Data available
Names: Lanning, Michael Lee, author.

Title: The court-martial of Jackie Robinson : the baseball legend's battle for civil rights
during World War II / Michael Lee Lanning.

Description: Guilford, Connecticut : Stackpole Books, [2020] | Includes index. |
Summary: "Eleven years before Rosa Parks resisted going to the back of the bus, a young
black second lieutenant, hungry to fight Nazis in Europe, refused to move to the back
of a U.S. Army bus in Texas and found himself court-martialed. The defiant soldier was
Jack Roosevelt Robinson, already in 1944 a celebrated athlete in track and football and
in a few years the man who would break Major League Baseball's color barrier. This was
the pivotal moment in Jackie Robinson's pre-MLB career. Had he been found guilty,
he would not have been the man who broke baseball's color barrier. Had the incident
never happened, he would've gone overseas with the Black Panther tank battalion-and
who knows what after that. Having survived this crucible of unjust prosecution as an
American soldier, Robinson-already a talented multisport athlete-became the ideal player
to integrate baseball. This is a dramatic story, deeply engaging and enraging. It's a Jackie
Robinson story and a baseball story, but it is also an army story as well as an American
story"—Provided by publisher.

Identifiers: LCCN 2019046248 (print) | LCCN 2019046249 (ebook) | ISBN
9780811738644 (cloth) | ISBN 9780811768627 (epub)

Subjects: LCSH: Robinson, Jackie, 1919-1972—Trials, litigation, etc. | African
American baseball players—Biography. | African Americans—Biography. | African
Americans—Civil rights—History. | Discrimination in sports—United States—History.

Classification: LCC GV865.R6 .L38 2020 (print) | LCC GV865.R6 (ebook) | DDC
796.357092 [B]—dc23
LC record available at https://lccn.loc.gov/2019046248
LC ebook record available at https://lccn.loc.gov/2019046249

♾™ The paper used in this publication meets the minimum requirements of
American National Standard for Information Sciences—Permanence of Paper
for Printed Library Materials, ANSI/NISO Z39.48-1992.

To Scott Howard

Contents

Author's Note

*T*he first African American Major League Baseball player was named Jack Roosevelt Robinson. His mother, siblings, and wife always called him "Jack." It was not until Robinson signed with the Brooklyn Dodgers that he became known as "Jackie." Because his world-wide fame is as "Jackie Robinson," that is the name used throughout this narrative.

In the following pages the reader is directed at various places to refer to Historical Perspectives located in the back of the book. These Historical Perspectives provide deeper insights into the racial conditions, places, and people during Jackie's time in uniform and his court-martial.

The analysis of, and conclusions about, the court-martial of Jackie Robinson are presented after a careful and lengthy study. However, not all readers will want to accept the author's translations and interpretations; some will want more direct, first-hand information. Therefore, this book includes as Appendix the complete witness statements made by the participants and the entire transcript of the trial to enable readers to make their own decisions.

Introduction

$\mathcal{O}$n April 15, 1947, Jackie Robinson, wearing Brooklyn Dodger Number 42, stepped onto the grass of Ebbets Field in New York City and changed Major League Baseball forever. Until that moment, "America's Pastime" had been an affiliation of all-white teams. Robinson was the first black to break the color barrier in any major American sport. It would not be his only "first."

Between the end of World War II and the Civil Rights Movement of the mid-1960s, Jackie Robinson became the icon of African Americans' quest for equality in the United States. His mere presence combined with his remarkable athletic abilities on MLB diamonds proved to the country that blacks and whites could compete and live together for the betterment of both races. He was the lone, unrivaled black leader until the emergence of the Reverend Doctor Martin Luther King, Jr. Even today, photographs of Jackie Robinson in his baseball uniform symbolize not only sports' willingness to move forward in race relations but also the country's awakening to the need to address the status quo.

Indeed, the groundswell for change was already well underway by the time the umpire called "Play ball!" that April afternoon. Jackie Robinson became a significant player in both the future of baseball and the future of African American rights. While finding his own way was indelibly linked with the history of his ancestors, he was able to coalesce the forces around him to shape a better world for himself and those who would follow, for he was a leader who stepped out front and out early.

On December 1, 1955—more than eight years after Robinson took his first turn at bat at Ebbets Field—Rosa Louise McCauley Parks refused instructions from a white bus driver in Montgomery, Alabama, to relinquish her seat to a white passenger and move to the "colored section"—the rear—of the vehicle. Her defiance, which generated nation-wide attention, led to a law suit (*Browder v. Gayle*) endorsed by the National Association for the Advancement of Colored People. A Federal District Court on June 5, 1956, found bus segregation unconstitutional under the Equal Protection Clause of the 14th Amendment to the U.S. Constitution. The United States Supreme Court affirmed the decision on November 13, 1956.

Despite the fact that Rosa Parks became the face of the Civil Rights Movement, she was not the first black to defy white rules regarding bus seating. More than ten years earlier, a young black man likewise refused to move to the rear of the bus. That young man was Second Lieutenant Jack Roosevelt Robinson, the date was July 6, 1944, and the place was Camp Hood, Texas. For that stance and his sequential protests, Robinson faced a General Court-Martial for his alleged disrespect to a superior officer and failure to follow a lawful command.

Whereas Parks's civil disobedience led to her being remembered as "the mother of the freedom movement" and "the first lady of civil rights," Robinson's trial in the closing days of World War II on a remote Army post in Central Texas received little news coverage. In those days, Jim Crow laws dictated behavior both in Southern civilian communities and on military installations. Robinson, who would go on to become one of the best known and popular athletes of all generations, was truly a man ahead of his time that pivotal day when he refused to give up his seat on a Jim Crow bus. While it did not bring him the attention or notoriety that the same act brought Rosa Parks, this experience affected him deeply and set the stage for him to become an African American hero and icon.

Although one of the least explored episodes about him, the court-martial of Jackie Robinson played a crucial role in his maturing process and in the development of his self-confidence. It demonstrated to him—as well as eventually to the rest of the world—that a black man could successfully and nonviolently stand up to white prejudices. That Robinson achieved the clarity of such maturity and confidence positioned him for everything that came after.

• *1* •

Racism

The Two-Headed Snake

$\mathcal{J}$ack Roosevelt Robinson was born near Cairo, Georgia, in Grady County, in the early years of the twentieth century. It was not a promising time for an African American to come into this world, especially into Southern Georgia. With the Civil War only a mere fifty years in the past, many former slaves and former slave owners were still living with, and holding onto, their vivid memories of the way of life that had been in their youth. Blacks and whites alike held fast to their resentments and grievances; all around them were ever-present reminders of the great loss of life and property during the war and the following Reconstruction, reminders that kept the wounds open for genera-tions. This was the situation into which Jackie Robinson was born, and he was inevitably influenced and shaped by the forces around him and the history that had come before him.

The victory by the Union forces over the rebel Confederates preserved the United States and freed the slaves, but those events in and of themselves did not instantly produce cultural or political equality—or even basic rights and security for the liberated blacks. Other than the absence of chains, African Americans continued to live very much like enslaved people. This standard of living was enforced by the formal laws of courts, the informal rules of the white majority, and the violence of the Ku Klux Klan via intimidation at best and lynching at worst.

That was the heritage that surrounded Robinson at the time of his birth. His was a life story that had been set in motion centuries before. At the time in world history when the first white settlers arrived on the East Coast of North America early in the seventeenth century, slavery was, and always had been, a common, wide-spread practice imposed on any group or race that fell under the control of a more powerful group or ethnicity. Tragically, America and Americans would be no exception. On August 20, 1619, a Dutch ship anchored off the Colony of Virginia to offer twenty individuals, recently captured on the African West Coast, to the colonists in exchange for provisions. Once those enchained individuals stepped ashore, the stage was set for national conflict and grief because a free people cannot rationally coexist with an enslaved one.

It took only forty-four years before the growing number of slaves in the colonies staged their first rebellion, which occurred in Gloucester County, Virginia, in 1663. Over the next 100 years, slaves rebelled more than 250 times. None of the uprisings, however, were successful, and the participants were executed or whipped and returned to bondage. The larger the number of blacks in the country, the more the whites feared losing control of their chattel. By 1775, the slave population had risen to 600,000—or 20 percent—of the colonial population of 3,000,000. Even though the economies of all the colonies owed much to the institution of slavery, indentured blacks composed about 40 percent of the total population of the Southern colonies where agriculture was particularly dependent on their labor. This was the backdrop of the Robinson family. (Historical Perspective 1.)

The half-century between the end of the Civil War and the turn of the century was filled with racial realignment on the parts of all Americans. It was a tumultuous time, a violent time, a dangerous time. It was expectations set against realities, the powerful challenged by the impoverished, traditions rocked by change. These shifts left Americans of all races reeling.

It was against such a backdrop that Jackie Robinson entered this world in the bloodiest months of racial violence to date in the United States. In 1919, thousands of black soldiers returned from combat in World War I, expecting better treatment as a reward for their service and sacrifices. Instead they found an ungrateful white population harboring the same old pre-war biases against them. Many of those mustering out of the service joined the half million or so other blacks who had already migrated from the South to the industrial Northeast and Midwest to fill jobs left open by whites inducted into the army. When white enthusiasm to put blacks back in their pre-war "place" collided with the African American demand for equality, the result was wide scale violence.

Still, on a day-to-day basis, Americans of all races found ways to coexist and work side-by-side. The post-World War I years were prosperous for both white and black workers. Jobs were plentiful and wages, even for blacks, were substantial. Then came the greatest equalizer of all—economic disaster in the form of the stock market crash of 1929 and the resulting Great Depression. Suddenly everyone, white and black, faced high unemployment, plunging incomes, and monetary deflation that would not totally recover until World War II.

Georgia to California

Fortunately for him, Jackie Robinson was born on January 31, 1919, into a strong family—at least on his maternal side. As the fifth of five children born to Mallie McGriff and Jerry Robinson, Jackie had older brothers Frank, Mack, and Edgar and sister Willa Mae to look out for him. Mallie's father and mother—Jackie's maternal grandparents—Washington McGriff and his wife Edna Sims, had been born slaves but did well after being freed. They lived on twelve acres they owned just south of Cairo in southwestern Georgia. Illiterate themselves but wise, the McGriffs emphasized education for their children. Mallie, the seventh of fourteen children, went to the local colored school through the sixth grade and, at age ten, taught her father how to read so he could study his Bible.

Cairo—pronounced "Cayro"—Georgia, founded in 1835 and later the county seat of Grady County, had a population in 1919 of about 1,900, 45 percent of whom were African Americans. (Historical Perspective 2.)

Jerry Robinson, Jackie's father and the eldest of eleven children, worked in the fields on a cotton farm owned by James Madison Sasser. His father Tony—Jackie's paternal grandfather—had crossed the border from the Florida panhandle in his youth and worked his entire life on the Sasser plantation. Neither Tony nor his wife could read or write.

Mallie McGriff and the handsome Jerry Robinson met at a Christmas dance in 1906 when she was only fourteen years old and he eighteen. They began to see each other, but the McGriffs disapproved of Jerry, not only for his age but also for what they considered his being a shabby prospect. They much preferred the son of a family who had come to Georgia from South Carolina and lived in the best tenant house on the Sasser farm. However, love trumped her parents' wishes and three years later Mallie married Jerry on November 21, 1909.

5

Jerry and Mallie moved into one of Sasser's tenant houses and went to work for the landowner at $12 a month. The couple was happy in the early months of their marriage as Jerry labored in the fields and Mallie tended a garden and took care of the house. Mallie, whose parents had taught her to plan and prepare for the future, was to understand that there was little future on $12 a month—especially since Sasser insisted that most of the income be spent at his company store.

Sasser differed little from Georgia landowners at the time, expecting the tenants' low wages to be spent at his facility, and he discouraged any kind of public meetings where they might organize. As a result, just as it had been in slave days, the church was one of the few places blacks could gather, worship, and socialize. During the Red Summer of 1919 and other periods of racial unrest, even these places became targets for burning and destruction.

Swine killing time in the fall also revealed Sasser's ideas on equality and further reinforced Mallie's thought that they were "not living high on the hog." The Robinsons and other black workers received only the scraps—feet, internal organs, and intestines for chitterlings.

Mallie believed that their present lives were not far removed from slavery and voiced her opinion to her husband and his employer. Both whites and blacks feared Sasser—a tall, powerful, rawboned man—but Mallie stood up to him and insisted that they become sharecroppers rather than working for wages. Sasser was not happy with the proposal but, because of the labor shortage, agreed to provide housing, land, seed, and fertilizer in return for one-half of the Robinson's crop.

The Robinsons prospered as sharecroppers—raising cotton, peanuts, corn, sugar cane, and potatoes and owning their own hogs, turkeys, and chickens. Mallie later recalled that she was happy with her life and lived the way she wanted to live. Jerry, however, tired of farm life and had a "roving eye" for other women. Three times he left Mallie and the farm only to return, usually after his money ran out. The couple would reconcile, have another baby, and then repeat the cycle.

Surviving family members today have conflicting opinions as to whether Jackie was born in his parents' home or that of his grandparents. All are in agreement that Dr. Arthur Brown Reynolds, a white physician, attended the birth. Of her five births, Jackie's was the only one assisted by a medical doctor. Apparently, the community's black midwives had either died or were ill from the Spanish flu, which was epidemic at the time. (Historical Perspective 3.)

The Robinsons chose Roosevelt as Jack's middle name to honor Teddy Roosevelt, the U.S. president from 1901 to 1909 who had charged up San Juan and Kettle Hills in the Spanish-American War supported by—and some say saved by—a black regiment on his flank. Roosevelt had been a great supporter of equal rights for African Americans, particularly during his first term. Pressure from white racists during his second term made him more conservative but he did condemn lynchings as well as oppose the segregation policies of President Wilson. Roosevelt died on January 6, 1919, and, with the birth of Jackie three weeks later, the Robinsons thought Roosevelt to be an appropriate middle name.

For his first eighteen months, baby Jackie lived with his parents in their tenant home. It is likely that he had little contact with whites, and he was too young to be aware of the racism and poverty that surrounded him in Southern Georgia. Jackie's arrival did little to help the deteriorating relationship between Jerry and Mallie with Jerry spending more and more time in Cairo, where it had become fairly common knowledge that he was having an affair with the married daughter of the respected Powell family who farmed land adjacent to that of Sasser.

On July 28, 1919, in the middle of cotton-growing season, Jerry told Mallie that he was going to Texas to visit a brother. Despite her suspicions, Mallie and the children bid him goodbye. They would never see him again. Rumors came to Mallie that Jerry had taken a northbound train rather than one to the west. Another rumor said he was working in a sawmill in Florida and the Powell daughter was with him. By the early 1930s when Mallie received a telegram from one of Jerry's relatives saying that he was dead, his demise had little effect on the family. Jack's older brother Mack, who was in high school when the telegram arrived, later recalled that it had been so long since they had seen or heard from their father that his passing "wasn't traumatic for us; we had no recognition of him."

Jackie was too young to have any memories of his father or even remember the telegram's arrival. In a Personal History Statement that he completed during Basic Training at Fort Riley, Kansas, years later, Jackie erroneously wrote that his father had died sometime around 1922 of natural causes.

After Jerry's departure from Georgia, Mallie had to determine how she was going to support her five children, especially because James Sasser was not happy to have lost one of his sharecroppers but still have his family living on his land and in his tenant house. He offered to have the county sheriff find Jerry and return him home, but Mallie refused. She also turned down a job as the Sasser family cook. Sasser told her, "You're about the sassiest nigger woman ever on this place." He then evicted her and the children from the tenant house to a much smaller, poorly maintained cabin.

With help from relatives, Mallie managed to gather their final crop and then found a job working for a nearby white family. By the end of the winter of 1920, Mallie realized how bleak life looked in Georgia. Race relations had worsened instead of improving after the Red Summer of 1919. The Ku Klux

Klan became larger and more active. Poll taxes and literacy requirements, combined with intimidation, prevented most blacks from exercising their right to vote. Other Jim Crow laws limited almost every aspect of their lives. A black farmer in southern Georgia was more like a serf in medieval Europe than a free person in America. And a black woman with five mouths to feed was several notches lower yet.

Mallie's opportunity to escape the prejudices and poverty came when her half-brother arrived from California in the spring of 1920. Burton Thomas, son of Edna McGriff from a marriage previous to Monroe Thomas, had moved to southern California after serving in World War I and was a great advocate of the region. He often said, "If you want to get closer to Heaven, visit California."

Mallie decided not to visit California but rather to move there. Mallie gathered up what funds she could—a little money from the last crop, a few dollars saved from her domestic job with the white family, some relatives' contributions, and perhaps a little extra from her white employer who sympathized with her situation. She also convinced relatives to join her who were willing to gamble on a better life in California—her sister Cora Wade, brother-in-law Samuel, and their two children; her brother Paul McGriff; and Mary Lou Thomas Maxwell, Mallie's half-sister and full sister of Burton Thomas.

Mallie and her extended family were not the only blacks in Georgia seeking freedom from the Jim Crow south. In 1920 alone, approximately 50,000 African Americans had joined the Great Migration in search of better paying jobs and a greater degree of freedom in the industrialized Midwest, North, and West Coast. The threat of the loss of cheap labor so disturbed southern whites that Macon and other towns in Georgia organized special police units to prevent blacks from moving away, using intimidation, beatings, and physical removal from trains. Like their neighboring counterparts, the white citizens of Cairo did not like the exit of their cheap workforce but took no action to prevent their exodus. On May 21, 1920, Mallie took her children and a few pieces of luggage in a borrowed buggy to Cairo where she met up with the rest of the relocating family members. At the scheduled time on the departure date, around midnight, the Number 58 train arrived. Mallie, carrying 16-month-old Jackie, and her mobile children—Edgar, 11; Frank, 9; Mack, 7; and Willa Mae, 5—boarded the dirty, segregated colored coach. With her entire fortune of $3.00 sewn into her undergarments, Mallie was undaunted by the conditions of the Jim Crow railcar. For the rest of her life, she called the railroad journey her "Freedom Train."

With virtually no money, the family ate what Mallie had packed at home for the trip and endured the hardships of the long train ride that took them across the Deep South and through the widest portion of Texas where rail stations had separate bathrooms and water fountains for whites and blacks. None of the Robinsons had any idea at the time, the role that Texas would play in baby Jackie's future.

Happily, the Robinsons' train took them on to Southern California— through Los Angeles and to Pasadena. Orange groves and the clean, prosperous towns so impressed Mallie that she wrote home that it was "the most beautiful sight of my whole life."

Burton had done well by Georgia standards, but he nevertheless remained on the low end of poverty by California norms. The group from Cairo moved into his three-room, cold-water-only apartment near the railroad station. A tin tub served both as a kitchen sink and bath. Cora, who was not in good health, kept the children, while Mallie looked for work. She soon secured a job as a maid to a white family with wages of $8.00 per week. Unlike Georgia, she was not required to work into the evening but rather returned home to her family in the late afternoons.

Mallie's new position did not last long because her employer lost his job and moved away. Within days, however, she found a similar domestic job with another white family named Dodges with whom she developed mutual respect and trust. Mallie remained in their employment for the next twenty years.

With increased money coming in, the Georgia group, as well as Burton Thomas, relocated out of the cramped apartment and into a separate house with a backyard. The house to which they moved was located at 45 Gloricta Street in northwest Pasadena. Mallie had managed to land her family in a place where the streets were lined with citrus and palm trees and where a significant portion of the area's small black population lived peacefully with its primarily white citizens.

Although Pasadena was far from southern Georgia, prejudices and oppression were a part of life for blacks living in southern California. Still, in its early years, Pasadena remained tolerate of blacks—partly because of Indiana abolitionists who had founded the town but mostly simply because there were few African American residents. The more blacks who arrived, however, the more restrictions whites wanted to place on them. (Historical Perspective 4.)

The first black in Pasadena had been a teamster who drove a head of cattle from Nebraska to Southern California in 1883. He stayed, bought a vineyard, and sent for his family. When the Robinsons arrived in 1920, African Americans numbered about 1,100 of the city's total population of 45,000. Blacks were not the only ones who suffered prejudices, for Chinese, Japanese, and Hispanic residents also encountered limitations. While there were no specific areas in which minorities were officially to reside, there were many parts of Pasadena where they were not allowed. Nearby towns of South Pasadena, Eagle Rock, and San Marino did not allow African Americans to be employed as domestics. By cutting off jobs usually filled by blacks, the cities naturally limited the number of African American residents. Glendale boasted that not a single Negro lived in their city limits.

Segregation increased rather than decreased with the passage of years. From the time of its founding in 1873 until Jackie Robinson departed for the army in the 1940s, Pasadena did not employ a single black policeman, fireman, schoolteacher, or city government official other than a few park and refuse workers.

The city also limited access to its public facilities with the best, or perhaps the worst, example being admittance to the city's only public swimming pool. When blacks and some white residents protested that the city restricted use of the Brookside Plunge in Brookside Park to "whites only," city officials initiated an "International Day" when the pool was open to everyone for one day of the week. This small gesture diminished with the city's promise to its white citizens that the pool would be drained and filled with "clean water" at the end of each International Day.

Thus was the backdrop for Jackie's formative years. Life was not easy during those first years in California for the Robinsons. In addition to living in the cramped apartment, the family often found food in short supply. Mallie received some welfare aid from the state, and her employer allowed her to take home the leftovers from meals. Still, the family frequently went hungry. The older children remember meals where the only food on the table was bread and sugar water.

There is no doubt that times were hard for the Robinsons, as they were for other blacks and many whites at the time. In later years, journalists and biographers emphasized Jackie's impoverished childhood as harsh and as poor as possible to reinforce his rags to riches stories. While his early years were tough, there is no doubt that his life in Pasadena was far better than it would have been if his family had remained in Georgia.

Despite the prejudices and restrictions of Pasadena, Mallie and her extended family, through hard work and dedication, thrived in California. By 1922, Mallie had managed to put aside sufficient funds to join Sam and Cora Wade in the joint purchase of a home at 121 Pepper Street on a previously all-white block just north of Glorieta Street. Family lore claims that a black real estate agent used his light-skinned niece as a front to buy the home and then selling it to Mallie and the Wades. However, local tax records show that two men, Charles R. Ellis and William H. Harrison bought the home in 1905 and sold it to Mallie Robinson and Sam Wade in 1922.

Regardless of how they acquired the home, the Robinsons and Wades soon found that their white neighbors did not welcome their extended black family. Initially other residents on the street offered to buy out Mallie and

Sam. Later someone burned a cross on their yard, and neighbors called the police when they thought the Robinson children made too much noise. Having come so far, Mallie was unwilling to be sidetracked by such diversions. She set out to win her neighbors' favor—if not their trust and friendship. She had her son Edgar do chores at no cost for the wealthiest person on the block who lived next door. Mallie also shared the fruits of her garden with her neighbors and, with the passage of time, found the acceptance she sought for herself and her children. Eventually, additional minority families moved onto Pepper Street.

After a couple of years, the Wades bought another home, leaving what Mallie called "the castle" to the Robinsons alone. Its five bedrooms offered space for all, and its backyard provided plenty of room for apple, orange, peach, and fig trees as well as a vegetable garden and pens for chickens, ducks, and turkeys. Most of the grounds were used for food production, but Mallie also raised flowers to beautify their home.

Mallie maintained her ties to Georgia and assisted several family members and friends in making their way west. When her father died in 1927, she helped bring her mother to Pasadena to live with her and later with the Wades. Jackie was fourteen when Edna McGriff died on July 25, 1933. For the rest of his life, Edna represented his ties to the Old South and to slavery as he listened to her stories that included explanations of the differences between a Negro and a nigger that he would quote at his military court-martial many years later.

During his life, Jackie Robinson had many mentors and supporters, the most important of whom were those during his coming of age in Pasadena. Mallie instilled in her children the importance of family, education, and religion. She emphasized courtesy, self-discipline, and standing up for what is right.

Not all was perfect at home or in Pasadena, however. After being apprehended for a minor infraction, the local police took Jackie and several friends to the station where they questioned them while denying them water for four hours. Finally, they brought in watermelons so they could laughingly take stereotypical pictures as the boys devoured the fruit. Jackie later recalled the incident as the "most humiliating day of my life."

Not happy in Pasadena, Jackie felt as if he did not belong there. Years later he said, "If my mother and brother and sister weren't living in Pasadena, I would never go back. I've always felt like an intruder there—even in school. People in Pasadena were less understanding in some ways than Southerners, and they were more openly hostile."

After the Wades moved out of the Pepper Street home, Mallie turned to Willa Mae to look after Jackie while she was at work. Although only three years older, Willa Mae saw to it that her baby brother had something to eat, and that he mostly stayed out of trouble. When Willa Mae started kindergarten at Grover Cleveland Elementary, Mallie had her take Jackie along with her. Willa Mae placed her brother in the school yard sandbox, instructed him not to wander off, and went to class. The school's teachers were not happy with the arrangement until Mallie met with them and explained that, if Jackie had to stay home, she would have to quit her job to take care of him. She would then have to go on relief, and, she said, it would be cheaper for the city to just let him come to school and play. Mallie then taught Jackie to say "Good morning, teacher," hoping that his charm and Willa Mae's responsible oversight would convince the teachers to allow the arrangement to continue.

After a year in the sandbox, Jackie returned to the school as a student. Then in 1926, two years afterward, Pasadena rezoned its school districts, placing the Robinson children in the Washington School system, which was a closer walk from Pepper Street. Jackie attended that elementary program and then graduated from Washington Junior High where he excelled at all sports but did not take his studies very seriously. He made mostly B's and C's—with more C's than B's as the years passed. Instead of studying, he preferred to play any game or sport available. His fellow students recall his great athletic abilities but also remember him to be so competitive and dedicated to winning that, no matter what the game, he was not very likable. When not engaged in sports, he mostly remained a loner.

Although Pasadena schools were integrated, all of Jackie's teachers were white. Two of them, Bernice Gilbert and Beryl Haney, especially liked what they saw in the young Jackie. Besides often providing him lunch, they developed an affection and friendship with him. Jackie and the two teachers maintained contact long after he became famous and no longer lived in Pasadena.

One of Jackie's earliest bad memories of Pepper Street occurred when, at eight years old, he was sweeping the front sidewalk of his home, and a neighbor girl shouted from across the street, "Nigger! Nigger! Nigger!" Too young to remember real discrimination when he left Georgia, Jackie was especially vulnerable to the prejudices and slights he received from the residents of Pasadena. Even small infraction made lasting impressions. Jackie and his friends, limited to one day in the public pool, often went swimming in the municipal reservoir. One day the police caught them and, with guns drawn, one of them shouted, "Looka there—niggers swimming in our drinking water!"

When not at school or playing sports, Jackie worked to supplement the family income as soon as he was old enough. He had a paper route, mowed lawns, and ran errands. In his free time, Jackie joined a group called the Pepper Street Gang. Composed of neighborhood blacks, Mexicans, and Japanese kids, the gang never committed vicious or violent crimes but got into more than their share of mischief, such as stealing fruit from street stands and orchards. The enterprising youths also stole golf balls from the local links hazards and then sold them back to the players.

In his biography, Jackie wrote that he "might have become a full-fledged juvenile delinquent if it had not been for the influence of two men who shared my mother's thinking." These two black men not only served as mentors, but also they were as close to father figures as Jackie had in his life. Carl Anderson, who worked as an automobile mechanic in a garage in the Pepper Street Gang's neighborhood, did not scold Jackie but rather pointed out how his crimes hurt his mother as well as himself. He also suggested to Jackie that he would get nowhere by following the crowd and that he should have the courage and intelligence to be his own man. Jackie wrote, "I was too ashamed to tell Carl how right he was, but what he said got to me."

The second man, Reverend Karl Downs, led the Scott United Methodist Church where Mallie had her children in the pews every Sunday morning. Jackie, who had not cared much for church until Downs arrived and initiated special programs for children, became so involved with the church and Reverend Downs that he quit hanging out with the Pepper Street Gang and even began teaching a Sunday School class. Jackie later wrote, "It wasn't so much what he did to help as the fact that he was interested and concerned enough to offer the best advice he could."

In addition to Anderson and Downs, Jackie's three older brothers were the other primary male influences on him. His eldest brother, Edgar, had a strange relationship with Jackie—and with everyone else, for that matter. Edgar was somewhat mentally challenged, but he loved speed—on roller skates, bicycles, or motorcycles. Jackie later wrote about Edgar, "There was always something about him that was mysterious to me." He added that the primary trait they shared was the way each, on occasion, would get angry and lose his temper.

Perhaps the greatest impact Edgar had on Jackie was not what he did but rather what was done to him. At the Rose Bowl Parade on January 2, 1939, Edgar set several chairs along the route to watch the festivities. Two policemen arrived to tell Edgar that he had to have a permit for the chairs. When he showed the officers that he had the required license, they muttered something about Negroes not having the kind of money necessary to buy a permit. They then beat him and arrested him for violating a city ordinance and for resisting arrest. Eyes blackened and arms bruised, Edgar received no medical treatment nor could he call home. The police did not release him until he pled guilty and paid a fine. Later efforts by Edgar and the local chapter of the National Association for the Advancement of Colored People to protest the incident were ignored. To Jackie the beating and arrest of his brother were just more examples of racism that exacerbated his bad feelings about Pasadena. There would be more cause for negative feelings as another brother reached adulthood.

Of his three male siblings, Frank showed the most concern for his little brother. Jack later recalled that Frank was mild and sweet-tempered but that "he was always there to protect me when I was in a scrap, even though I don't think he could knock down a fly."

Frank served as a good model for Jackie in showing him how to stay out of trouble by talking through conflicts rather than getting angry. He also demonstrated to Jackie that no matter how hard a black man worked, it was difficult for him to get ahead in Jim Crow Pasadena because the only employment Frank could find was lawn maintenance and tree trimming. He had so much difficulty making a living that he still lived at home with his mother even after he married and became a father.

It was Mack, his older brother by four and a half years, who had the greatest influence on Jackie. Mack excelled in track and field to set several Pasadena broad jump and the 200-meter-sprint high school records. Jackie attended all his brother's meets and, for the first time, saw the adoration and attention given sports stars. Despite a heart murmur, Mack continued training after high school and earned a place on the 1936 U.S. Olympic Team. In that year's games, held in Berlin, Adolf Hitler walked out of the stadium after African American Jesse Owens won the 100-meter dash, besting the Nazi leader's Aryans. Hitler was not there later to see Mack come in a close second to Owens in the 200-meter dash, earning the Silver Medal.

Mack noted that the U.S. Olympic officials segregated white and black athletes in different hotels. He also said that the local Germans treated him better and with more respect than the whites back in Pasadena and that he received no reception or parade welcoming him home. A columnist in the *Pasadena Post* wrote in 1938 about Mack's Olympic performance and the rising local fame of Jackie. The piece said, "In many places they would be given the key to the city. Here we take them in stride, for granted. Never have they received their just due, from their own home citizens."

After the Olympics, Mack enrolled in the University of Oregon where he helped the school win national collegiate and Amateur Athletic Union track titles. He dropped out of the university in his senior year to return home to support his family. In addition to not receiving recognition in Pasadena for his Olympic silver medal, Mack also faced the city's same Jim Crow restrictions in employment. When he applied for a job with the municipal services, officials gave him a broom and pushcart, assigning him duties of a night shift street sweeper. On cold nights he often wore his leather U.S.A. Olympic Team jacket. When a judge ordered Pasadena to integrate its public swimming pool, the city retaliated by firing all its black employees, including Mack. Pasadena eventually rehired Mack, but he continued in minimal maintenance positions.

When Mack's wife gave birth in 1940 to their second son, who was mentally disabled and could not speak, the couple prepared to place the child in an institution. Mallie stepped forward and said she would care for the boy and took him into her home. With Mack, as well as Jackie and all her children, Mallie remained the family's greatest protector, supporter, and influence. In the meantime, Jackie watched how the members of his family fared.

• 3 •

The Athlete Emerges

$\mathscr{I}$n 1935, Jackie graduated from Washington Junior High School and enrolled in John Muir Technical High School, an institution that had originally been a vocational training facility but that had recently joined the other Pasadena high schools in offering a full range of academic subjects. During his years at John Muir Tech, Jackie matured as an athlete and elevated his reputation as a competitor and winner. He also realized from the experiences of his brothers that the opportunities for black Americans were few outside of athletics. In addition to pushing himself harder in a multitude of competitions, he began closely following professional sports in the newspapers and on the radio.

During his four years at John Muir, Jackie excelled in football, basketball, baseball, and track, all the while singing in the school's glee club. As he matured physically and mentally, Jackie dominated every game in every sport. He quarterbacked the football team; he became known for the prowess of both his offense and defense on the basketball court. Jackie won the Southland Class A broad jump, and, during one baseball season, moved from his usual shortstop position to catcher to help his team. In 1936 his baseball talent gained him a place on the annual Pomona tournament all-star team. Joining him were future Major League Baseball Hall of Fame members Ted Williams of San Diego Hoover High School and Bob Lemon of Long Beach Wilson High School.

In addition to playing on the integrated teams at John Muir, Jackie also participated in competitions limited to African Americans only. The same year that he made the Pomona all-star baseball team, he also won the junior boys' single championship at the annual Pacific Coast Negro Tennis Tournament.

The *Pasadena Post* regularly carried articles and even pictures of Jackie's sports accomplishments. One of their stories called him the "snake hipped quarterback," but writers also showed their racial bias by referring to him as the "dusky Jack Robinson." Other newspapers called him the "Midnight Express" and the "Dark Demon." The *Pasadena Star-News* mostly downplayed or ignored the accomplishments of blacks, but, near the end of Jackie's high school career, the paper had to acknowledge his gifts. One story conceded that "for two years [he] has been the outstanding athlete at Muir, starring in football, basketball, baseball, and track."

In his autobiography Jackie said about his time at John Muir, "I enjoy competition and I was aggressive in my determination to win. Often I found myself being singled out by the other players. They decided that I was the best man to beat. I enjoyed having that kind of reputation, but I was also very much aware of the importance of being a team man, not jeopardizing my team's chances simply to get the spotlight."

Jackie graduated mid-year from Muir and on January 31, 1937, celebrated his eighteenth birthday. On February 1 he enrolled in Pasadena Junior College, a facility still recovering from an earthquake in 1933. As it rebuilt with many new buildings, PJC gained the reputation as one of the best, and later the most beautiful, campuses in California and the country. There were only about seventy blacks in its student body of 4,000, which ensured little racial tension on campus. Classrooms and facilities were opened to all students, regardless of race. The single exception was dance classes where blacks could only register as couples rather than as individuals.

During his first semester at PJC, Jackie excelled at track but finished second in sprints and the long jump behind his brother Mack who was preparing for the 1940 Olympics. For once, Jackie did not mind being an "also ran" because he enjoyed his brother's company and the opportunity to learn from him. In baseball, Jackie still lacked home run power, but he managed to regularly get on base where he displayed his speed and skill in stealing bases.

During his first track season, Jackie met Jack Gordon who would become his best friend at PJC and stay close to him for the rest of his life. Gordon, somewhat smaller and lighter skinned than Robinson, later recalled, "Jack was kind of shy at times. I guess he didn't have the personality to get along with most people. He didn't talk much; he wasn't outgoing. He never pushed himself on you." Gordon helped Jackie get over much of his shyness as the pair became known as "Little Jack and Big Jack."

Football season did not begin well for Jackie that fall. His first day of practice went well with Jackie leading the team as quarterback. On the second day, however, he limped from the field with a chipped bone in his right ankle that required him to wear a cast for the next month. The PJC Bulldogs lost all four games during Jackie's absence. When he returned, they began a winning streak that continued for Jackie's entire stay at PJC. Although the ankle injury seemed minor at the time, it would play a significant role in Jackie's future in the U.S. Army.

Jackie suffered from racism, both on and off the field, while playing for the Bulldogs. He frequently heard racist insults from opponents, such as "get the nigger." In one instance, an opposing player for Long Beach Junior College punched Jackie in the face after the final whistle, setting off a melee that involved players and spectators alike. On one road trip Jackie and other blacks were refused service at a roadside restaurant. On another occasion, the team hotel in Phoenix turned the black athletes away. His white teammates were mostly supportive, at least after a time, and walked out of places that did not accept blacks.

But that was not the case early in the year. The new coach had brought with him several Oklahoma players who did not wish to play with blacks. However, the coach stood his ground in demanding they all play as a team. As quarterback, Jackie helped bring the two races together by spreading the scoring plays around to include the Oklahoma players and showing his appreciation for their blocking.

He later said, "That convinced me that it was smart to share the glory. That in the final analysis white people were no worse than Negroes for we are all afflicted by the same pride, jealousy, envy, and ambition."

Jackie was a master of multitasking before it became a common term. On May 8, 1938, he participated in a track meet in Claremont where he broke his brother Frank's broad jump record. He then hurried from the track facility, jumped into a car that raced him to Glendale—changing into his baseball uniform on the way—and joined his PJC team in the third inning of their Southern California Junior College Baseball Championship game. Upon arrival, Jackie took over at shortstop and led his Bulldog team to victory. He was awarded the title of the Southern California Junior College Baseball Most Valuable Player with a batting average of .417 and a record of stealing twenty-five bases in only twenty-four games.

A week after his double-athletic performance, Jackie participated in a match at Brookside Park on March 14 between a Pasadena all-star team and the Chicago White Sox who were in town for spring training. Jackie had two hits and made three dramatic fielding plays, one of which not only robbed American League batting champion Luke Appling of a hit but also turned the effort into a double play.

Jackie's performance so impressed Jimmy Dykes, the White Sox manager, that he said, "No one in the American League can make plays like that. If that kid was only white, I'd sign him right now."

But, of course, Robinson, although in his prime, had no chance of joining the White Sox or any other Major League team. Baseball at the time, although it claimed to be the National Pastime, remained the most segregated professional sport in the United States. Its claim would have been more accurate if it said it was the "Whites' National Pastime."

This was no news to Jackie. He later said, "Growing up, I really gave no thought to becoming a baseball player. There was no future in it for colored players. I was really shooting at becoming a football, basketball, or track star. But I didn't think much of a chance existed for me in baseball."

Jackie closed out his PJC career by leading the Bulldog basketball team to the conference championship. The Pasadena Elks Club awarded Jackie its Most Valuable Player of the Year trophy. PJC also honored him for his leadership off the athletic field. The student body elected him to the Lancers, a service organization that monitored and maintained control at school assemblies and other student gatherings. On January 27, 1939, just before his departure from PJC, the college presented Jackie and nine other students gold pins, making them members of the Order of the Mask and Dagger for performing "outstanding service to the school and whose scholastic and citizenship record is worthy of recognition."

Pasadena Junior College had proven to be a great transition period for Jackie. While there he not only honed his athletic skills, but also he learned how to get along with—and succeed against—competition on the playing fields and in the classrooms of a predominately white society. He fought racism by setting the example in athletic achievements and interacting rationally with his white teammates and fellow students. He learned that standing up for his rights, while also adhering to the system, led to success and a reluctant acceptance.

• 4 •

UCLA and Rachel Isum

$\mathcal{H}$is athletic accomplishments at Pasadena Junior College brought Jackie Robinson to the mixed-reaction attention of major colleges in California, along the West Coast, and across the country. Some schools flatly overlooked him because they had no desire to integrate not only their sports teams specifically but also their universities as a whole. Other institutions feared that opponents would not schedule them if they had Negroes on their teams. A few, however, were eager to sign Jackie to play for them in his final two years of eligibility, and they presented him with some interesting offers.

Jackie's following his brother Mack to the University of Oregon would not have been surprising, but Jackie thought that the school was too far from home. He wanted to be near his mother so he could take care of her. That left the Southern California institutions from which to choose. Stanford University expressed a serious interest but Jackie said no. Then the school offered to pay Robinson's tuition at an East Coast institution so he would not be a sports opponent. A smaller California school offered to pay both Jackie's and his girlfriend's tuition if he enrolled.

Jackie quickly narrowed his choices down to the two largest local universities. The University of Southern California fielded powerhouse teams with winning records and national recognition. It had the reputation, however, of recruiting black athletes only as tokens, keeping them on the bench instead of in the game. That left the University of California at Los Angeles as a perfect fit. Their football team already had two black stars—half-back Kenny Washington and receiver Woody Strode—so Jackie would not be an anomaly. And as fate would have it, all their sports teams had done poorly the previous year so the athletic department was desperate for superior players regardless of color. The fact that Jackie could live at home with his mother and drive the

20

short distance to the UCLA campus every day tipped the scales in making his decision.

On February 15, 1939, Jackie enrolled in UCLA. The university, established as a four-year school in 1924, had grown to a student population of nearly 10,000. African Americans numbered fewer than fifty even though the school had no official racial barriers. Black students were discouraged from attending university socials or parties other than the black Sphinx Club, the provider of the only social activities for African Americans. The university's faculty did not have a single black professor or administrator, and its host city of Westwood did not allow black residents.

Jackie did not play any university sports during his first semester at UCLA. He did not intend to be "just a ballplayer" but rather he strove to become a good enough student to enable him to find a good job upon graduation. Furthermore, beginning in the fall, he planned to play only football and compete in the long jump during track season. His goal was to make the 1940 U.S. Olympic Team in the long jump as had his brother Mack.

Robinson stayed with his plan as he took English, French, math, physiology, and physical education classes that first fall. He was not a star in the classroom as he was on the sports fields, but nonetheless his grades were sufficient to keep him in good academic standing. Other than playing on a black basketball team in a statewide tournament of Negro fraternities, in which Jackie scored twenty-five points in one game, he stayed away from sports to concentrate on his coursework.

The new year began fine for the Robinson family. Jackie was doing well in school, and his mother was making enough money to purchase the house next door at 133 Pepper Street. Mallie moved into the new house, leaving the old one to Jackie, Willa Mae, Edgar, and Frank and his family. Then tragedy struck the family on July 10 when a car crossed the path of Frank's motorcycle on Orange Grove Boulevard. He died the next day. Jackie had lost his greatest fan and mentor.

While adjusting to the loss of Frank, Jackie found other parts of his world changing during the summer of 1939. The 1940 Summer Olympics, officially known as the Games of the XII Olympiad, were originally scheduled to be held in Tokyo, Japan from September 21 to October 6. When war broke out between Japan and China, the Games were rescheduled for Helsinki, Finland, but the outbreak of World War II in Europe canceled that venue as well. With no one having any ideas when peace and the Olympics would be restored, Jackie decided to go ahead and play other sports at UCLA. It was an excellent decision for him as well as for the university.

In his first year of sports as a UCLA Bruin, Jackie became the university's first athlete to letter in all four major sports—football, basketball, track, and baseball. He, along with Washington and Strode—the "Gold Dust Trio" as the press labeled them—went undefeated with six wins and four ties in 1939. In their final football game of the season, the team drew the largest crowd to attend a football game up until that time. Some 103,352 people watched UCLA and USC battle to a scoreless tie.

Jackie led the Bruin basketball team as its, and the conference's, high scorer during the 1939–1940 season. Ironically, his poorest performance in college was on the baseball diamond where he went into one of several slumps to finish with a dismal .097 batting average. His fielding also suffered as he tied with a teammate for the most errors committed. However, Jackie bounced back during track season, winning his conference championship in the long jump at the Los Angeles Coliseum and going on to win the NCAA title in Minneapolis, Minnesota. By the end of his first year at UCLA, the press had begun calling Robinson "the Jim Thorpe of his race."

Robinson completed the school year with nothing lower than a C in his primary courses and earned easy A's in his physical education classes. For the first summer since childhood, Jackie did not play organized sports during the summer of 1940. Instead he worked in the property department of Warner Brothers film studio, a job likely secured for him by the UCLA athletic department.

Back on campus for the 1940 football season, Jackie continued to dazzle the crowds, his opponents, and the press. He set the national punt return record with an average of twenty-one yards and earned the title of third leading passer in the state. The Bruins football team, however, did not fare as well collectively as Jackie did individually, winning only one while losing nine. UCLA had simply not been able to recruit superior athletes to support their star player. According to the Associated Press, the Bruins were the nation's biggest disappointment of the season. Jackie was not only dissatisfied with the team record but also frustrated when he made only the honorable mention All-American team. Some observers believed that slight resulted from his team's losing record; others thought that racism had influenced the selection.

Jackie would later say that his greatest accomplishment in the fall of 1940 was meeting freshman coed Rachel Annetta Isum. Dedicated to athletics, he had had little time for or interest in dating because he was shy around the opposite sex. Except for mixed doubles tennis, Jackie had little interaction with black women other than family members, and, not wanting to agitate any prejudices, Robinson had completely avoided relationships in high school and college with white girls. Jackie later said, "I could count on one hand the number of girls I went out with before Rachel." This changed when his best friend Ray Bartlett introduced him to his future wife.

Before they met, Rachel knew about Jackie from his sports exploits and assumed he would be cocky and arrogant. She was in for a surprise. In her book about her husband, Rachel wrote, "When we met, I was immediately drawn to him. He was impressive—a handsome, proud, and serious man with a warm smile and a pigeon-toed walk. And he felt drawn to me as well, but we were both shy and intent on reaching the goals we had set for ourselves. For me getting a degree was my highest priority. I would let nothing interfere with it. Still our relationship blossomed. We casually met in the parking lot and other public places until I invited him home to meet my family. My mother saw the best in him, my father was jealous, and my brothers in awe."

Rachel's father, Charles Raymond Isum, was a second-generation black Californian. At the time his daughter met Jackie, Raymond had recently retired after working for the *Los Angeles Times* as a bookbinder. His early retirement was the result of a severe heart condition acquired in World War I when gassed by Germans while serving as a U.S. Army sergeant.

In his future father-in-law, Jackie encountered another level of prejudice. Jackie's relatives thought Raymond disapproved of Jackie because he was "too black"—racism not being limited to whites alone. Many African Americans were just as quick to judge fellow blacks by the degree of darkness of their skin as whites were to judge them for being black at all. In fact, many black college elite fraternities and sororities had what they called the grocery bag test—pledges darker in color than a grocery bag were not admitted.

Those who knew Raymond Isum well would have doubted that he felt, or expressed, objections over Jackie's dark complexion. A native of Atlanta, he was known for his pride in his race and fair play. Whatever his feelings, he did not prevent his daughter from seeing Jackie. The two men, however, never developed a close relationship before Raymond's death on March 6, 1941.

Rachel's mother, Zelle Jones, who grew up in the Southwest where her prosperous family owned a café, pool hall, and theater as well as land in Nogales, Arizona, on the Mexican border, found Jackie perfectly acceptable for her daughter. Zelle herself had attended college at Tuskegee Institute in Alabama before settling in California with Raymond. After her husband's retirement and around the time she met Jackie, Zelle worked as a self-employed caterer while also working in the employee's cafeteria of the Los Angeles Public Library.

The meeting of Rachel with Jackie's family also went well. Rachel later remembered that they were friendly and that Mallie was gracious and kind, writing, "Right from the beginning I could tell that there was no competition or conflict with her. She thought of me the way my mother thought of Jack. Here's a girl in the church, she doesn't drink or smoke, a good student, going into nursing, no other boyfriends. Everything that she would have wanted for

Jack—that was me. And I could relate to her very well, in her own struggle, what she had gone through just to be there."

Jackie and Rachel both knew that they were meant for each other but that they still had much to do and accomplish as individuals before they could unite as a permanent couple. They remained dedicated to each other in a committed, but apparent chaste, relationship for the next five years.

• 5 •

Early Stances against Racism

$\mathcal{O}$n both the Pasadena Junior College and University of California at Los Angeles campuses, Jackie let his performance on the sports fields and courts be his spokesperson. He was not an agitator nor did he protest injustices. At PJC, Robinson did not join the all-black club "Armulites," but he did hang out with the small number of African Americans. However, he encouraged his friends to spread out more across the campus and interact with the white students.

Jackie's racial pride and opposition to racism and Jim Crow treatment increased and solidified during his time at PJC and UCLA. Some of the changing attitudes proved beneficial to him; other aspects, not so much. By the spring semester of 1941, Jackie had been involved in several incidents that led to arrest and punishment.

Although Jackie and the Pepper Street Gang had been into much mischief as children and frequently detained and questioned by the local police, Robinson had no criminal record until he was a student at Pasadena Junior College. On January 22, 1938, Jackie and a friend, Jonathan Nolan, were on their way home in Jackie's car when Nolan began to loudly sing a popular suggestive tune of the day, "Flat Foot Floogie." A policeman heard Nolan's singing and pulled the car over. When the policeman began to berate Nolan, Jackie stood up for his friend and a verbal confrontation followed.

Jackie learned, or relearned, very quickly that a white policeman had far more power than a black motorist. The policeman took them to the station, locked them up, and did not offer either one access to a telephone. As a result, Jackie and Nolan spent the night behind bars. At a hearing three days later, police court judge Kenneth C. Newell sentenced Jackie to ten days in jail but suspended the incarceration for eight months on the condition that

25

he avoid arrest for the next two years. Although the records do not provide an explanation for the judge's ruling, it is likely he suspended the jail time because of Jackie's having no prior record and especially because he was a well-known athlete.

On September 5, 1939, police once again arrested Jackie. This time Robinson had been driving home from a softball game in Brookside Park with Ray Bartlett and several other friends riding on the running boards of his car. According to Bartlett, a white man pulled alongside and said something about "niggers." Bartlett reached over and slapped the man with his ball glove. Both cars then pulled to the side of the street. Bartlett and the white man were about to fight when blacks in other cars and from the neighborhood began to surround the two would-be fighters. By the time a policeman arrived, the white man had backed off and said he did not want to fight. As the policeman waded into the crowd, most bystanders began to melt away or openly run from the confrontation. According to the police report, the crowd numbered "between 40 and 50 members of the Negro race." Only Jackie stood his ground. Bartlett, who later explained that he was more scared of his strict mother than the police, slipped away as the officer approached. According to Bartlett, "So I withdrew. But not Jack. He just wouldn't back down. He was very stubborn."

Robinson remained the only one for the policeman to arrest. He recalls, "I found myself up against the side of my car with a gun-barrel pressed unsteadily into the pit of my stomach."

Jackie never explained just why he stayed when others ran. Maybe he, as Bartlett said, was "stubborn" or he just did not want to abandon his automobile. Perhaps he welcomed the opportunity to confront a policeman because of their treatment of his brother at the Rose Bowl Parade the previous January.

Whatever the reason, Jackie was back in jail facing charges of hindering traffic and resisting arrest. The charges were all the more serious because of his two-year suspended sentence from his previous infraction. This time, however, Jackie had more support. Coaches at UCLA and friends in Pasadena came to his aid, posting his $25 bail and retaining an attorney, described by the press as "prominent in sports circles in the state," who petitioned city officials for leniency.

On October 18, the case was heard before Judge Hebert Farrell of Alhambra who was filling in for Judge Newell, the adjudicator of Jackie's previous offense. Judge Farrell accepted the prosecutor's and Jackie's decision to change his plea from not guilty to guilty and fined him $50. When a reporter asked the prosecutor about Jackie's suspended sentence, he explained, "[T]he police court had no right to suspend a sentence for more than six months." The *Pasadena Star-News* reported that the verdict had been influenced by "the prominent sports attorney" who requested "the Negro football player be not disturbed during the football season."

In his Personal History Statement completed during Basic Training at Fort Riley, Robinson responded "yes" to the question, "Have you ever been arrested, indicted, or convicted for any violation of law other that a minor traffic violation?" In providing details, he took some liberties in writing, "Pasadena, Calif. Blocking sidewalk. 1939. Fight was on corner where a group of coloreds were watching fight between a white and colored fellow. I was arrested along with some others but was the only one taken in. Case never came before court because of nature of offense."

Robinson was resentful about what he considered "bigotry of the meanest sort," but he also later acknowledged, "I got out of trouble because I was an athlete." Newspaper articles about the incident—with headlines such as "Gridiron Phantom Lives Up to Name"— bothered Jackie because he thought they made him appear to be a thug instead of a man standing up for his rights. Baseless rumors circulated that Jackie had been accused of robbery and that he was often in trouble with the police with multiple arrests and confinements. Jackie said, "This thing followed me all over and it was pretty hard to shake."

The truth about Jackie's interaction with the police is best explained by Hank Shatford, a *Pasadena Junior College Chronicle* reporter while Robinson was on campus and later an attorney and Pasadena superior court judge. When asked about Jackie and the police, Shatford said, "They didn't consider Jack as a rabble rouser. Not at all. It's just that Jack would not take any stuff from them. Jack never wanted to be regarded as a second-class citizen. He rebelled at any thought of anybody putting him down, or putting any of his people down. He wanted equality. And he had a temper. Boy, he could heat up pretty fast when he wanted to! When he felt he was right and the other guy was wrong, he didn't hesitate. He was in there. But he also had an extremely warm side to him that I saw all the time."

· 6 ·

After College

$\mathcal{B}$y the end of basketball season at UCLA in his senior year, Jackie had become disgruntled with school. His failure to make the first team All American in football and the poor records of his teams on the gridiron and basketball court were discouraging. Although Jackie worked part-time as an assistant janitor in a campus building and at a used textbook store in Westwood, Jackie felt that he did not sufficiently contribute to his mother's finances. Lastly, and perhaps most importantly, Jackie had come to the conclusion that education would not help a black man get ahead in a Jim Crow world.

Jackie would later write, "I could see no future in staying in college, no real future in [professional] athletics, and I wanted to do the next best thing—become an athletic director. The thought of working with youngsters in the field of sports excited me."

UCLA coaches, his mentor Karl Downs, his mother, and Rachel all attempted to talk Jackie out of leaving school before graduation to no avail. Rachel said, "I tried to talk him out of it. He was so close to finishing. He put it all on Mallie, that he wanted to help her financially, because she was still working so hard. But I think he would have left in any case. He had had enough."

Doing the "right thing" was always important to Jackie. On March 3, 1940, he went into the UCLA registrar's office and formally withdrew from the university. Instead of being a "dropout," he departed with an "honorable dismissal."

Then Jackie looked for work. The Broadway Clowns, a traveling basketball team organized in 1934 by former Harlem Globetrotter Al "Runt" Pullins, offered Jackie a job. So did a professional baseball team in Mexico. Jackie turned down both offers. In addition to their low wages, Jackie was well aware that there was no chance to advance to the major all-white professional teams.

Pat Ahern, the athletic director for the National Youth Administration who knew Jackie and his sports accomplishments, offered him a job as assistant athletic director at their NYA camp at Atascadero, California, about a six-hour drive north of Los Angeles. Jackie accepted the position of organizing sports activities for students at the camp, founded in 1935 as part of President Roosevelt's New Deal programs to combat the Depression, so that their time out of class was productive as well.

Jackie enjoyed his time with the NYA group members, a mixture of races who came from poverty and difficult backgrounds—many having been in trouble with law enforcement before coming to the camp. Jackie saw a lot of his teenage self in his students and appreciated both their situations and his time with them. No one expressed concern about a black man being in charge of white teens. The only overt racism he experienced was being turned away from a camp dance.

World events soon overtook the purpose of the NYA. With World War II already raging in Europe and Asia and the likelihood of the United States joining the conflict, war-related industries and other employers were in need of manpower. With jobs abundant, the NYA no longer had purpose. By summer the NYA began closing their program and turning over the facilities to the U.S. Army.

Jobless, Jackie accepted an invitation to join a college all-star football team in Chicago for a gridiron game with the Bears—the reigning National Football League champions. On August 28, before a crowd of 98,000 at Soldier Field, the college all-stars held their own until near the end of the game when the Bears scored three quick touchdowns. Jackie caught a 36-yard pass for a touchdown, causing a Bear defensive player to say after the game, "The only time we worried was when that guy Robinson was on the field."

After the game, most of the college all-stars went from Chicago to teams in the all-white National Football League. Jackie, however, returned to Southern California where he joined the Los Angeles Bulldogs in a match against the Hollywood Bears before a crowd of 10,000 at Gilmore Stadium. Both teams were predominantly white except for Jackie playing with the Bulldogs and former UCLA teammate Kenny Washington playing for Hollywood. This game was important for Jackie in two ways. One, it was his first time to get paid to play football. Two, he reinjured his right ankle—the one that he had initially hurt at PJC. Not only would this cause him to leave the game early but also that ankle injury would be an important factor in his future.

Despite that recurring ankle injury, a week later Jackie accepted an offer to play for the Honolulu Bears of the Hawaii Senior Football League. His old friend Ray Bartlett also agreed to play for the Bears and sailed with Jackie aboard the SS *Matsonia* to the Islands. In addition to a salary of $100 per game, the Bears promised the players jobs as construction workers near Pearl Harbor when they were not practicing or playing. According to Bartlett, "We could use the extra money, because we were both trying to help our mothers. But because the construction job involved defense, it also meant we wouldn't be drafted, at least not yet."

The *Honolulu Advertiser* greeted Jackie with a full-page photograph of him on the gridiron and informed its readers of the arrival of the "Century Express." An advertisement encouraged readers to come to the games and "See the Sensational All-American Half-Back Jackie Robinson." While the fans were enthusiastic, the Waikiki hotels were not so welcoming to Jackie and Bartlett. Turned away from accommodations because of their color, they had to rent an apartment in Honolulu's Palama Settlement district.

The Bears worked out and played their games at night because of the day-time tropical heat. This left ample time for their construction jobs. Jackie did not take to the manual labor and quickly got crosswise with his foreman. According to Bartlett, Jackie either quit or was fired after a few days on the job.

The Honolulu Bears played a six-game schedule against other island city teams and those from army and navy units. Jackie performed well early in the season with 20,000 paying to see his first game. As the season progressed, however, Jackie's ankle injury slowed his running abilities and the Bears' overall performance. By the final game of the season on December 3, the Bears drew a paying crowd of only 600.

Jackie was more than ready to return to California to see his mother and Rachel. He boarded the homeward-bound SS *Lurline* on December 5, 1941. Two days later, Jackie was playing poker with fellow passengers when the crew began painting the portholes black. The captain informed his passengers that the Japanese had bombed Pearl Harbor and that they would sail in blackout the remainder of the voyage to avoid a submarine attack.

The *Lurline* made it safely into Los Angeles, and Jackie, having moved back in with his mother on Pepper Street, looked to take advantage of recent events in the job market. African American leaders had pressured President Franklin Roosevelt into providing measures for fair and equal employment for black workers. In June of 1941, the president signed Executive Order 8802, banning discriminatory employment practices by Federal agencies and all unions and companies engaged in war-related work. The order also established the Fair Employment Practices Commission to enforce the new policy.

With the executive order and the need for workers to fill the expanding industries preparing for war, Jackie quickly found a job with Lockheed Aircraft as a truck driver with a salary of $100 per month. He was happy to contribute to his mother's household expenses, but he knew that he would soon have to make a decision about the draft, military service, and his future.

· 7 ·

African Americans and
Military Service

$\mathcal{T}$he draft, and the military as a whole at the outbreak of World War II, presented Jackie Robinson and other African Americans with much the same situation as had previous conflicts engaged by the United States. Since the founding of the nation, blacks had fought for their own personal freedom as well as that of their fellow Americans. African Americans contributed to the success of the Revolutionary War that gained the country—though not its slaves—independence. Blacks played a significant role in preserving the Union and in securing their own freedom during the Civil War. African American soldiers fought Native Americans on the vast western plains, participated in the charge up San Juan and Kettle Hills in the Spanish-American War, and helped defeat the Germans on the European battlefields of the First World War.

However, in every previous conflict, the United States initially denied or discouraged the enlistment of African Americans into the uniformed services. As the battles intensified and lengthened, the country called upon its blacks to fill the ranks, but, in most instances, restricted them to support duties rather than combat positions. Units were segregated with all-black enlisted soldiers led by an all-white officer corps. With few exceptions and despite their service and sacrifice, by war's end, African Americans enjoyed no more rights and recognition than before the conflict. (Historical Perspective 5.)

In 1940, the U.S. Army had a total of five black regular army officers. Three of these were chaplains. The other two rotated between the four segregated black regiments, as the Professor of Military Science and Tactics at the all-black Wilberforce University in Ohio and as the military attaché to Liberia. Originally there had been three black officers for the position in Liberia, a country established and run by freed slaves from America, but one died from disease in the harsh African tropical climate. None of the services planned to commission additional blacks as officers.

Despite their continued mistreatment, blacks readily volunteered and accepted being drafted into the armed forces at the outbreak of World War II. Many African Americans saw the military as a means of bettering themselves and their race. Some readily accepted the time-honored tradition of the military offering of travel and adventure as well as a regular paycheck, lodging, and subsistence—even if the pay was low, the lodging possibly a fox hole, and food from a can. There were a few, no doubt, who liked the idea of legally fighting and killing whites—even if they were Germans. Most, however, felt as Jackie Robinson later wrote, "Like all men in those days, I was willing to do my part."

Many white Americans, though, did not have confidence in the service of African Americans. In 1942, Assistant Secretary of War and post-war President of the World Bank, John J. McCloy, said, "If the United States does not win this war, the lot of the Negro is going to be far, far worse than it is today. Yet there is an alarming large percentage of Negroes in and out of the army who do not seem to be vitally concerned with winning the war."

The general consensus among African Americans about World War II was that they would approach it at a Double V campaign—Victory over the Axis powers in Europe and in the Pacific and victory over racism and segregation at home. Jackie said of the Double V campaign, "I was in two wars, one against a foreign enemy, the other against prejudice at home."

• 8 •

2nd Lt. Robinson

$\mathscr{D}$espite being "willing to do his part," Jackie Robinson had some reservations about entering the army. When he registered for the draft at Pasadena Longfellow Elementary School—prior to his going to Hawaii and the attack on Pearl Harbor—he had declared that he was his mother's sole means of support in hopes of receiving a deferment. Jackie also hoped after returning to California that his job in the defense industry might defer, or at least delay, notice from the draft board. He also had concerns that his injured ankle might not stand up to the physical aspects of basic training.

In March 1942, Jackie participated in a workout with the Chicago White Sox in Pasadena's Brookside Park. Sox's manager Jimmy Dykes told reporters that he supported integrating Major League Baseball and that Robinson would be an asset to any club. He did not need to add that breaking baseball's color line was, however, still impossible.

Concern about playing baseball, taking care of his mother, and holding his defense industry job all became mute when Jackie received a notice dated March 23 from his local Draft Board that read, "Greeting: Having submitted yourself to a Local Board composed of your neighbors for the purpose of determining your availability for training and service in the armed forces of the United States, you are hereby notified that you have been selected for training and service in the Army." It further explained that his service was for "the duration of war plus six months."

So on April 3, Jackie reported to the Pasadena National Guard Armory from where he was transported to Fort MacArthur in San Pedro. There he received uniforms, immunizations, and a physical exam. The physical did not note any problems with his ankle and recorded him to be six feet tall and weighing 180 pounds. Jackie also signed allotment papers sending $22 of his monthly salary of $50 to his mother.

After four days of initial processing, Jackie and other inductees boarded a train to Fort Riley, Kansas, where he joined B Company, 8th Training Squadron, Cavalry Replacement Center for thirteen weeks of basic training. Kansas, settled in the mid-nineteenth century by abolitionists and "free staters," was generally tolerant of blacks, but Fort Riley, which enforced segregation policies—despite a black regiment on post—had a population from across the country, including some officers and enlisted men who could not or did not set aside their prejudices and racism when they put on a uniform.

Jackie's natural athleticism served him well in basic training. He hit 196 out of 200 targets on the rifle range, earning an Expert rating with the M-1 rifle. The training staff rated his character as "excellent."

While in basic training, Jackie became aware of the Cavalry Officers Candidate School conducted at Fort Riley. With his performance in basic, his physical skills, and his nearly completed college degree, Jackie seemed to be a prime candidate for OCS. He applied but was not admitted. Jackie later wrote, "The men in our unit had passed all the tests of OCS, but we were not allowed to start school; we were kept sitting around for at least three months, and we could get no answers to our questions about the delay."

The delay came from Fort Riley officials not knowing just what to do with the black OCS applicants. No official regulations barred African Americans from OCS or from their becoming officers. Unofficially, however, the general consensus, including the opinions of senior commanders who did not approve of black officers, was they were not capable of handling the responsibilities of a commissioned officer. Secretary of War Henry L. Stimson said, "Leadership is not imbedded in the Negro race yet and to try to make them commissioned officers to lead men into battle—colored men—is only to work a disaster to both."

While waiting on the decision about attending OCS, Jackie remained assigned to B Company, 8th Training Squadron, Cavalry Replacement Center. He cleaned stalls, groomed horses, and assisted in administering vaccinations. He also had time to ride the horses on trails in the post's training areas. His medical records show that on January 21, 1943, he was treated for "[f]rostbite, moderate severity, both hands, accidently incurred while riding horse January 16, 1943 at the Cavalry School Range, Fort Riley, Kansas." The report concluded that the injury was in the line of duty.

In the spring of 1943, Jackie attempted to join the camp baseball team only to be told that the officer in charge had proclaimed, "I'll break up the team before I'll have a nigger on it."

Stable duty and a segregated baseball team did not make for rewarding days, but one good thing did happen while Jackie waited on word about OCS. Joe Louis, the Heavy Weight Boxing Champion of the World arrived on orders at Fort Riley. Born in Alabama as the grandson of former slaves and at that point the best known and most popular—or at least most accepted—black person in America, Louis found a friend in Robinson. The two golfed, rode horseback, and sparred together.

Along with most of the country, Jackie had followed Louis' climb up the ladder. He knew when the Associated Press selected him as "Athlete of the Year" for 1935 and when Louis suffered his first professional loss in the ring on June 19, 1936, to German fighter Max Schmeling. Jackie had been proud when Louis knocked out James Braddock on June 22, 1937, in the eighth round.

Jackie was still in high school when Max Schmeling arrived in New York City for a rematch with Louis in June 1938. (Historical Perspective 6.) The fight was broadcast by radio to millions of listeners throughout the world, with announcers reporting on the fight in English, German, Spanish, and Portuguese. The fight lasted only two minutes and four seconds. Schmeling managed only a couple of ineffective punches the entire short fight. Louis knocked down the German three times and on the third knockdown, Schmeling's trainer threw in the towel.

While Jackie finished high school and attended college, Joe continued with his fights. One was a charity bout for the Navy Relief Society against Buddy Baer on January 9, 1942, which raised $47,000 for the fund. The media widely reported his contribution to the Navy Relief Society, adding to his popularity among white Americans. Not all African Americans were so impressed when one of their own contributed to a navy that restricted black men to duty as mess boys.

The day after the Relief fund fight, Louis voluntarily enlisted in the U.S. Army as a private at Camp Upton on Long Island. Newsreel cameras recorded his induction, including a staged scene in which an induction clerk asked, "What's your occupation?" Louis replied, "Fighting and let us at them Japs." (Historical Perspective 7.)

Instead of fighting the Japs, though, Louis performed exhibition bouts and conducted enlistment campaigns as a member of the Special Services Division before reporting to Fort Riley where his path intersected with Jackie's in a fateful way.

Louis's greatest impact on Jackie, one that influenced his new friend's army career and helped him later break the Major League color barrier, was in taking advantage of the contacts Louis had made in his boxing career. When Jackie told Louis about how he and other African Americans were being kept from attending OCS, the boxer contacted Truman K. Gibson, a Washington, D.C. attorney and assistant to William Hastie, civilian aide to the Secretary of War. Gibson flew to Fort Riley and met with Robinson, Louis, and other black soldiers as well as post officials.

The Cavalry OCS at Fort Riley admitted Robinson and several other African Americans a short time later in November 1943. Before his entering OCS, the army recognized Jackie's good performance and character while assigned to the stables by promoting him to corporal.

Joe Louis departed Fort Riley and, because he and Jackie had become such good friends, made a courtesy call on Rachel while he was on leave and brought her up to date on Jackie's life in the army.

Jackie did well in the thirteen-week-long OCS course, which was one of the few parts of the army of that period that was totally integrated. White and black candidates were housed in the same buildings, studied, trained, and dined together. Jackie was popular with his fellow candidates, both black and white.

On January 28, 1943, Jackie and seventy-seven other candidates graduated and received their commissions as second lieutenants, just a day after they had been honorably discharged from enlisted status. Special Orders No. 19 included a list of the seventy-eight new lieutenants from towns, large and small, all across the United States. The orders contained no designation of race, and there is no record stating the number of blacks in this first integrated Cavalry OCS. Estimates range from "a handful" to a half dozen.

Subsequent orders on the same date stated that the new officers would "report to the Commandant, the Cavalry School, for temporary duty pending assignment to permanent duty status." A letter from Commandant of the Calvary School added, "This commission to continue in force during the pleasure of the President of the United States of the time being, and for the duration of the present emergency and six months thereafter unless sooner terminated."

Jackie orally and in writing swore an oath of office: "I Jackie Roosevelt Robinson, 01031586, having been appointed a 2d Lieutenant in the Army of the United States, do solemnly swear that I will support and defend the Constitution of the United States against all enemies, foreign and domestic; that I will bear faith and allegiance to the same; that I take this obligation freely, without any mental reservation or purpose of evasion; and that I will well and faithfully discharge the duties of the office upon which I am about to enter, so help me God."

The Oath of Office was the same for all officers with no differences for whites and blacks. Each man who took the oath and pinned the gold bar of a second lieutenant on his collar was an officer and worthy of being treated as such. Unfortunately, Jackie would soon discover that, while the color of all second lieutenant bars were the same, black officers did not necessarily receive treatment equal to white ones.

Biographies of Jackie and Louis contain little about his success in OCS and the apparent equal treatment of the candidates by the army. The books on both men do, however elaborate on some accounts of various degrees of veracity. Biographers, in order to make their stories more interesting and marketable, on occasion have been known to embellish or even make up stories. Such was the case of Jackie's time immediately after graduation from OCS. Supposedly a confrontation between Jackie and a superior officer occurred shortly after he was commissioned. At least that is what appeared in an early book about Louis's time at Fort Riley and was repeated as fact in several later accounts. According to the story, Jackie intervened when a white officer called a black soldier "a stupid nigger son of a bitch." Jackie either verbally or physically assaulted the white officer, depending on the source.

The story continues by elaborating about Truman Gibson's return to Fort Riley to lobby the commanding general against punishing Jackie, including how Gibson plied the general with a generous gift of alcohol and a gold watch. There is no evidence whatsoever that the confrontation took place or that Gibson returned to mediate. The whole episode was a made-up "good story." But, because the tale had been written down, other writers—ones either too lazy to research the facts or with an agenda to make Jackie a hero—simply repeated the account without question.

While the story of his confronting a bigoted officer is certainly not true, Jackie did take some extraordinary efforts to gain equality for his troops after joining Company B of the Cavalry School Provisional Truck Battalion. In his first assignment as an officer, he had two distinct responsibilities. First, as a platoon leader, his duties in the segregated unit included supervising truck drivers, the maintenance of their vehicles, and their transportation support for the Cavalry School. He performed well in this primary assignment. In his second duty as the moral officer, he came into conflict with post officials.

Several of Jackie's soldiers complained to him about the limited seating at the snack bar in the Post Exchange. Only a few seats were designated "Colored Area," and black soldiers often had to stand while seats remained empty in the white section. Jackie called the camp Provost Marshal, a major, to seek resolution to the problem. The conversation became heated after the major said that changing the seating arrangement "might adversely affect the morale of the white troops." Jackie remained respectful, properly showing deference to the major's rank by ending each sentence with "Sir."

After a lengthy conversation, the major, unaware that he was talking to a black officer, said, "Lieutenant, let me put it to you this way. How would you like to have your wife sitting next to a nigger?"

In his autobiography, Jackie wrote, "Pure rage took over; I was so angry I asked him if he knew how close his wife had ever been to a nigger. I was shouting at the top of my voice."

Jackie had made the phone call from his battalion headquarters building and surely many of the troops, and likely the unit's commanding officer, overheard Jackie's end of the conversation. When the major hung up on him, Jackie went to see his battalion commander, a white lieutenant colonel, to explain the conversation and the problem with seating at the PX snack bar. He later learned that his battalion commander then sent a sizzling letter to the camp commanding general. In describing the incident in his book, Jackie wrote, "He put in a strong request to change the seating situation and recommended that the provost marshal be disciplined for his racist attitude."

Seating at the PX remained segregated, but more seats were allocated to blacks. The provost marshal must have been counseled because he was much more respectful when Jackie had to stand up to him again—this time about one of his truck drivers being in trouble. Jackie was recorded as saying that he was grateful for the support of his battalion commander. More importantly, the incident made an impression on Jackie. He said, "He proved to me that when people in authority take a stand, good can come out of it."

The token addition of snack bar seats did not mean that racism relaxed across the post. When Jackie again attempted to join the post baseball team, the coach told him that he would have to play on the post colored team. Both the coach and Jackie knew that there was no such thing as a colored team. Angry and disappointed, he walked away.

That fall, another coach invited Jackie to join the post football team. What he did not tell the young lieutenant was that Jackie would be allowed to compete only against teams that agreed to African American opponents. The University of Missouri, the season's first game for the Fort Riley team, was one of those who refused to play against blacks. Jackie wrote in his autobiography, "They made it quite clear to the army that they would not play a team with a black player on it. Instead of telling me the truth, the army gave me leave to go home. Naturally I was delighted to leave, but I knew I would never play on that team."

Robinson spent much of his furlough in northern California where Rachel had transferred to the San Francisco School of Nursing after her UCLA days. She also worked as a riveter on the Lockheed Aircraft night shift. So, Jackie walked around the city during the day, waiting for her to get out of class. At night, because he had little money, he slept in his car. He wrote, "I was so happy to be reunited with her, and when my leave was over, I knew we'd be together forever once the war was over."

When he visited his family and friends in Pasadena, Jackie made quite an impression in his cavalry uniform's dark jacket, riding britches, highly polished boots, and a wide-brimmed campaign hat. The primary person he wanted to impress, however, remained Rachel to whom he offered an engagement ring. She accepted, but she was still in no rush to be married.

Rachel had her own ambitions, wanting a career beyond that of wife. She said, "I had come to realize how dominated I had been by my family all my life, how they had shaped my thoughts, my goals, and my very being. Now I was in nursing school, which was terribly demanding and regimented. I could see that marriage was going to be another force, maybe more powerful, keeping me in place, with me trying, striving hard, as usual, to be the best wife I could be, just as I tried to be the best child, the best young lady, the best student I could be. I could see marriage suffocating, I was not eager to rush into it."

Other concerns were also in Rachel's mind. She worried about Jackie being sent to combat and about what was going on within her own family. In later writings, she said, "Enough had already happened in my family's history of military service for me to consider war a personal, potent, and destructive force." In addition to her father's being gassed in World War I, her older brother Chuck, who had become a Tuskegee airman, had been shot down over Yugoslavia and was being held in a German prisoner of war camp. Her younger brother Raymond was serving in the Pacific.

When Jackie returned to Fort Riley, he went to the football coach. In relating the meeting, Jackie wrote, "I said that I had no intention of playing football for a team which, because I was black, would not allow me to play in all the games." The coach, a colonel, countered that he could order Jackie to play. Jackie agreed that he could be ordered to play but added that he could not be ordered to play well. With the colonel's permission, Jackie left the team.

Jackie had another reason for leaving the squad. Shortly after his return from California, he had reinjured his right ankle—the one that had troubled him during this college years—while negotiating an obstacle course. Each time the ankle began to feel better over the next two months, he hurt it again, either during military training or while playing sports.

· 9 ·

Medical Issues

*W*hile Jackie was adjusting to his change in rank from an enlisted man to an officer and recovering from his most recent ankle injury, the Army was in motion adapting its units to function more efficiently in the modernizing world, actions that would impact Robinson and his immediate future. On December 9, 1943, Jackie and sixteen other lieutenants received new orders. They were to report to the 2nd Cavalry Division at Fort Clark, Texas, just outside of Brackettville, near the Rio Grande, a post guarding the Mexican border since 1852.

Jackie arrived at Fort Clark in the midst of modernization changes and the reorganization that the 2nd Cavalry was undergoing in converting from its original 1921 horse-mounted mission to its becoming an infantry unit. Along with its sister unit, the 1st Cavalry Division—an organization that would become known as the "First Team" that led the way in every future U.S. conflict to remain on active duty today—the 2nd Cavalry was dismounting and turning in its horses. The 1st Cavalry was all white and quickly filled its ranks to be combat ready and deploy to the Pacific Theater in the summer of 1943. Meanwhile the 2nd Cavalry, an integrated division with black enlisted soldiers and mostly white officers, never enjoyed full strength until the draft inducted a sufficient number of black soldiers to fill their ranks. Yet, even with the buildup and overseas orders, the 2nd Cavalry would soon become a footnote in history. (Historical Perspective 8.)

On December 21, the 2nd Cavalry assigned 2nd Lt. Robinson to Troop F of its 27th Cavalry Regiment. Jackie's stay with that unit was brief, but he had sufficient time at Fort Clark to observe that Mexicans in Texas were treated little better than blacks. Referred to as "wetbacks" whether they were in the United States legally or illegally, Hispanic Americans did have the advantage over African Americans in that they were thoroughly integrated into the Armed Forces. Non-citizen Hispanics also found readily available employment because of the Mexican Farm Labor Agreement, initiated on August 4, 1942, which brought workers across the border to work in the fields and orchards in the Bracero (Spanish meaning "manual laborer") Program, an effort to replace Americans—black and white—called up by the draft.

When Jackie reported to Troop F, preparations for deployment to North Africa were underway, including requiring soldiers of the 27th Regiment to pass rigid physical tests. Jackie's injured ankle worsened and precluded his passing the test and his assignment to a berth on a boat to North Africa. Instead, his medical condition produced transfer orders on January 4, 1944, back to the Cavalry Replacement Pool at Fort Riley with temporary assignment in route to Brooke General Hospital in San Antonio for evaluation of his injury.

Jackie's short stay at Fort Clark did not merit a mention in either of his autobiographies. Nor did he include learning while on the border that his mother was ill or his efforts to get leave to visit her. That latter piece of information comes from a single piece of paper in his military personnel file that is a copy of a telegram from his sister Willa Mae saying, "Mother is very sick. Please come home immediately." Other than marked "Received" and date-stamped January 4—the same day Jackie received orders to report to Brooke General Hospital—the paper reveals nothing.

As ordered, Jackie reported to Brooke General Hospital "for observation and treatment." His medical history and physical findings stated, "This 24 year old 2nd Lieutenant, with 1 9/12 service (12 months as officer), was admitted to this hospital 5 January 1944, to the Medical Service. He transferred to the Orthopedic Service on 27 January 1944.

"Patient gives a history of having sustained an injury to the right ankle in 1937 while playing football at Pasadena, Cal. He was in a cast for several weeks and recovered in about 6 weeks. He next injured the ankle in 1941 playing football in Honolulu, as a civilian. He recovered in about 2 weeks. His next injury was in September 1943 while on obstacle course at Ft. Riley, Kansas. Since that time the ankle had given him considerable difficulty in that it is painful and swells following excessive walking."

"Physical examination is essentially negative. X-ray examination shows an old, ununited fracture of the medial malleolus of the right ankle with some evidence of traumatic arthritis."

On January 28, 1944, the Brooke General Hospital Disposition Board met to make recommendations about Jackie's health, treatment, and future. Records show that the Board reviewed the medical history and findings and concluded that Robinson's medical problems "existed prior to entrance on active duty." This was important, as it would prevent Jackie from someday filing for a veteran's disability claim regarding his ankle that was not a service-related injury.

The findings continued, "The Board is of the opinion that this officer is physically disqualified for general military service but is qualified for limited service. He is not qualified for overseas duty at this time. The Board recommends that he be discharged from the hospital and assigned to temporary limited service. It is recommended that his assignment be such that he will not encounter calisthenics, marching, drilling or other duties requiring strenuous use of the right ankle, and that on or about 28 July 1944 he be reexamined with a view to determining his physical fitness."

Jackie reported to the Cavalry Replacement Center at Fort Riley on February 7, 1944, to face new concerns—not about his ankle or his next assignment but rather about his relationship with Rachel. Through letters and phone calls, they discussed her intention to join the United States Cadet Nurse Corps, a program authorized on March 29, 1943, by the Nurse Training Act—also known as the Bolton Act—to provide "for the training of nurses for the armed forces, government and civilian hospitals, health agencies, and war industries through grants to the institutions providing the training."

Rachel saw the Cadet Nurse Corps as an opportunity because its purpose was to ensure that the country had enough nurses to care for its citizens at home and abroad during the war. Because it was non-discriminatory and welcomed women of all races, she was interested.

Although cadet nurses wore uniforms, they had no commitment to join the military upon graduation. The cadet pledge, considered a statement of intention rather than a binding contract, stated, "At this moment of my induction into the United States Cadet Nurse Corps of the United States Public Health Service, I am solemnly aware of the obligations I assume toward my country and toward my chosen profession; I will follow faithfully the teachings of my instructors and the guidance of the physicians with whom I work; I will hold in trust the finest traditions of nursing and the spirit of the Corps; I will keep my body strong, my mind alert, and my heart steadfast; I will be kind, tolerant, and understanding; above all, I will dedicate myself now and forever to the triumph of life over death; As a Cadet nurse, I pledge to my country my service in essential nursing for the duration of the war."

Rachel was motivated not only by her own patriotism but also by other factors. For one, she later explained, "I was broke as a student. I had no money, and I could earn none in the current student ways. When I was not working in the hospital, I was in class; there was no time. The Corps paid a stipend of twenty dollars a month." Remembering the damp, cold San Francisco winter, she added, "I also liked the big, warm flannel coat they gave you; I really wanted that heavy coat."

Jackie had a low opinion of women in uniform, assuming they were sexually promiscuous predators taking advantage of GIs far from home. About his reactions, he later wrote, "I shook with rage and youthful jealousy." Although Rachel had made no commitment to enter the armed forces after graduation, Jackie demanded that she cease and desist with her interest in the Corps or break off their engagement. Rachel, determined to earn her nursing degree, responded by returning his engagement ring via the U.S. Postal Service.

While Jackie tried to deal with the broken engagement, Fort Riley officials—without regard to his "limited service" status—set the course of his future based on their needs rather than his. With the backdrop of successful "island hopping" occurring in the Pacific and preparations in progress for the Allies' invasion in Europe, more men and officers, black as well as white, were needed at the front or with units preparing to deploy overseas, Jackie among them.

Lieutenant Robinson was ordered to report to Camp Hood, Texas, on April 12, 1944. It would be a decision that would change Jackie's life and the future of Major League Baseball forever. Had he not received those orders, Jackie himself might have gone the way of a footnote in black athletics as his Fort Clark unit had in army history.

· 10 ·

Camp Hood, Texas

$\mathcal{T}$he Camp Hood, Texas, that greeted Jackie offered outstanding opportunities and facilities for blacks, including officers, for their training prior to their deployment to combat overseas. Still, in all likelihood, the place was as ill-prepared for Lieutenant Robinson as he was for the camp and the nearby now-military town of Killeen. Originally established in 1881, Killeen lay about halfway between Waco and Austin as a railroad stop shipping cotton, wool, and grain. Killeen had remained fairly small and isolated until it became a military boom town of carpenters, construction workers, contractors, and soldiers and their families with the establishment of the military installation. Locals were happy to profit from the boom while also resenting the loss of the surrounding farm and ranch lands to the military.

What had been, in pre-war years, 300 farms and ranches as well as three villages was now the huge camp of more than 50,000 acres and two airfields that had the capacity of housing and preparing 95,000 troops for combat. It provided space for 4,000 German POWs as well.

Many locals in the Killeen area resented the huge influx of soldiers, especially African Americans. Killeen and Camp Hood had all the prejudices and Jim Crow practices of other southern camps. The racial superiority of whites over Indians, Mexicans, and blacks was commonly believed and practiced by residents of Killeen as well as Texans as a whole. In the years between the Civil War and World War II, Texas lynched 493 individuals, the third most of any state. To their credit, "only" 352 of those lynched were black, with 141 of the others being white or Mexican. (Historical Perspective 9.)

Camp Hood, in addition to its mission as the army's only facility to train tank destroyer personnel, provided training for infantry units and officer candidates. While the best defense against a tank is a tank itself, there were never a sufficient number of tanks in the U.S. Army to defend against or attack the German panzers. Tank destroyers, both towed and mechanized, were a cross between a tank, an artillery gun, and a bazooka and had the single purpose of destroying enemy tanks.

Named in honor of West Point graduate John Bell Hood, who had earned fame as a Confederate general commanding the Texas Brigade in the Civil War, the camp's rolling hills with limestone outcroppings and cedar brush provided excellent training areas for infantry and tank destroyer units. Naming of a new camp in honor of a man who fought as a rebel against the United States in the Civil War was not limited to Texas. In a continued effort to maintain the unity of the states and to make amends for the abuses of Reconstruction, installations all across the South bore the names of generals who had fought for state rights and to preserve the enslavement of blacks.

When Jackie arrived in Texas, he found a state ruled by Jim Crow and a military post totally segregated, which meant segregated facilities and services for black soldiers as well as officers and with black units being assigned to the poorest barracks in the most undesirable area of the post. Shortly after Jackie's arrival, he went to the white officer's club to cash a check only to be turned away at the door.

Fortunately for Jackie, he was assigned to the 761st Tank Battalion, an outstanding unit activated on April 1, 1942, at Camp Claiborne, Louisiana and recently transferred to Camp Hood for additional training before deployment to the European Theater.

Known as the Black Panthers, the 761st was an all-black battalion with the exception of its commander Lt. Col. Paul L. Bates and a half-dozen other white officers. Before leaving Louisiana, the battalion had lived up to its motto—"Come out fighting"—when its black soldiers had mounted their tanks to attack their white opponents in a riot that involved the Military Police. Col. Bates had persuaded his black soldiers to stand down before the situation had gotten completely out of control.

Col. Bates, a thirty-four-year-old Western Maryland College economics major and football player, had earned the respect of all of his command— white and black—by setting high standards that he demanded be met. The unit trained rigorously to master tank fire and maneuvers in the field and its soldiers set the example with highly shined boots and sharp uniforms in camp. Bates' black soldiers trusted him to look out for their welfare both in the field and in garrison, and he encouraged his soldiers to channel their resentment of racism and Jim Crow laws into hatred for the enemy.

Jackie joined Company B of the 761st as a platoon leader in charge of five M-4 Medium tanks (known as Shermans) and about twenty-five soldiers. While second lieutenants stereotypically had a reputation for being a bit arrogant and ignorant, Jackie displayed wisdom when faced with the daunting challenge of leading men in areas he himself did not understand. Upon arrival at his platoon, he met with his non-commissioned officers and admitted his inexperience. He told them that, having been trained as a horse soldier, he knew nothing about tanks and armored warfare. He was, however, willing to learn.

In his autobiography, Jackie wrote, "I had no knowledge, background, or experience in whatever it was a tank battalion did. I decided there was only one way to solve my problem and that was to be very honest about it. I went to the top sergeant of my platoon and told him that I knew nothing about tanks and would depend on him for guidance. I called all the men together and leveled with them. I said that I wasn't going to kid them. It would be up to them to get the job done and let me know whatever it was I could do to help. I never regretted telling them the truth. The first sergeant and the men knocked themselves out to get the job done. They gave that little extra which cannot be forced from men. They worked harder than any outfit on post, and our unit received the highest rating."

In addition to his platoon duties, Jackie acted as Company B's morale officer. On a unit level, he organized company softball and baseball teams to increase the battalion's morale, and on a personal level, he set the example by following his religious practices and beliefs—including rarely being profane— by dressing well both in uniform and in civilian clothes, and by comporting himself as an officer who understood and appreciated his enlisted men. Fellow officers found Jackie to be a private person whose leadership not only gained the respect and support of his enlisted men but also impressed the battalion commander.

In early May, Col. Bates requested that Jackie remain with the battalion when it deployed to the European Theater, though both men knew that he would first have to get his limited duty status changed to being fit for overseas duty. On May 25, 1944, the 761st sent a request to the Camp Hood Hospital for an examination "to determine the physical qualification for overseas service" of 2nd Lt. Robinson.

Camp Hood Hospital officials determined that they had no authority to change the "limited duty" status issued by a General Hospital (Brooke). As a result, on June 21, Jackie was transferred to McCloskey General Hospital in Temple, Texas—25 miles to the east—for "further observation, treatment, and recommendation for type of duty."

McCloskey General Hospital, a recently activated facility, was already one of the army's largest general hospitals and one that specialized as a center for orthopedic cases, amputations, and neurosurgery as well as serving as a major maternity ward where as many as fifteen babies were born each day to military wives. (Historical Perspective 10.)

Jackie's examination results at McCloskey reflected the same conclusions that had been reached at Brooke General Hospital in San Antonio the previous January: "Injury, secondary result of, fracture right ankle, manifested by pain, swelling, and crepitation on prolonged use of ankle, ankle injured 1937 and 1941 while playing professional football in Los Angeles and Honolulu."

On June 26, 1944, the McCloskey Disposition Board reviewed the medical report and stated, "The Board is of the opinion that this officer is still unfit for general duty but is fit for limited military service. The Board recommends that this officer appear before an Army Retiring Board for consideration or reassignment to permanent limited military service. This officer is fit for overseas duty." This report is somewhat confusing in its conflicting findings; however, in the final analysis it meant that Jackie was fit for overseas service but only in a limited capacity. The Board also passed the final decision to the Retiring Board for final disposition.

Jackie remained attached to McCloskey pending the meeting and findings of the Army Retiring Board, but he made frequent trips back to Camp Hood to visit the 761st Battalion. It was on one of these journeys that Jackie's future in the army and in Major League Baseball hinged. The event that would elevate him to becoming an icon in the Civil Rights Movement began inauspiciously.

• *11* •

Back of the Bus

$\mathcal{O}$n June 6, 1944, an Allied army went ashore on the beaches of Normandy, France, and U.S. forces continued their successful Pacific Ocean island-hopping campaign to liberate the Philippines. America's enemies had reached their high mark, and although a long, bloody road lay ahead, there was a glimmer of final victory in sight.

Back home, however, the daily routine duties of stateside soldiers continued. With his attachment to McCloskey General Hospital, Jackie had ample off-duty time to visit his old unit and friends. So, on the evening of July 6 at about 5:00 p.m., he boarded a commercial bus for the half-hour ride to the Camp Hood Central Bus Station from where he took another bus to the Colored Officers Club. In his autobiography, Jackie says he had made the trip "to talk with some of my friends" but found "the whole outfit had gone off on maneuvers."

Jackie stayed at the club for a couple of hours, talking with officers he knew though he did not then—or ever—drink alcoholic beverages. When he boarded the military bus to go back to the Central Station, from where he would catch the civilian Southwest Bus Company's bus back to McCloskey, he saw Mrs. Virginia Jones, the very light-skinned wife of a fellow lieutenant, sitting about halfway down the aisle. Jackie sat beside her and began talking. The bus had gone only a few blocks when, according to his autobiography, Jackie remembered, "The bus driver glanced into his review mirror and saw what he thought was a white woman talking with a black second lieutenant. He became visibly upset, stopped the bus, and came back to order me to move to the rear. I didn't stop talking, didn't even look at him; I was aware of the fact recently Joe Louis and Ray Robinson had refused to move to the backs of buses in the South. The resulting publicity had caused the army to put out regulations barring racial discrimination on any vehicle operating on an army post. Knowing about these regulations, I had no intention of being intimidated into moving to the back of the bus."

Jackie was on firm ground. The army had indeed taken action on discrimination issues as a result of a commotion created by Joe Louis and fellow boxer Ray Robinson when they had not been allowed to use the telephone at the Camp Sibert bus station near Gadsden, Alabama, after missing their ride. MPs had escorted them to the Office of the Provost Marshal. Only after Louis threatened to "call Washington" were the two released.

The Army was in the process of publishing War Department Order Number 97. That order would read, "Transportation—Busses, trucks or other transportation owned and operated either by the Government or by a governmental instrumentality will be available to all military personnel regardless of race. Restricting personnel to certain sections of such transportation because of race will not be permitted either on or off a post, camp, or station, regardless of local civilian custom." Although the order was not yet official, many African Americans were aware of its pending publication. According to his later writings, Jackie was among those who knew it was coming.

Requiring blacks—soldiers or civilians—to sit in the back of buses had recently become a national issue. An angry white bus driver had shot and killed a black passenger in Durham, North Carolina, who had refused to move to his bus's rear. When a white jury acquitted the driver, it gained all that much more attention.

While the army's on-post regulations supposedly desegregated buses, Jim Crow laws in Texas and other southern states still ruled transportation off of the military installations. As a result, many Camp Hood bus drivers continued to force blacks to the back of the buses. In response, the commanders of the 761st and other segregated battalions often dedicated their own trucks to transport their soldiers around the camp and into town.

On this particular July evening, the bus driver backed down, but Jackie's problems and his temper escalated once they reached the Central Bus Station. The driver reported the incident by pointing out Jackie to his dispatcher, reportedly saying, "There's the nigger that's been causing the trouble." Jackie angrily responded with profanity, causing a group of white soldiers and civilians to gather around. Two MPs arrived and quickly dispersed the small crowd. Showing proper courtesy to Jackie—one of them calling him "Sir"—they asked him to accompany them to the MP station. Things deteriorated further upon their arrival there when someone referred to Jackie as "a nigger lieutenant."

According to witnesses, Jackie's temper swelled as he shouted that if anyone called him a nigger again, he "would break them in two." The situation got no better with the arrival at the MP Station of the Assistant Provost Marshal, Captain Gerald Bear, and the Camp Officer of the Day, Captain Peelor L. Wigginton. Both Bear and Wigginton, being rear echelon officers, likely had a natural resentment toward the combat arms branches of artillery, infantry, and Jackie's branch of cavalry. From what happened next, one could safely assume the two officers also had some prejudices toward African Americans.

The bus driver and dispatcher, as well as several civilians, demanded action against Jackie. The Provost Marshal, whom Jackie quickly determined was a Southerner, showed more respect to the enlisted MPs than to himself as an officer. Without listening to Jackie's side of what had occurred, according to some accounts Capt. Bear ordered the lieutenant out of a room. Other eyewitnesses said that Jackie was so angry by this time that he had refused to leave and had begun interrupting the questioning of witnesses. Both the Provost Marshal and the Duty Officer later claimed that Jackie conducted himself in a "sloppy and contemptuous" manner that was not the proper demeanor of an officer and gentleman.

Capt. Bear called in a civilian stenographer and, in the early hours of July 7, began taking sworn statements from those involved. More than a dozen civilian employees, enlisted MPs and soldiers, as well as Bear and Wigginton recorded their accounts. Only Jackie's statement (Appendix A) supported his side of the story. Mrs. Jones did not give a statement that night.

In Jackie's autobiography, he said his "first indication that I might be up against a tougher situation than I thought" was when he gave his statement to Capt. Bear and the civilian stenographer. He wrote, "I didn't know whether she was his secretary or aide or what. But she was doing all the talking, asking all the questions. They were real, nice, objective questions like, 'Don't you know you've got no right sitting up there in the white part of the bus?' It wasn't bad enough that she was asking that type of question. She wasn't even pausing long enough to hear my answer. At one point she snapped that one of my replies made no sense. I became very annoyed. In the back of my mind was a serious question as to whether she was the proper person, legally, to question me anyway. So I replied sharply that if she would let me finish my sentences and quit interrupting, maybe my answers would make sense. At this point, traditional Southern chivalry for wounded white womanhood took over; Capt. Bear came out of hibernation to growl that I was apparently an uppity nigger and that I had no right to speak to that lady in that manner." Bear would later deny under oath that there was any conflict between the stenographer and Robinson. There is also no collaborating evidence to Jackie's later recall that he used the phrase "uppity nigger."

Capt. Bear, however, would become the primary person to elevate a minor disagreement over bus seating to the army's most serious level of court-martial. Jackie suspected his motivations came from more than seating arrangements and continued with his story, writing, "The captain was very annoyed because I wouldn't back down. He began to rave. I interrupted him asking, 'Captain, tell me, where are you from anyway?' He stormed that that had nothing to do with it, that he wasn't prejudiced, that back home he owned a laundry, that he employed a number of blacks—and all the rest of the stuff that bigots talk when confronted with the charge of being bigots."

After the completion of the statements, the MPs transported Jackie back to McCloskey. Word about a drunken black lieutenant nearly causing a riot at the Camp Hood Bus Station had swept across that post and reached Mc-Closkey before Jackie reached the hospital. A doctor advised Jackie to take a blood test to prove he had no alcohol in his system. If he did so, the results did not reach his medical records file. Jackie informed Lt. Col. Bates about what had happened. Bates recommended Jackie take leave to San Francisco in hopes the incident would "blow over" in his absence.

Jackie took leave and had what he wrote was "a joyous reunion" with Rachel. He said, "When Rae got home from work every evening, I was right there waiting." The two renewed their plans to marry, but not until Rachel completed her nursing degree and Jackie was out of the army.

Upon his return from leave to McCloskey General Hospital, Jackie found that the bus station incident had not "blown over" but rather had escalated with Captain Bear and other MP officers initiating General Court-Martial charges. Jackie began preparing his defense.

• *12* •

The Charges

$\mathcal{T}$he Continental Congress established the first Articles of War on June 30, 1775, to govern the conduct of the Continental Army. With the ratification of the United States Constitution in 1789, Congress assumed responsibility for regulating the army and navy. In 1804, that august body enacted the Articles of War containing the rules and regulations for governing the United States Armed Forces, rules that—with only minor revisions and language updating—remained in effect for more than a century. On June 4, 1920, Congress made additional revisions and additions to the Articles of War. The Articles include not only many crimes punishable under civilian law (e.g., murder, rape, larceny, assault, etc.) but also offenses that affect good order and discipline. Those unique military crimes include such offenses as desertion, absence without leave, disrespect towards superiors, failure to obey orders, dereliction of duty, wrongful disposition of military property, drunk on duty, malingering, and conduct unbecoming an officer. The document also includes specific provisions to punish misbehavior during times of war, including aiding the enemy, spying, and espionage. It also provides three types or levels of court-martial to try alleged offenders.

These are the Articles of War under which Jackie faced charges. The first type of court-martial, the Summary Court-Martial, consists of one commissioned officer who may try only enlisted personnel for non-capital offenses. These are usually only minor aggressions. The second level, Special Court-Martial, is an intermediate trial of members of the military who are accused of non-major offenses. A Special Court-Martial consists of no fewer than three members and a military judge, or an accused may choose to be tried by a military judge alone. The third type, General Court-Martial, mandates that the panel be composed of no fewer than five officers, and that this level is for the most severe offenses, primarily felonies. There are also various Non-Judicial actions for minor offences as well as Letters of Reprimand.

Officers are not subject to Summary Court-Martial but can be tried by Special or General Court-Martial. Although Jackie's alleged offenses were of a minor caliber, Camp Hood officials nevertheless pursued a General Court-Martial.

The names of those who prepared the actual charges are not on the military forms, but, whoever they were, they no doubt wanted the maximum findings and punishment for the black man who had dared to stand up for his rights. They "stacked" the charges by listing every possible violation and specification (Appendix B). The initial Charge I of Violation of the 63rd Article of War, Specification 1 accused Jackie of disrespect to Captain Wigginton with Specification 2 accusing him of disrespect to Captain Bear.

Charge II, Violation of the 64th Article of War, Specification 1 accused Jackie of willfully disobeying an order from Captain Bear to be seated and Charge III, Violation of the 95th Article of War, Specification 1 accused Jackie of vulgar language to a civilian, Milton R. Renegar. Specification 2 under the article accused Jackie of wrongful obscene language to civilian Elizabeth Poitevint, and Specification 3 charged wrongful use of "vile, obscene, and abusive language in a public place to wit the Central Bus Station."

After the proposed charges were prepared, they were reviewed by the Office of the Staff Judge Advocate. There is no record of staff deliberations, but it is likely they considered the following: The charges were obviously "stacked" to achieve maximum charges against the accused. Some of the witness statements were taken after midnight in the early morning hours of July 7, 1944, while others were taken later in the day. (Historical Perspective 11.) At that time, most of the witnesses were still angry at what had occurred, and some had openly vocalized their prejudices.

In the bigger picture, however, there were more important matters facing the entire army and country. The clouds of war hung over the participants— and many would soon be committed to battlefields around the world. Allied troops were moving off the Normandy beaches toward Paris, two million Soviet troops were closing on Warsaw, the few surviving Japanese were surrendering on Saipan, and American band leader Glenn Miller was preparing for his first concerts for GIs on the European mainland. How important was it that a black lieutenant had gotten angry over his treatment by a white civilian bus driver, an MP captain, and the Officer of the Day?

• 13 •

The Statements

$\mathcal{I}$n an Army camp, someone is always responsible for all activities occurring between the end of the duty day and reveille the next morning. That person is Officer of the Day (OD) who is generally selected through roster rotations at the facility's headquarters. In addition to the headquarters' OD, each battalion and larger unit also has an Officer of the Day rotating from their own rosters. On the July night of the bus incident, Capt. Peelor L. Wigginton (often misspelled as Wiggington)—the Camp Laundry Officer—had drawn the extra duty of Camp Hood OD. His primary assignment in charge of a laundry, unfortunately, was not a military occupational specialty highly respected by combat arms branches, yet another complicating factor in the multifaceted situation.

Capt. Wigginton's statement (Appendix C) is by far the most lengthy of all of the witnesses' testimonies. As the Camp Officer of the Day, he was the first officer to arrive at the MP station when the confrontation started. He immediately began questioning the participants, and then he called Capt. Bear to request that he come to assist.

Wigginton did an adequate job of questioning Robinson and other witnesses. In his statement, he reported that Robinson told him, "that he had boarded the camp shuttle outside the colored officers club, and saw a colored girl, a Mrs. Jones, wife of an officer on this post, sitting about half-way down the isle [sic] of the bus; he sat down with her and before arriving at the next stop the bus driver asked him to move to the rear of the bus. Lt. Robinson then told the bus driver that he was the equal of anyone, and would not move; the bus driver then told the Lt. that if he did not move he would make plenty trouble for him when they arrived at the Central Bus Station." At the bus station, according to Wigginton's statement, the driver asked the dispatcher to

55

call the MPs, at which point Robinson admitted he said, "If you don't quit fuckin' with me I'll cause you plenty of trouble."

Wigginton also noted that Robinson had refused to provide his name to the bus driver whom he had called a "damn civilian." Wigginton stated that Robinson said that PFC Ben W. Mucklerath and several others, who had gathered at the Bus Station, had called him a nigger and that a white lady threatened to report him to the MPs because of his language. Mucklerath said that he had not called Robinson a nigger and that he had heard the Lieutenant say to the white lady, "I don't care if you do report me, and if you don't quit fuckin' with me you'll get in trouble." Robinson then interrupted Mucklerath saying, "Captain, private, you, or any general calls me a nigger, and I'll break him into [sic]."

Wigginton's statement continued, "While he was talking to me and while I was talking to him, Lt. Robinson was leaning on the high desk in the interior of the Sgt. of the Guard Room, in a very disrespectful manner. His attitude in general was very insolent, disrespectful, and smart-elec [sic], and certainly his actions were unbecoming to an officer and a gentleman, particularly in the presence of the enlisted men together with other officers."

According to the Camp OD, Robinson continued to interrupt after Capt. Bear arrived. "Captain Bear finally ordered the Lt. to stay in the outer room of the Guard Room and wait until he was called. He directly disobeyed this order and returned to the swinging door between the two rooms and attempted to start another argument with Captain Bear. Captain Bear ordered him back to the room and told him to sit down in a chair and wait until he was called. Lt. Robinson walked back into the room but did not stay there."

Wigginton's statement concluded, "From time to time, Captain Bear, who was conducting the investigation, asked Lt. Robinson material questions which covered the issue. Lt. Robinson's attitude during this time was very disrespectful, and insolent. At one time during the questioning Captain Bear asked the Lt. about when and where he used profane language in the presence of ladies, and the Lt. stated that the only time he used profane language was when he told the bus driver to 'stop 'fuckin' with me.'"

It is noteworthy that while Wigginton displayed no overt signs of racism, he did refer to Mrs. Jones as a "colored girl" in his statement. In the 1940s, the words "colored" and "Negro" were acceptable references to African Americans. Calling a black adult woman a "girl" or a black adult male a "boy," however, were not acceptable and showed the bigotry of the speaker. Also, both the whites and blacks involved in the incident should not be judged by today's standards. In the 1940s, African Americans—civilians and soldiers alike—lived in a segregated society where a vast number of whites continued to believe that blacks were inferior. Prejudices and racism still prevailed, but having a white man, especially an enlisted soldier, calling a black officer a nigger was not at all acceptable even then.

Captain Gerald M. Bear, Camp Hood Assistant Provost Marshal, arrived at the MP Guard Room shortly before midnight and asked Wigginton for a briefing on what had occurred. In his statement (Appendix D), he said, "Lt. Robinson kept continually interrupting Captain Wigginton and myself and kept coming to the Guard House door-gate. I cautioned and requested Lt. Robinson on several occasions to remain at ease and remain in the receiving room that I would talk to him later. In an effort to try to be facetious, Lt. Robinson bowed with several sloppy salutes, repeating several times, 'OK, sir, OK, sir,' on each occasion. I then gave Lt. Robinson another direct order to remain in the receiving room and be seated on a chair, on the far side of the receiving room."

Bear concluded, "Lt. Robinson's attitude in general was disrespectful and impertinent to his superior officers, and very unbecoming to an officer in the presence of enlisted men."

The most important part of Bear's statement is that he ordered Robinson "on several occasions to remain at ease." This would become a critical part of the future trial.

The bus driver, Mr. Milton N. Renegar, a local civilian, in his statement given to Captain Bear on July 8 (Appendix E) said that at the 172nd Street Bus Stop "some white ladies, maybe a soldier or so, and a colored girl and a colored Second Lieutenant got on the bus. The colored girl and the colored Lt., whom I later learned to be 2nd Lt. Jack R. Robinson of the 761st Tank Battalion, sat down together about middle ways of the bus. On that particular run I have quite a few of the white ladies who work in the PXs and ride the bus at that hour almost every night. I did not say anything to the colored Lt. when he first sat down, until I got around to bus stop #18, and then I asked him, I said, 'Lt., if you don't mind, I have got several ladies to pick up at the stop and will have a load of them before I get back to the Central Bus Station, and would like for you to move back to the rear of the bus if you don't mind.' When I asked him to move to the rear he just sat there, and I asked him to move back there the second time. When I asked him the second time he started cursing and the first thing he said was, 'I'm not going to move a God damned bit.' I told him that I had a load of ladies to pick up and that I was sure they wouldn't want to ride mixed up like that, and told him I'd rather he would either move back to the rear or get off the bus, one of the two. He kept on cursing and saying that he wasn't going to get back, and I told him that he could either get back or he'd be sorry of it when I got to the Bus Station, or words to that effect."

On arrival at the Central Bus Station, Renegar stated, he told the dispatcher to call the MPs because everyone on the bus was angry. He said, "I had asked the Lt. in a nice way to move and he had refused. One of the ladies who was riding said, 'I don't mind waiting on them all day, but when I get on the bus at night to go home, I'm not about to ride all mixed up with them." The "them" is an obvious reference to blacks.

The bus driver said that, after he told the dispatcher to call the MPs, "this White lady asked me if I was going to report the Lieutenant and I told her 'yes', and she said, 'well if you don't I am.'" At that time the colored Lieutenant said to the lady, "you better quit fuckin' with me." Renegar then claimed Robinson called him a "son-of-a-bitch" but continued that Robinson had actually said to an MP, "I don't know why that son-of-a-bitch wanted to give me all this trouble." Renegar also seemed angry that Robinson had continued to talk and curse after he had told him to "hush." He concluded, "The only time I heard the colored girl who was with him say anything was when he started to leave with the MP's and she just asked him what the trouble was."

In many later accounts, including Jackie himself in his autobiography, the possibility that Renegar thought that Robinson had sat in the middle of the bus beside a white woman are incorrect. Although Mrs. Jones had a light complexion, Renegar refers to her three times as a "colored girl" as opposed to the "white ladies" who worked in the PXs in his statement.

Pfc. Ben W. Mucklerath, Company D, 90th Regiment, IRTC, was at the station waiting for a bus back to his barracks when he witnessed the initial confrontation incident. In his statement (Appendix F) he said, "I was sitting down on a seat along side of the Bus Station building. I saw a white lady step off the bus and start into the bus station. A colored Lt. also got off the bus and was directing obscene language at her, he said, 'You better quit fuckin' with me.' That's all I heard him say at that time. He said this in the presence of a large number of ladies and children, and it was plainly heard by those present. I then heard the white lady say to the colored Lt. whom I later learned to be 2nd Lt. Jack R. Robinson, 'I'm going to report you,' and the Lt. repeated a second time, what he had just said to her."

Mucklerath seemed to be anxious to become a part of and to escalate the incident because the next thing he did was call the MP headquarters. "When I went outside again the MP patrol car had already arrived. I asked the driver of the patrol car if he had a colored Lt., and the Lt. turned to me and said, 'You better quit fuckin' with me.' He also said to the MP driver, 'There's no God-damned son-of-a-bitch going to tell me where to sit.'"

He continued with his statement, saying that he had heard Robinson "using some very obscene and vulgar language; I distinctly heard him say 'son-of-a-bitch.' . . . His conduct, generally, was very unbecoming to an officer and a gentleman." He added that when he arrived at the MP Station, ". . . the colored Lt. turned to me and said, 'If I ever see you again, I'll break you in two.'"

In his statement, Mucklerath then said, ". . . this colored Lt. interrupted me two times and had to be called down by Captain Wigginton. I was interrupted when he threatened me, and he accused me of calling him a damn nigger."

At the conclusion of Mucklerath's statement, he again claimed, "I had not at any time called the Lt. a nigger."

Mucklerath comes across as very angry in his statement. He is upset that a "colored lieutenant" would use profanity around a "white lady." Mucklerath also appears to be enjoying his situation as an enlisted man being able to make accusations against an officer, particularly a black officer. Although Mucklerath signed the statement as being in his own words, it was recorded by Capt. Bear's stenographer who may very well have embellished Mucklerath's report, such as "His conduct was very unbecoming to an officer and a gentleman."

The dispatcher for the Southwestern Bus Company, Mr. Bevlia B. Younger, stated (Appendix G) that he called the MPs at the request of the bus driver and then he heard "a colored Lieutenant whom I later learned to be 2nd Lt. Jack R. Robinson, in a loud and boisterous voice make the remark, 'what is the matter with you fuckin' people around here, you can't fuck me in this manner.'"

When the MPs arrived, Younger stated, he told them, ". . . the trouble was with a nigger Lt., the nigger Lt., hearing the remark, resented being called so—and informed Cpl. Elwood that, 'no God-damned sorry son-of-a-bitch could call him a nigger and get away with it.'"

Younger's statement is the most openly racist of all the witnesses in that he seems to have no problem with calling Robinson a nigger. He also demands that "something be done about the colored lieutenant," and that the "feeling was very high" and there "was a great deal of nervous tension shown among the ladies and white soldiers present."

Mrs. Elizabeth Poitevint stated (Appendix H) that she got on the bus at Stop #23 after working at PX #10 and saw a colored girl sitting about "middle ways of the bus" and that a colored second lieutenant got on and sat beside her. At the next stop, she continued, ". . . some white women, most of them with their babies, got on the bus. The driver came back to the colored Lt. and said, 'Lieutenant, will you move to the back of the bus so these people can sit down?' The colored Lt. said, 'I certainly will not. I paid my fare and I don't intend to move out of this seat.'"

Poitevint stated that the driver and the lieutenant continued to argue on the bus and again when they reached the Central Station. At the station, she testified, she said to the driver, "If you want any witnesses as to what he has done to you, you can call on me, because I've heard everything he has said. Then the Lt. turned to me and said, 'Listen here you damned old woman, you have nothing to say about what's going on. I didn't want to get into this, they drafted me into this, and my money is just as good as a white man's.' And I told him, I said, 'Well, listen buddy, you got to know where you should sit on the bus.'"

Mrs. Poitevint, who had to serve black soldiers in her PX job, then stated, "I had to wait on them during the day, but I didn't have to sit with them on the bus." She then continued to note the argument saying the bus driver was very polite and the colored lieutenant hateful, profane, and threatening. She added, "I am sure that no one called him a nigger because I was there all the time."

The statement by Mrs. Poitevint also records comments of the driver and Robinson not included or supported in other statements. Her personal feelings about blacks are apparent in her words about having to wait on them in the day "but I didn't have to sit with them on the bus."

Mrs. Ruby Johnson, another PX #10 employee, added little new about the incident in her statement (Appendix I). She did state, "At that time the bus driver asked the colored lieutenant if he would move to the back of the bus, the Lt. said, 'No, I'm going to sit here, I'm not going to move to the back of the bus.'" Mrs. Johnson makes no mention of Jackie using profanity.

Cpl. George A. Elwood (Appendix J) was the driver for MP Motor Patrol 6 when he was sent to the Central Bus Station "to investigate a disturbance caused by a colored lieutenant." He stated that on his arrival, the Dispatcher, Mr. Younger, came over and told him that a colored Lieutenant had been giving a lot of trouble and using a lot of profane and vulgar language. He added, "Then the Lt. came over to the patrol car and said that he was tired of the 'God-dammed sons-of-bitches trying to push me around,' and said that, 'by God he wasn't going to stand for it anymore.'"

Elwood continued, ". . . a white soldier whom I learned to be Pfc Mucklerath, came over to the pick-up and asked me if I got that nigger lieutenant. Right then the lieutenant said, 'Look here, you son-of-a-bitch, don't you call me no nigger. I'm an officer and God damn you, you better address me as one.'"

At the MP station, Elwood stated, ". . . later when I return to the Guard Room, Captain Wigginton, the Camp OD, was trying to explain the situation to Captain Bear and the colored Lt. interfered and he wouldn't be quiet, and I distinctly heard Captain Bear tell the Lt. to be at ease and wait outside the Sergeant's of the Guard Room. This Lt. interrupted continually and when Captain Bear would speak to him he would bow from the hips and give him a very sloppy salute, and had sort of a smart smile on his face all the time, and he said, 'OK, sir,' two or three times, and this was very disrespectful considering his manner. Finally, Captain Bear told him to go sit down on a chair in the corner back away from him and had Sgt Painter stay out there and see that he stayed down in the chair. The colored Lt. had a smart attitude and was very disrespectful toward the officers and the MP's present."

Sgt. William L. Painter, as the MP Sergeant of the Guard, had dispatched Elwood to the Central Bus Station. Painter stated (Appendix K) that, after they arrived at the MP Station, he questioned Mucklerath and Robinson. He reported, "I asked them what the trouble was and Pfc. Mucklerath started to tell me what it was all about, and Lt. Robinson interrupted him and told him, 'if I ever see you again I'll break you in two.' Then the soldier, Pfc. Mucklerath, told me he wanted that to be a matter of record and that he wanted me to get the name of all the witnesses who heard Lt. Robinson threaten his life. . . ."

Painter further stated, "Pfc. Mucklerath did not at any time, in my presence, call the Lieutenant a nigger."

About Robinson, he stated "His attitude, generally, was very insulant and disrespectful toward Captain Wigginton and the MP's present. Captain Bear, Assistant Provost Marshal, arrived and asked what the trouble was, and Captain Wigginton started to tell him and the Lt. interrupted Captain Wigginton. Captain Bear asked the Lt. to be at ease and step away from the Guard Room door and not interrupt them. Lieutenant Robinson would salute Captain Bear in a bowed manner, and exaggerate the salute as though he were making fun of Captain Bear. His attitude was very smart-alec [sic], and he paid no attention to Captain Bear and Captain Wigginton's orders and continually interrupted them. Captain Bear told Lt. Robinson to stay in the outer office of the Guard Room, and instead Lt. Robinson went outside of the guard room and talked to the driver of a jeep belonging to the OD, 761st Tank Battalion. I witnessed Lt. Robinson refuse to obey the direct orders of Captain Bear and Captain Wiggington, to be quiet and to stay in the outer office of the Guard Room."

The statement (Appendix L) of the MP Corporal of the Guard, Eugene J. Henrie, mirrors that of Sgt. Painter and adds little. He did state, "I did not at any time hear Pfc Mucklerath say anything disrespectful to the Lt. nor call him a nigger."

Acting Cpl. Elmer S. Feris, an MP at the station, overheard the conversations with Mucklerath and Robinson. His statement (Appendix M) supports those of Painter and Henrie.

Captain Edward L. Hamilton, the MP duty officer, stated (Appendix N) that he was at the station with the witnesses and another officer, 1st Lt. George Cribari. He stated, "While making his statement Lt. Robinson was very disrespectful and discourteous to Capt. Bear in his attempts to be facetious. During his statement, while referring to a Pfc calling him a 'nigger,' Lt. Robinson turned to Captain Wigginton and stated, 'If you, Captain,' and pointed to me and Lt. Criberi, 'or you, or you, should call me a nigger, I would break you in two.'" He went ahead to state that any General or anyone else who called him a nigger, he would break them in two. This threat was made in the presence of four officers, one enlisted man, Sgt. Howard C. Hyatt, MP, and Miss Wilson, stenographer. This was very unbecoming, and his manner of conversation was very unbecoming to an Officer of the United States Army."

First Lieutenant George Cribari, a Medical Corps officer, was apparently just visiting Hamilton at the MP Station and had no role in the official proceedings. In his statement (Appendix O) that is typed below that of Hamilton's, Cribari said, "I have read the above statement of Captain Edward L. Hamilton, and any statement I could make would be identical in substance."

The statement of Pvt. Walter H. Plotkin (Appendix P) mirrors that of his fellow MPs at the station. In fact, it is so similar that it appears to be rehearsed, or perhaps he listened in to the others giving their statements and parroted their words.

Pvt. Lester G. Phillips, a soldier in the Student Regiment who accompanied the MPs to their station from the bus facility, also said in his statement (Appendix Q) that Robinson had cussed and "used vulgar language in the presence of a large number of ladies." Phillips also felt that it was necessary to include, "I did not hear anyone call this colored Lieutenant a nigger, and did not hear anyone say anything at all to him."

• *14* •

The Investigation

$\mathcal{S}$omewhere in the review of the charges and statements, the Camp Hood Staff Judge Advocate determined that the original charges against Robinson were not only stacked but also that some of the specifications would be difficult to prove. Getting a conviction of an officer, by his fellow officers, for using "vulgar, obscene, and abusive" language to a civilian bus driver in the presence of "ladies" as being "conduct unbecoming an officer and gentleman" would be all but impossible—especially considering that evidence existed showing that Robinson had been called a "nigger" on several occasions. Cuss words were no strangers to anyone on an army camp—male or female—given that famed army leaders such as Lt. Gen. George Patton and other senior leaders were known for their "salty" language.

Apparently, the Judge Advocate Office also determined that disrespect to Capt. Wigginton, if displayed, was a result of the interaction between Robinson and Bear. This left only two charges (Appendix R): disrespect toward Capt. Bear and failure to follow a lawful order from Capt. Bear. While the reduction in the number of charges and specifications might appear to benefit Robinson, the emphasis downplayed the cause of the incident, that is, of Jackie's being told to go to the back of the bus and of his being called "nigger."

What had begun as a confrontation between a black officer and a white civilian bus driver who told him to go to the back of the bus had now become an official matter of a black officer being disrespectful toward and not following the orders of a white superior officer. Although Capt. Bear, with the camp's Judge Advocate Office's assistance, had prepared the original charges, only Robinson's commander could formally recommend a General Court-Martial. According to nearly every account, including a much later interview with his widow, Col. Bates refused to sign the charge sheet. Camp Hood

63

officials countered by transferring Jackie to the 758th Tank Battalion, whose commander readily signed the charges.

This version of events makes for a good story, but there is no evidence to support the claim. It is more likely that Jackie was transferred to the 758th because the 761st was already in the process of moving to East Coast ports for deployment to the European Theater. With Jackie, still on limited duty from his ankle injury and pending court-martial, the transfer would have been more administrative than punitive or based on racial prejudices. The question of the transfer is further confused by the fact that Col. Bates remained behind at Camp Hood to testify at Jackie's trial before joining his battalion on its way to Europe.

Jackie returned from his leave in California to find that court-martial proceedings were progressing. Correspondence from the 5th Armored Group, Camp Hood, and the XXIII Corps on July 10 and 14 stated, "While the officer concerned was a member of the 761st Tank Bn. at the time the alleged offense was committed, this Headquarters is informed he has been reassigned to the 758th Tank Bn., 5th Armored Group."

Camp Hood officials were also well aware that they had on their hands a situation that might bring negative national attention. On July 17, only ten days after the incident and in the midst of the investigation, Col. E. A. Kimball, commanding officer of the 5th Armored Group, made a telephone call to Col. Walter L. Buie, the chief of staff of the XXIII Corps. Upon the completion of the call, Buie recorded a typed summary (Appendix S) of their conversation. Such a summary, or Memorandum for the Record, is extremely unusual between staff officers and commanders. Its primary purpose is for the person making the summary to protect himself in possible future investigations.

Buie wrote that Kimball said, "I have a case here involving a colored officer who got in trouble in connection with a bus. . . . This is very serious case, and it is full of dynamite. It requires delicate handling."

According to the memo, Kimball had continued by saying that an "Inspector" (someone from the Officer of the Inspector General) should be brought in to investigate. Buie had responded that none was available and asked if Kimball's headquarters could investigate it on their own.

The memo shows that Kimball responded in the affirmative but added a statement that contained the status of racial relations at Camp Hood at the time. According to Buie's summary, Kimball said, "The bus station situation here is not good, and I am afraid that any officer in charge of troops at this Post might be prejudiced."

There were likely many similar conversations to those of Buie and Kimball at various levels at Camp Hood and at XXIII headquarters. None, however, were recorded or otherwise have survived the passage of time.

Courts-martial proceedings are generally viewed by those outside the military as being kangaroo courts with little protection or rights for the accused. Jackie reinforced this perspective in his book when he wrote, "Anyone who knows about the Army court martial system can tell you it's loaded mostly in favor of those bringing charges."

Actually, that conclusion is not factual. Courts-martial of the period were indeed "loaded," not at the trial itself but rather through a meticulous administrative, investigative, and review process before accusations ever went to trial. A pre-trial investigation procedure, similar to a civilian Grand Jury, occurred before charges could be advanced. There were also strict rules regarding "command influence" to prevent commanders from making verbal or written comments on their thoughts on the guilt of the accused. Guilty verdicts and punishments were reviewed by the chain of command in what would compare to an appeal process today.

In the Robinson case, on July 17 an initial Charge Sheet was prepared listing Jackie as the accused and thirteen witnesses as having made attached sworn statements for the prosecution. No witnesses were listed for the defense. On the same date—July 17—Jackie was placed under arrest at McCloskey General Hospital. Later stories would exaggerate this part of the process as his being placed in arm and leg chains and taken to a jail cell. In reality, as a commissioned officer, his arrest merely meant that he was restricted to the hospital grounds—no locks, no chains, no bars on doors. He was also free to travel with no escort from the hospital to Camp Hood as a part of the investigation.

Jackie had not been standing idly by even before his arrest. On July 16, he handwrote a letter on McCloskey General Hospital stationary (Appendix T) to Truman Gibson, now an assistant to the Secretary of War, asking for advice and help. Still being the "good soldier," Robinson wrote, "I don't want any unfavorable publicity for myself or the Army but I believe in fair play." Later in his letter he repeated, "I don't mind trouble but I do believe in fair play and justice."

Gibson forwarded the letter within the War Department with the notation, "This man is the well known athlete. He will write you."

Robinson also wrote to the NAACP summarizing his situation and requesting legal assistance. The NAACP responded that they would be unable to help because of the large number of similar requests they had received. A fellow black officer, writing anonymously to the National Association for the Advancement of Colored People (NAACP) said that they should investigate the situation to reveal ". . . just how rotten the whole business is" and added that the situation was ". . . a typical effort to intimidate Negro officers and enlisted men."

Other black officers wrote to African American newspapers, including the *Chicago Defender* and the *Pittsburgh Courier,* seeking publicity of the pending trial. Still others wrote to their congressmen and senators asking them to investigate.

None of these efforts had any influence on the pending court-martial. Military justice, unlike its civilian counterpart, moves quickly and decisively. Most of the responses to Jackie's requests for assistance arrived after the trial ended, resulting in the army's merely responding with the court-martial verdict and with no other details. The black newspapers, despite their circulation and influence, were weekly rather than dailies, and the trial concluded before they could mount any amount of significant coverage.

Despite requesting legal support from outside sources, Robinson accepted the Defense Council, 2nd Lt. William A. Cline, that the Army appointed to him. Cline, born in 1912, about 190 miles southeast of Camp Hood in Wharton, Texas, attended Texas College of Mines, Columbia University, and the University of Texas at Austin before graduating from the Cumberland University Law School in Tennessee. He then joined his father's law practice in Wharton where he mostly practiced contract and administrative law before the war. Although too old for the draft, Cline volunteered for the army shortly after Pearl Harbor. Instead of being trained as a staff judge advocate, he earned a commission at the Field Artillery Officers Candidate School. Assigned to Camp Hood in a tank destroyer battalion scheduled for deployment to North Africa, the unit converted to an amphibious tank battalion for the invasion of Sicily after the fighting in Africa ceased. During the transition, XXIII Corps detailed Cline to court-martial duty.

He and Jackie apparently developed a relationship in the short time before the trial. In a later interview, Cline recalled that, when he first learned of his appointment as defense counsel, he went over to Jackie's quarters to discuss the case. According to Cline, he had a lengthy visit but at the time Jackie still thought the NAACP was going to send legal help. Cline remembered telling Jackie that outside assistance was a good idea because, he said, "I came from just about as far South as you can get."

In one visit with Jackie, Cline took along his son who was a huge football fan and wanted to meet the UCLA hero. Cline also said that Jackie talked a lot about his mother and Southern California.

In his biography, Jackie wrote, "My first break was that the legal officer (Cline) assigned to defend me was a Southerner who had the decency to admit to me that he didn't think he could be objective. He recommended a young Michigan officer who did a great job."

Jackie likely made the decision to seek additional military assistance after Cline's admission and when it became apparent that the NAACP was not going to provide legal representation and he did not have sufficient financial means to hire a civilian attorney.

That young Michigan lawyer Cline recommended as additional counsel was 1st Lt. Robert H. Johnson. Although Johnson was a University of Michigan Law School graduate, he was serving as a white infantry officer in the segregated 679th Tank Destroyer Battalion. Otherwise, little is known about him at the time except through Jackie's comments in his autobiography and through the trial records where he took a major part in examining and cross-examining witnesses.

Camp Hood officials referred the charges against Robinson and statements from the witnesses to Major Henry S. Daugherty of the 5th Armored Group, then serving as the Article 70 of the Articles of War investigating officer. While his responsibilities resembling those of a civilian grand jury—that is, to determine if sufficient evidence existed to refer the case to court-martial by applying the binary system of yes or no to reach the ultimate decision—Daugherty had the primary role of taking charge of the witnesses and their statements. In reviewing the documents he received, Major Daugherty realized that a statement from an important witness was missing. Mrs. Virginia Jones, the woman Robinson had sat with on the bus, had not gone to the MP Station, and, thus, she had made no statement. On July 19, Daugherty directed Capt. Bear to secure Mrs. Jones's story of the incident. In his statement of that same date (Appendix U), Bear said, "Attempts had been made previously to obtain the name of the person in order that we could obtain a statement from her regarding the incident. Shortly after learning her name I proceeded to Belton, Texas (20 miles to the east), and contacted Mrs. Virginia Jones."

According to Bear, "She informed me that she had received a call from Lt. Robinson, and that she expected him to come along on the bus to Belton to see her. She was expecting him to arrive when I talked with her. She told me that Lt. Robinson had told her that he wanted to talk to her before she went before the investigating officer. Mrs. Jones further stated that she wanted to talk to Lt. Robinson before making a statement to anyone. She refused at that time to make a statement before discussing it with Lt. Robinson."

Apparently, Mrs. Jones did talk with Robinson because later in the day she gave her statement (Appendix V) to Bear. For the record, she said, "I got on the bus first and sat down, and Lt. Robinson got on and came and sat beside me. I sat in the fourth seat from the rear of the bus, which I have always considered the rear of the bus. The bus driver looked back at us, and then asked Lt. Robinson to move. Lt. Robinson told the bus driver to go on and drive the bus. The bus driver stopped the bus, came back and balled his fist and said, 'Will you move back?' Lt. Robinson said, 'I'm not moving,' so the bus driver stood there and glared a minute and said, 'Well, just sit there until we get down to the Bus Station.' We got to the Bus Station and Lt. Robinson and I were the last two to leave the bus. The bus driver detained Lt. Robinson and demanded to see his pass. Lt. Robinson said, 'My pass?', and the bus driver said, 'Yes, I want to see your pass.' Lt. Robinson asked him what did he mean wanting to see his pass, and we then got off the bus. A woman walked up to Lt. Robinson and shook her finger in his face and said, 'I'm going to report you because you had a right [sic] to move when he asked you to.' She stood there and argued with Lt. Robinson awhile, and I don't remember what all was said. Lt. Robinson did not say anything at first and then he said, 'Go on and leave me alone.' So she walked into the bus station, and about that time the crowd around the bus driver and Lt. Robinson thinned out, and the bus driver said something to the Lt. which I did not hear."

Mrs. Jones concluded, "I did not hear him say anything vile nor vulgar at any time, nor he did not raise his voice."

Over the next three days, Daugherty conducted the Pre-trial Investigation. In his report dated July 20, 1944, Daugherty wrote that he had investigated the charges dated July 17 against Lt. Robinson "in accordance with the provisions of Article of War 70." Preprinted provisions of the form stated, "I informed the accused of the nature of the charges alleged against him; of the names of the accuser and all witnesses, so far as known to me; of the fact that the charges were about to be investigated; of his right to cross-examine all available witnesses against him and to present anything he may desire in his own behalf, either in defense or mitigation; of his right to have the investigating officer examine available witnesses requested by him; and that it was not necessary for him to make any statement with reference to the charges against him, but that if he did not make one it might be used against him."

The report then stated, "In the presence of the accused, I have examined all available witnesses and documentary evidence under direct and cross examination testimony." Daugherty then listed the thirteen witnesses who had been examined, followed by three who were not called to testify because Jackie had made it known that he did not desire to cross-examine them. The original statements of all the witnesses were attached to the cover sheet.

In paragraph 8 of his report Daugherty stated, "Trial by General Court Martial is accordingly recommended."

In his final paragraph, Daugherty wrote, "In arriving at my conclusion, I have considered not only the nature of the offenses and the evidence in this case, I have likewise considered the age of the accused, his military service, the necessity for preserving the manpower of the Nation in the present emergency, of salvaging all possible military material, and the established policy of the War Department that trial by general court-martial will be resorted to only when the charges can be disposed of in no other manner consistent with military discipline."

Daugherty did not record or make notes on his questioning of the witnesses as it was not required under the provisions of Article of War 70. At the subsequent trial Jackie testified that several of the witnesses gave somewhat different accounts to Daugherty than to Capt. Bear.

On July 20, Daughtery completed his report and forwarded it to the headquarters of the 5th Armored Group commander, Col. E. A. Kimball. Despite being the one who had said in his telephone conversation on July 17, that he was afraid "that any officer in charge of troops at this Post might be prejudiced," Kimball indorsed the report on July 24 by writing "trial by General Court Martial recommended." He forwarded the case to the Commanding General, XXIII Corps.

The Judge Advocate of XXIII Corps, Lt. Col. Richard E. Kyle, reviewed the documents and forwarded them to the Commanding General of XXIII Corps on July 25. His report stated that he had "carefully examined the charges and all accompanying papers" against 2nd Lt. Robinson and found "the charges are appropriate to the evidence." He then wrote, "I recommend trial by general court martial."

Kyle then added a paragraph of "Instructions to the Trial Judge Advocate, military language for prosecutor." It said, "Trial will be expedited, but under current policy, accused will not be brought to trial within five days after service of charges without his consent, unless military necessity requires such action."

This was not a "rush to judgment" but rather a reflection of the times. The war was reaching its peak in Europe and in the Pacific, and the Army needed the trial to take place before witnesses and court personnel were transferred from Camp Hood.

• 15 •

The Court-Martial

$\mathcal{A}$t 1:45 p.m. on August 2, 1944, 2nd Lt. Jack R. Robinson appeared before a General Court-Martial at North Camp Hood, Texas. The setting was a newly-built pine administrative building identical to many at Camp Hood and to dozens at other military installations across the United States. Windows of the building were open and a few fans stirred the air, but there was no cooling the 103-degree temperature, which was the high temperature reached in the month of August in Central Texas.

The legal rationales for the charges against Jackie were simple. The army can efficiently and effectively operate only when it maintains a high degree of discipline and military order. Disrespect by a subordinate to a superior officer, or the failure to follow a lawful order by a superior officer can erode the leadership and affect the performance of an entire unit.

The charges against Jackie included both disrespect for and failure to follow orders from a superior officer. To convict Robinson of disrespect toward a superior officer, the Army had to have evidence to meet the following criteria—that such behavior or language had been directed toward that officer; that the officer toward whom the acts, omissions, or words were directed was the superior commissioned officer of the accused; that the accused then knew that the commissioned officer toward whom the acts, omissions, or words were directed was the accused's superior commissioned officer; and that, under the circumstances, the behavior or language was disrespectful to that commissioned officer.

To convict Robinson of failing to obey a lawful order required the following—that a member of the armed forces issued a certain lawful order; that the accused had knowledge of the order; that the accused had a duty to obey the order; and that the accused failed to obey the order.

While the outcome of a court-martial can and usually is—consequential, for sure, some accounts of Jackie's trial reported that he could receive the death penalty for failing to obey a lawful order if convicted. That was far from factual because that threat of death applied only to disobedience in combat situations. It was certainly not a consideration in this case. Nevertheless, Jackie faced serious punishment if convicted—possibly the forfeiture of all pay and allowances, and confinement for one or two years. As an officer, he could be dismissed from the service—the officer equivalent of a dishonorable discharge.

On that hot August afternoon, the court consisted of nine officers, appointed by Special Orders Number 120 and subsequent amendments from headquarters, XXIII Corps dated June 10 "for the trial of such persons as may be properly brought before it." The orders, as written, stood in effect for an indefinite period, generally sixty to ninety days.

Colonel Louis J. Compton acted as the president of the court-martial board while Major John H. Shippey served as its "Law Member," meaning the attorney who could advise Compton and the board on legal questions. With the exception of Shippey, who served at the XXIII Corps Headquarters, all the board members were assigned to field artillery or tank destroyer units at Camp Hood. In other words, eight of the board members were Robinson's combat branch peers.

The court-martial orders also named the other participants in the proceedings. First were the Trial Judge Advocate, or Prosecutor, 2nd Lt. Milton Gordon and his assistant 2nd Lt. Knowles M. Tucker. Next named were the Defense Council, and his assistant 1st Lt. Joseph C. Hutcheson. Hutcheson, however, had been excused earlier by the appointing authority because of other pressing duties. This was not a disadvantage to the defense because Robinson had already been working with additional counsel Lt. Johnson.

The Record of Trial of the General Court-Martial said, "The accused stated he desired to be defended by regularly appointed defense counsel (Cline), assisted by 1st Lt. Robert H. Johnson, 679th Tank Destroyer Battalion, as his individual counsel."

The court officers sat behind a long table at the front of the room facing the defense on their right and prosecution to their left. Col. Compton, as president of the board, sat in the center with the other officers sitting on either side of him decreasing in alternating in rank until the most junior officers were at the table ends. Everyone except Jackie was familiar with the proceedings as each had served on two or three courts-martial per week since appointment.

Some reports on the court-martial mention that at least one of the Court Members was "a southerner" but offer no proof. Major Mowder graduated from Jackie's alma mater of UCLA. Little else is known about the composition of the board other than their names, ranks, and units. From unit photographs of the era it can be confirmed that Captains Carr and Campbell were African Americans.

When officially opened, the court-martial followed prescribed proceedings. (The entire Trial Transcript is at Appendix Y.) Second Lt. Gordon, as the Trial Judge Advocate, handled the initial introductory remarks from a pre-printed, fill-in-the-blank form entitled "Record of General Court Martial" as directed by Appendix 6 of the Manual for Court-Martial. The form included the Organization of the Court, both present and absent, the identification of Robinson as the accused and his request for counsel that included his appointed defense, Cline, assisted by Johnson. Gordon then went through a series of questions to ensure that members of the court were not aware of any person or thing that might be grounds for challenge from the board. Following all negative responses, Gordon stated for the record that he had no challenges of the board members.

Gordon then turned to Cline, the Defense Attorney, and informed him that he had "the right to challenge any member or members of the court for cause, or any one member, other than the law member, peremptorily." Cline responded that he had no challenges. Robinson then also had the opportunity to challenge any member, which he chose not to do.

The members of the court were then sworn and the charges against Jackie for disrespect to Capt. Bear and failure to follow a lawful order from Bear were read. An affidavit from Maj. Daugherty, swearing that he had investigated the original charges, was presented to the court followed by an indorsement from XXIII Corps, referring the charges to a General Court-Martial. The Court then called upon Jackie to plea to his charges, and he responded "Not Guilty" to each of the charges and specifications.

Gordon, not wishing to make an opening statement, then called 2nd Lt. Howard B. Campbell, 758th Tank Battalion, as his first witness. This was merely a procedural action to allow Campbell to positively identify Robinson as a member of this unit and to verify for the record that he, the accused, was present in the courtroom.

The prosecution next called its primary witness Capt. Gerald M. Bear. In response to the prosecutor's questions, Capt. Bear testified that Capt. Wigginton had asked that he take charge of the investigation when he arrived at the MP Station on the night of the incident. One of his first acts, he told the board, was to say to Lt. Robinson, "You go outside of the guard room, and wait out in the receiving room." According to Bear, Robinson went into the receiving room but then leaned back toward the guard room through a half-gate door separating the two. Bear described Robinson as being "in a slouching manner with his elbows on the gate" and continually interrupting while he and Wigginton were trying to talk. Bear stated that, each time of the several times that he told the lieutenant to get away from the door, Robinson bowed and said, "O.K. sir. O.K. sir." Bear related that, when saying this, the defendant had "kind of smirked or grimaced his face."

Bear then testified, "Finally, after that went on for some time, I told Sgt. Painter to place a chair on the far side of the room, and then I said, 'Lieutenant, you go over and sit down in that chair on the far side of the room and you remain sitting there until I call you, do you understand that,' and he said 'O.K. Sir, O.K. Sir, O.K. Sir.'"

When asked if this had been a direct order to Robinson, Bear responded in the affirmative. Bear then testified that, when he walked out of the building to arrange other witness statements, he found Robinson outside talking to the driver for the 761st Tank Battalion Officer of the Day. He continued, "I said to Lt. Robinson, 'Lieutenant, go back in that room and remain in that room, remain sitting, do you understand that;' and he reluctantly went back inside." Bear then went on to state that Robinson's way of walking and his speech tone were not proper and that he "continued to act in a contemptuous and disrespectful manner." Bear said, "In fact I had lost control of the lieutenant."

When asked for elaboration about his statement that he had lost control of Robinson, Bear responded that the lieutenant was argumentative while giving his statement, talked rapidly to the stenographer, and even resorted to "baby talk." He added that Robinson argued about being transported back to Temple in an MP vehicle until Captain Wigginton interrupted and said, "'Lieutenant, I have heard enough of this argument and your conversation, and you're manner, and if you do not go, I am going to lock you up for insubordination and disrespect to your superior officer.'"

In its cross-examination, the defense attempted to show that Robinson's interruptions while giving his statement were efforts to ensure the records were accurate. This was also an attempt to reveal Bear's anger and possible prejudice toward a black officer. When this tact mostly failed, the defense had Bear admit that he had only been an investigating officer at Camp Hood for less than a month. Bear countered this admission by stating that he had served in the same position for ten months previously in "the Alexandria area."

Having made little progress questioning Bear's credibility, the defense attempted to show that Bear's statements during the investigation differed from what he had just said on the stand. The defense established that, according to his statement made the night of the incident, he had told Robinson to "remain at ease and remain in the receiving room" rather than having given him a direct order to do so, as he had testified before the court.

Later in the cross-examination, the defense asked Bear if anything occurred after Robinson's statement had been typed "that made you angry or caused you to reprimand the accused?"

Both the Court President and the Law Member interrupted the proceedings to determine what the defense was trying to bring into the court. The defense counsel responded, "I am attempting to bring out whether or not there was an atmosphere there, the background of this whole case should be before the court, and I do understand that I am limited to what was brought out on direct examination."

When the Law Member said, "The witness may answer," the Defense asked of him, "Is it proper on cross examination to interrogate the witness as to his bias and prejudice? That is the purpose of my examination at this time."

At this point the Prosecution argued, "No bias or prejudice has been shown." The Law Officer disagreed and said, "Let the witness answer the question."

Bear answered, "I do not recall reprimanding him about his statement, or talking to him about it at all after it had been typed."

Unable to get the details of the incident at the bus station on the record at this time, the defense turned the examination of Bear back to the Prosecution. The Prosecutor's first re-direct was to "a question asked by Lt. Johnson." This reference to the additional counsel is important in the transcript because it is the only time the name of the defense counsel appears. All the other references to the defense are introduced by the letter Q, leaving no identification of which of the Defense Counsels posed the question. This statement by the Prosecutor indicates that Johnson performed the "heavy lifting" of cross-examination while Cline likely handled the later introduction of the character witnesses.

The Prosecutor in his re-direct established that Bear's instruction to Robinson "to go out and remain at ease" had been a direct order and that Jackie had responded, "O.K. Sir."

On his recross-examination the Defense attempted to show that Bear's order for Robinson to remain outside resulted in a long wait and this was not the proper treatment of a fellow officer.

A lengthy segment of testimony next focused on the type of "arrest" made before Robinson returned to McCloskey Hospital and how he was transported there. Bear stated that he put Robinson "in arrest in quarters" to be sure he returned to McCloskey and that Robinson was transported by an MP pick-up truck with two or three MP escorts because at the late hour the buses had ceased to run.

The Defense then asked Bear if it were true that he answered "No" when asked the next day if Robinson was supposed to "be in arrest in quarters." The Law Member sustained an objection by the Prosecution that it was immaterial.

Bear stepped down and the Prosecutor called Capt. Peelor L. Wigginton who gave a lengthy statement that closely mirrored that of Capt. Bear—to the point that it appeared to have been rehearsed. The quartermaster officer continued until the defense halted Wigginton with an objection that the witness was reaching a conclusion when he said about Robinson, "I did not think he acted at all like an officer should do."

After the Law Officer replied, "Let's skip the opinion," he himself proceeded to ask questions about Jackie's behavior. Wigginton's testimony again closely resembled Bear's, including that Robinson had been ordered to remain in a chair in the outer room only to go outside the MP Station.

The Defense opened its cross-examination by asking why Robinson's statement had been the last to be taken. After the Law Member overruled an objection by a member of the court, Wigginton simply answered "No." Wigginton then denied that his testimony in court differed from that in his questioning by Maj. Daugherty and confirmed that at no time had he placed the defendant under arrest. The Defense then asked multiple questions about the reports that he (Wigginton), Bear, and the stenographer had become angry with Robinson when he asked to have his statement corrected.

When the Law Member said he did not see the purpose of the cross-examination, the Defense responded, "I am trying to determine the bias and prejudice of the witnesses on this basis."

With these words, the Defense had brought up "the elephant in the courtroom." Was this court-martial more about the color of the defendant's skin than about his conduct at the MP Station?

The Prosecutor responded, "I object to bringing any foreign matter into this case on any such basis."

Apparently, the Law Member had no desire for the trial to turn in that direction and ruled by saying, "What transpired as between this witness and the legal stenographer and in the absence of the accused, is not material and is not proper cross-examination."

With the failure to introduce the question of racial bigotry and bias, the Defense turned the witness back to the Prosecution who asked several questions about conversations between him and Bear. When Wigginton answered that he was merely briefing the MP captain on what had occurred before his arrival, the prosecution rested their case.

The defendants in a court-martial, as well as in a civilian court, are not required to testify, and it is generally advisable that they do not do so. If the defendant in court-martial makes a sworn statement, it opens up cross-examination questions by the Prosecutor and Court Officers. In a court-martial, the defendant can make an unsworn statement that is not subject to cross-examination but its content is not considered evidence in the same sense as a sworn statement. The Law Member carefully explained the rights of the accused to testify and defined the differences between a sworn and unsworn statement. Robinson responded, "Yes, sir," when the Law Officer asked if he understood his rights and if he desired to make a sworn statement.

Robinson identified himself and provided background information about his hometown and his time that he had been in the army. He explained that after arrival at the MP Station he had told Wigginton what happened at the Bus Station. He admitted that he interrupted when Pvt. Mucklerath gave his statement, but, he testified, he did so only to refresh the private's memory to ensure a correct statement.

Robinson said that when Capt. Bear arrived, he tried to follow him through the guard room, but the MP officer said, "Nobody comes in the room until I tell them." When Robinson asked why Pvt. Mucklerath was in the room, Bear responded that he was a witness.

Jackie continued, "Captain Bear sat down and Captain Wigginton started to tell him the story, and he started in with the story that Private Mucklerath had told him that I had said if I ever saw him again I would break him in two, and I told them that what I had actually said was that if he ever called me a nigger again I would break him in two; that I was in the MP truck and Private Mucklerath came up and said, 'Did you get that nigger lieutenant' and that was when I made that remark."

The Defense interrupted its own witness to ask, "Lieutenant, do you know what a nigger is?" Robinson responded, "I looked it up once, but my Grandmother gave me a good definition, she was a slave, and she said the definition of the word was a low, uncouth person, and pertains to no one in particular; but I don't consider that I am low and uncouth, I looked it up in the dictionary afterwards and it says the word nigger pertains to the negroid or negro, but it is also a machine used in a saw mill for pushing logs into the saws. I objected to being called a nigger by this private or by anybody else. When I made this statement that I did not like to be called a nigger, I told the Captain, I said, 'If you call me a nigger, I might have to say the same thing to you, I don't mean to incriminate anybody, but I just don't like it.' I do not consider myself a nigger at all, I am a negro, but not a nigger."

The defense then switched the questioning about Capt. Bear's claims that Robinson "leaned on the door and saluted him in a sloppy manner." Robinson denied that he had done so and pointed out that Capt. Wigginton had said the same in his interview with Maj. Daugherty during the Article 70 investigation, adding, "I don't know why he has now changed his story."

A lengthy question-and-answer period then ensued with Robinson saying that Bear had never given him a direct order to sit in a chair and, when told to go back into the room, that he did so. Robinson admitted to interrupting statements but claimed he did so, not to be "impudent," but rather to ensure the accuracy of the testimony. When asked how he was treated by his fellow officers at the MP Station, Robinson replied that Capt. Bear "was not polite at all" and that he was "very uncivil toward me; and he did not seem to recognize me as an officer at all; but I did consider myself an officer and felt that I should be addressed as one."

Robinson acknowledged that he might have talked fast while giving his statement but explained that reports of his later slow speech pattern, and his manner of speech, had been greatly exaggerated. He also said the stenographer had become agitated after she had typed his statement and that he had marked through parts concerning Capt. Bear's questions about his playing football as not being relevant. He also made several other changes that brought the stenographer's response, "If you had completed your statement it would have made sense."

Robinson replied that it would have made sense if she had properly recorded Bear's question. The stenographer responded by picking up her purse, saying "I don't have to make excuses to him" as she walked out of the room.

After Bear had convinced the stenographer to retype the statement for his signature, Robinson testified that he and the MP captain discussed how he was to return to McCloskey Hospital. Robinson testified that when told he might "get in trouble with the buses," he had "told him that I would not, that I abided by Texas Law, but that I knew there was no Jim Crow rule on Post and the bus driver had tried to make me move to the rear, and I told him that I would not move back."

The Defense then asked, "Just where were you sitting at that time with the reference to the front and rear of the bus?"

Before Jackie could respond, the Prosecutor rose from his seat and said, "I object to this line of testimony, for it has nothing to do with this specification; what happened on the bus, or this testimony about what happened has no place in this case."

The Law Member responded, "I do not see materiality of it; the objection is sustained."

This ended the Defense's questioning of Jackie. He had not only denied the claims of being insubordinate and failing to follow a lawful order but also—more importantly—he had brought up the failure of Bear and Wigginton to treat him as a fellow officer, or even as a fellow officer who happened to be black. Robinson had also entered in the record that he had been called a nigger and that the stenographer had revealed her personal prejudice by saying, "I don't have to make excuses to him." Unfortunately for the Defense, the Prosecution objected to mention about the incident of Robinson's being told to move to the back of the bus. The Law Officer's sustaining the objection determined the direction that the trial would take—that testimony about a white bus driver ordering a black officer to the back of the bus would not be admitted.

Then the Prosecutor cross-examined Jackie. Although he could have avoided further mention of racial actions and words, the Prosecutor chose to clarify some things before the Defense could do so. He had Robinson establish that Mucklerath, Painter, and Elwood were at the MP Station and then asked if Mucklerath called him a nigger. Robinson responded in the affirmative and then said that this was in the presence of Elwood but not Bear.

When asked if anyone else insulted him in any way, Jackie said that while Bear had not called him a nigger, he had "said very angrily that I was not to come in there" in reference to the orderly room.

The questioning then switched to the subject of Robinson's interrupting Bear while the latter took statements from the witnesses. Jackie again admitted that he had interrupted but only, he said, to ensure "some important things get in." He added that, when Bear told him to stop interrupting, he had complied and left the room.

Asked if he thought Wigginton was lying about what he testified to on the witness stand, Robinson answered, "Yes, he was." He then added, "I talked with Captain Wigginton at the investigation, and he did not testify that way at the time." Further questioning brought out that Wigginton had never insulted Robinson, had never called him a nigger, and treated him like a gentleman. When asked if Bear had treated him like a gentleman, Robinson responded, "I don't believe Captain Bear did."

Another lengthy question-and-answer session then occurred about whether or not Jackie had had his hands in his pockets, whether or not he knew how to properly salute, and whether or not he had had control of his mental faculties. When asked if he had anything to drink that night, Jackie answered in the negative, but then added that "evidently they figured that I had."

Robinson testified that Bear had never ordered him to any specific place, that he had slowed down his speech when told to do so, and that he did not sneer or grimace while giving his statement. He admitted to arguing with Wigginton and then Bear about whether or not he was under arrest for his transport back to McCloskey Hospital. Although threatened with arrest, Jackie testified that that action had never taken place.

When the Prosecutor finished his cross-examination of Robinson, a Member of the Court asked Jackie about the location of a chair in the receiving room and, specifically, if he was told to "get away from the door" until he was called. Jackie responded, "Not to my knowledge."

The Defense then called Lt. Col. R. L. Bates, commander of the 761st Tank Battalion. When asked about Robinson's reputation in the community, camp, post, and station, Bates began, "Particularly with the enlisted men, he is held in very high regard; he is a well-known athlete."

Apparently not wanting Jackie's national athletic reputation to be entered into the record, the Prosecutor objected on the grounds of the answer being not responsive. The Law Member sustained the objection.

When the Defense called for a shorter answer to his question, Lt. Col. Bates responded, "It is excellent." Bates answered further questions by saying his personal evaluation of Robinson was "excellent" and that he had a "good" reputation. He continued that Robinson was an "excellent" soldier and one whom he would like assigned to his command. Bates concluded that he would be satisfied to go into combat with the defendant.

The Prosecution had no cross-examination for Bates, and the Defense called Capt. James R. Lawson. As Robinson's former company commander in B Company of the 761st Tank Battalion, Lawson testified that Robinson had a "good reputation" and that he comported himself as an "excellent" soldier. Lawson said he would like to have Robinson back in his command. Two lieutenants from the 761st followed Lawson to the stand and gave similar answers about Robinson's reputation and abilities as a soldier.

When the Defense had no further witnesses, the Prosecution called 1st Lt. George Paul Cribari, a medical officer assigned to Camp Dispensary N. Once the Prosecution established that Cribari was at the MP Station accompanying Capt. Wigginton at the time of the incident, he questioned the medical officer about Capt. Bear's treatment of Robinson, inquiring about any show of animosity or antagonism toward Robinson during his questioning for his statement. He then stated that Robinson was "rude" to the MP captain, placed his hands in his pockets, and grimaced or grinned when told to slow his speech when giving his statement.

In the Defense cross-examination, Cribari volunteered that he was "an innocent by-stander, merely witnessing the disrespect of one officer to his superior." The Defense objected to the statement and the Law Member ruled the objection was proper. The statement, however, had been made and remained in the Court Record. The Defense then established that Cribari had only heard Bear tell Robinson one time to slow his speech while giving his statement.

The Court, apparently seeing Cribari as being reasonably neutral despite appearing as a witness for the Prosecution, had several questions. The members had him define what he considered "rude" and show how he saw Robinson place his hands in his pockets. He then demonstrated the defendant's exaggerated slow speech when giving his statement, further elaborating on his observations of "rudeness" on the part of the defendant. The Defense was allowed then to establish that Robinson had said to Cribari, "I haven't got a chance."

The Prosecution called Cpl. George A. Elwood of the Military Police Enlisted Detachment at Camp Hood. Elwood testified that he observed Robinson interrupt the conversation of Wigginton and Bear and heard the MP captain tell the defendant to go into the outer office and sit in a chair until called upon. He added that Robinson sat in the chair for a while before going outside to talk to a jeep driver. Elwood said that when told to sit in the chair Robinson said "Yes, sir, yes sir mockingly and with a smile on his face."

In the cross-examination by the Defense, Elwood said that enlisted witnesses were not told to leave the room and that Robinson had, at least for a while, sat in the chair. Elwood admitted that Bear was in his chain-of-command but denied that they had rehearsed his testimony.

The Prosecution, apparently anticipating the next questions by the Defense, asked in his Re Direct Examination if Bear or Wigginton had used any abusive language toward the defendant. When Elwood answered no, the Prosecution asked if he had heard Private Mucklerath use the word "nigger" and again received the answer of "no."

After no one had any further questions of Elwood, the Prosecution called Private First Class Ben W. Mucklerath and asked him if he had ever called Robinson a "nigger." Mucklerath responded "No" and the Prosecution passed him to the Defense whose first cross-examination question was, "Do you recall Lt. Robinson telling you if you ever called him a nigger he would break you in two?" Mucklerath answered, "Yes, sir" and said he had no idea why Robinson had said that. The Defense further questioned Mucklerath about his asking at the Bus Station, "Do you have the nigger lieutenant in the car?" Again, Mucklerath denied ever using the word "nigger" at any time. The Prosecutor then rested.

The Defense re-called Cpl. Elwood to the stand. After he established that Elwood knew Mucklerath, the Defense asked, "Did he ever ask you at any time if you had a nigger lieutenant in your car?"

Elwood answered, "Yes, sir, he did at the bus station."

In his cross-examination, the Prosecution violated the axiom that one should never ask a question to which the inquirer does not know the answer when he asked Elwood, "To your knowledge, could Lt. Robinson have heard him ask that question?

Elwood responded, "Yes, sir, I guess he could."

The Prosecution, having no desire to further pursue that line of questioning, said he had no further witnesses. The Defense and Prosecution made their closing arguments. The trial transcript does not include these remarks.

The Verdict

$\mathcal{T}$he complete court-martial of Jackie Robinson—including opening proceedings, testimonies, closing statements, and deliberation—took only four hours and fifteen minutes.

There is no record what portion of that time the nine-member Court spent in deliberation nor how many votes they took before they reached their decision. At 6:00 p.m., the Court announced, "Upon secret written ballot, two-thirds of the members present at the time the vote was taken find the accused of all specifications and charges: Not guilty; and therefore acquits the accused."

Other than the witness statements and the transcript of the court-martial, sparse records exist about what actually occurred on the bus, at the Bus Station, during the investigation, or at the court-martial. Neither the witnesses, investigating officer, prosecutor, nor court members left any accounts about their participation, nor were they later interviewed to seek their thoughts before their disappearance into the fog of history.

Other than Jackie, Capt. Cline was the only trial participant to later sit down for an interview. Despite Lt. Johnson's participation, Cline as the lead defense counsel received, or took, most of the credit for the conduct and results of the court-martial, primarily because he simply lived longer to tell the tale. Johnson died in 1951 while Cline lived into the twenty-first century and gave several interviews about the trial before his death. Unfortunately, Cline offered little additional substance to the story. The passage of so many years had him confusing the facts and mis-remembering details of the trial. The only mention he made of his co-counsel, Johnson, was to say that he was assisted by "another fellow."

Cline did say in a 2012 interview that the testimony of Lt. Col. Bates "had a big effect on the court's acquittal of Jackie." In the same interview, Cline said that one factor that weighed heavily in the verdict of not guilty was that Jackie, as a cavalryman in a tank unit, was a combat officer while the military witnesses, Bear, Wigginton and others against Jackie were from the rear service branches of military police and quartermaster.

On a personal note, Cline said, "All during the trial, every time we'd get a break, or something, Jackie'd run back to the telephone and I guess he'd call Rachel, or his mother, I don't know who he was calling, but he'd go call 'em on the telephone, and when it was over he was very appreciative and thanked me. But I never had any contact with him after that."

There is no mention in the court-martial transcript of any breaks, but there must have been some during a more than four-hour trial. While Jackie certainly must have been grateful for Cline's and Johnson's representation, he made no mention of them by name in either of his books or in his many interviews during the subsequent years.

The verdict must have been a great relief to Jackie, but there is little record of his thoughts about the trial. In his first autobiography written in 1948, he has only two sentences about his time in the army and makes no mention of his court-martial. Twenty-four years later, in his 1972 autobiography, Robinson devotes only three pages to the incident at the bus station and a single page to his court-martial. His memories of the trial were vague, maybe deliberately so, in his later writings and interviews.

While the witness statements and trial transcripts offer the basic facts, they are only words written on the page. Neither the demeanor of the participants, their tone of voice, their level of anger, nor any other emotion is revealed. In addition to the inability to see what was "in the hearts" of the participants, there are also other important missing items including the closing arguments by the prosecutor and defense.

In reading the trial transcript several distinct issues arise. First, neither the Law Member nor the Prosecutor had any desire for the trial to become an issue of Robinson being told to move to the back of the bus or for it to become a racial incident with Jackie being called a "nigger." This guidance likely came from the senior camp Judge Advocate who may have received the recommendation from Col. Kimball, the 5th Group Commander. The memo of Kimball's telephone conversation with Col. Buie at XXIII Corps, is proof of his knowledge and concern of the case, but as the commander he would have been extremely careful not to exert command influence on the board members, or for it to appear that he was doing so.

The most puzzling part of the transcript testimony is that of Cpl. Elwood and Pvt. Mucklerath. Elwood initially testified that he did not hear Mucklerath use the word "nigger." Mucklerath then testified that he never called Robinson a nigger. When asked why Robinson would have told him if you ever called him a nigger "he would break you in two" Mucklerath said he had no idea what he was thinking.

Elwood, upon being re-called by the defense, countered his own witness statement when asked about Mucklerath, "Did he ever ask you at any time if you had a nigger lieutenant in your car?" This time, Elwood responded, "Yes, sir, he did at the bus station."

When asked if Lt. Robinson could have heard this declaration, Elwood responded, "Yes, sir, I guess he could."

Perhaps Elwood's first statement referred to not hearing Mucklerath use the word "nigger" at the MP Station but admitted in the second that he had heard him do so at the Bus Station. Whatever his reason, this was the trial's final testimony. Just why the prosecutor let this damning impeachment evidence go unchallenged is unknown. Likely, he wanted to "cut his loses" and not to risk further adverse testimony to be heard. It is also interesting that neither the prosecutor nor Law Member attempted to stop this line of questioning.

The trial transcript concludes, "Closing arguments were made by the defense and prosecution." However, these arguments are not included. Two reasons could possibly explain this omission. One, closing arguments were generally lengthy narratives, making it difficult for the court reporter to transcribe them accurately, and, two, closing arguments are not evidence but rather summations of what was presented during the court-martial. They are not considered as testimony for review by high levels in the event of appeal.

The only account directly referring to the contents of the closing arguments is in an article that appeared in *American Heritage* magazine in 1984 by Jules Tygiel. According to Tygiel, Robinson later recalled, "My lawyer summed up the case beautifully by telling the board that this was not a case involving any violations of the Articles of War, or even of military tradition, but simply a situation in which a few individuals sought to vent their bigotry on a Negro they consider 'uppity' because he had the audacity to exercise right that belonged to him as an American and a soldier."

This claimed portion of the defense's closing argument has often been repeated in subsequent books and articles but, unfortunately—despite being inspiring and compelling—no evidence exists that proves it is true. Tygiel did not include it in his 1983 book entitled *Baseball's Great Experiment*. Nor does Robinson make any mention of it in either of his two autobiographies. Furthermore, Cline, the Defense Attorney who would have most likely made the comments, did not offer any details about the closing arguments in the several interviews he did before his death. There also is no record or claim that Capt.

Johnson might have made the statement. If Tygiel had documentation of the closing arguments, he took it to his grave when he died in 2008.

Ignoring the probability that Cline or Johnson did not actually present such an eloquent argument, the statement nevertheless stands as an excellent summary of what occurred in the aftermath of a black man refusing to move to the back of the bus on the evening of July 6, 1944, at Camp Hood, Texas. Whether fact or legend, the condensed version of the incident is compelling.

The prosecutor did a reasonably good job of using the testimonies of Bear and Wigginton to show that Robinson had been somewhat uncooperative, if not out and out insubordinate. Missing, however, was any explanation about why Robinson had been transported to the MP Station in the first place. Also, Bear admitted in his testimony that he had "lost control" of Robinson, an admission a superior officer rarely makes. It is also noteworthy that while Jackie confessed in his statement to using profanity—not a crime—at the Central Bus Station, there were no accusations that he had done so at the MP Station.

Other than getting Elwood to testify that Mucklerath had referred to Robinson as "a nigger," the most effective cross-examination by the defense created doubt about whether or not Bear had ever clearly issued a direct order to begin with. Robinson's own testimony countered much of Bear's and comes across in the trial transcript as calm and professional. Testimony by Robinson's commander and senior officers from the 761st Tank Battalion about Robinson's good character must have been influential. Their stating that they would willingly go into combat with him has no higher recommendation. Although not directly enumerated, the trial manuscript alludes to Bear's and his stenographer's becoming angry with Robison for his lack of respect to the "white woman."

Voting by the Court-Martial Board is by secret ballot and results in announcements only of guilt or acquittal. For Jackie to have been found not guilty would mean that at least four members of the nine-member board voted in his favor and against the allegations. Whether the vote was five to four for conviction or acquittal, or nine to zero, or some unknown combination, was a moot point. What is a fact is that the Court did not have two-thirds of its members voting for a guilty verdict.

In final analysis, it must be noted that the participants sat for four hours in a hot room listening to complaints of relatively minor infractions that rarely reached the level of General Court-Martial, a body that more often heard cases of desertion, physical altercations, robbery, and even murder. The Board Members had taken a half day away from training their units that would be in combat within a few months with the Allies advancing across Europe toward Germany and facing the Battle of the Bulge. As soldiers of all ranks exclaimed at the time, "Don't you know there is a war going on, buddy?"

The most important part of the story about the court-martial of Jackie Robinson was not that he was put on trial but rather that he lived in a time when his refusal to move to the back of the bus would create such a legal ordeal, a time when one American would presume to tell another to move to the back of the bus, a time when racial prejudices were blatant and pervasive.

Jim Crow laws ruled the South, racial injustices permeated the North and East, and all minorities suffered discrimination in the West. The military was fraught with the attitudes that the servicemen brought with them.

However, race relations and prejudices of the time should not be judged by the standards of today. Black soldiers, especially black officers, in great numbers were novel in the armed forces. Racism and the whites' sense of superiority toward blacks had been instilled for generations. Fair and equal treatment of African Americans was something still in the distant future.

While those beliefs and practices, now oftentimes seemingly shocking and inexcusable, were abhorrent, passing judgment misses the point. To understand Jackie Robinson—his life and his successes—one must understand rather than condemn the times in which he lived. If anything, understanding what he endured and triumphed over makes him even more impressive.

The court-martial of Jackie Robinson serves as a good example of the racism of the period and at the same time exhibits the efforts of the army to reach a degree of fairness. Although tried for offenses caused by, or at least influenced by, racism, justice was served with the court-martial verdict of not guilty on all charges.

Final Army Days

$\mathcal{T}$he time Jackie spent waiting for his court-martial had not been idle. With his unit subject to overseas deployment, Jackie again had had to deal with his fitness status regarding his injured ankle.

On June 26, 1944, Jackie had appeared before the McCloskey General Hospital Disposition Board that was evaluating his latest medical examination to determine if he was physically able to accompany the 761st Tank Battalion in its deployment overseas.

The Deposition Board recorded that its diagnosis was unchanged from that of Brooke Army Hospital—Robinson suffered from lingering pain and swelling from prolonged use of his ankle due to injuries suffered playing football in 1937 and 1941. "The Board is of the opinion," the record said, "that this officer is still unfit for general but is fit for limited service. The Board recommends that this officer appear before an Army Retiring Board for consideration of reassignment to permanent limited military service. This officer is fit for overseas duty."

This ambiguous evaluation had left Jackie confused. He was "fit for overseas duty" while at the same time being recommended for "permanent limited military service." Also, the referral to the Retiring Board meant that Jackie could also be considered for a medical discharge.

On July 21, two weeks before his court-martial, Robinson had appeared before the Retiring Board at McCloskey Hospital to determine if he should be "retired from the Service of the United States." The six officers and their Recorder asked the questions.

The first question was from the Recorder who asked Robinson if he desired to be retired from the service. Jackie responded, "No, sir."

To the question, "Do you consider your disability permanent?" Jackie again answered, "No, sir."

The Recorder had then introduced Robinson's Report of Physical Examination and the findings of the Disposition Board. After a brief discussion, the Retiring Board had announced that it agreed with the Disposition Board. It had found Robinson "incapacitated for active duty" but to be returned to his unit in "a limited service status." The entire Board meeting had lasted only fifteen minutes, after which Jackie had returned to Camp Hood to prepare for his court-martial.

Following his acquittal, Robinson reported to the 758th Tank Battalion—the unit to which he been transferred in order to have its commanding officer recommend the court-martial. At the battalion's location at North Camp Hood, Jackie was assigned to B Company. Neither he nor any of the other soldiers made any record of their feelings about this assignment. Jackie surely must have been displeased because he was again reporting to the man who authorized his trial. On the other hand, the unit may not have been eager to welcome him back. With the 758th in the process of preparing for overseas deployment and the Army experiencing a shortage of lieutenants, having a "limited duty" one fill a slot would not have been readily acceptable.

Even though the court-martial was over, it was not in the past. While Jackie faced post-court-martial assignment difficulties, the Army endured dozens of inquiries about the event, inquiries from the War Department in Washington, D.C., questions from the NAACP, information requests from a multitude of others. Senator Sheridan Downey (D, CA), as one of those concerned, wrote letters to the War Department requesting information. These correspondences, known as "Congressionals," are given great and immediate attention, as senators and congressmen are the ones who make budget decisions. By the time the letters were received, however, the court-martial had already occurred. Both Camp Hood and the War Department simply responded, "Lt. Robinson was tried by court martial on August 3, 1944 and acquitted on all charges."

Robinson's stay with the 758th Tank Battalion did not last long. On August 19, orders transferred him to the 659th Tank Destroyer Battalion also located at North Camp Hood. Instead of preparing for deployment overseas, the 659th was in the process of transferring its assets and personnel to other units to meet its date of disbandment on December 1. This assignment was likely in response to the 758th Battalion's not wanting an officer on "limited duty" taking one of its lieutenant's positions.

Although Jackie had professed to the Retiring Board a few weeks earlier that he wanted to remain in the army, his court-martial and unit transfers had changed his mind. In his biography, he wrote, "I was pretty much fed up with the service. So I did something which is very much frowned upon in GI procedure. I sent an airmail special delivery letter to the Adjutant General's office in Washington, D.C. This was in violation of the standard procedure of going through your own company, battalion, regiment, and division headquarters. On the way up, such correspondence, if it ever reaches its intended destination, can get marked up with disapproving notations from your superior officers. The disapproving endorsements have great weight with the top brass which is very likely to turn down any request you make which is not favorable in the eyes of your superiors. I bypassed all that."

Jackie's letter (Appendix W), dated August 25, 1944, referenced the findings of the Army Retiring Board at McCloskey Hospital that placed him on limited duty and said, "In checking with the Special Services Branch I was told that there were no openings for Colored Officers in that field. I request to be retired from the service and be placed on reserve as I feel I can be of more service to the government doing defense work rather than being on limited duty with an outfit that is already better than 100% over strength in officers."

Robinson did not receive a response to his letter to the Adjutant General before receiving orders on September 19 to report to the segregated 372nd Infantry Regiment at Camp Breckinridge, Kentucky—another army camp named after a Confederate army general. This transfer was unrelated to either his court-martial or his letter to the Adjutant General; rather it was part of the preparation of the disbandment of the 659th and the preparation of the 372nd for deployment to the Pacific. He was not singled out as nine other African American lieutenants stationed at Camp Hood also were on the transfer orders with Robinson. It is unlikely, however, that any of the Camp Hood leadership were particularly unhappy to see him go.

From Camp Breckinridge on September 29, Jackie once again wrote to the War Department Adjutant General. In his letter (Appendix X) he referenced his previous correspondence and said, "Since that time I have been transferred to an infantry unit, and to do duty with this organization would only further aggravate my injury." He concluded by again requesting he be placed on inactive status.

This time Jackie forwarded the letter though proper channels. His company commander prepared a 1st Indorsement on September 30 that merely stated "Forwarded." This second letter, with the company commander's indorsement, went no further because actions were proceeding in reference to Jackie's first letter.

On September 26, with no reference to Jackie's request not having been submitted through proper channels, the War Department Adjutant General sent a message down the chain of command, stating "Inasmuch as Lieutenant Robinson does not desire to be retained on active duty in a limited service capacity, it is desired that orders be issued relieving him from active duty."

The Adjutant General's message passed through the various appropriate headquarters until October 17 when Jackie received orders releasing him from the 372nd at Camp Breckinridge, effective October 21. He was then assigned to Camp Wheeler, Georgia—still another camp named after a Confederate general. In the meantime—while his orders for him to revert to inactive status were processed—he was granted leave to go home to California. On November 18, 1944, Robinson received his orders relieving him from active duty with an honorable discharge.

· 18 ·

The Negro Leagues

*J*ackie Robison left the army with mixed feelings. He was proud that he had graduated from Officers Candidate School to be commissioned a second lieutenant and that he had been successful in improving the equality of black soldiers at Fort Riley. At Camp Hood, he had done what he thought was right in standing against Jim Crow rules about moving to the back of the bus, and he was satisfied that the army had done the right thing in finding him not guilty in the resulting court-martial. He did not, however, ever express regrets about not joining his fellow officers and soldiers of the 761st Tank Battalion in their deployment to the European Theater and their valiant fight across Germany.

During the post-war years and during his baseball career, Jackie occasionally mentioned his service as an officer and his honorable discharge, but it was not until his autobiography in 1972 that he made any mention of his court-martial—and even then covered it in only a few brief pages.

Despite his downplay of his military service and his court-martial, both made a significant impression and impacted Jackie's thoughts and future. He had learned that he could stand up to Jim Crow laws and use the system to fight bigotry and prejudices. That was a lofty and noble purpose, but it was not a job—nor did it provide an income.

November 1944 found Jackie unemployed and back with his mother on Pepper Street in Pasadena with his job skills only as a soldier or an athlete. He quickly decided to make use of the latter. He reconnected with contacts he had made in the army and in Los Angeles to rejoin the workforce. One of those was a man he had met before his taking leave from Camp Breckinridge when he had walked by a ball field and observed a black soldier throwing impressive curve balls to a friend. Jackie had stopped and introduced himself to Ted Alexander, who had played in the Negro

Leagues for the Kansas City Monarchs before the war. Alexander had explained that, with many ballplayers called to active military duty, the Negro Leagues were looking for talent.

Jackie knew little about the Negro Leagues, it being doubtful that he had ever seen one of their games. Still, it sounded like a good job opportunity to him as well as the chance to play ball. With Alexander's assistance, Jackie sent a letter to Thomas Y. Baird, who co-owned the Monarchs with founder J. L. Wilkinson. Baird expressed interest in Jackie and offered him $300 per month if he made the team. Jackie successfully countered for $400 and agreed to join the team in Houston for spring training in April.

The possibility of playing for the Monarchs held both positives and negatives for Jackie. On the good side, he had a job, and that job was playing baseball. On the bad, he would be on the road and away from California. Rachel remained in nursing school in San Francisco and was not happy with Jackie leaving again for a job halfway across the country. In her biography, she wrote, "The war forced us to endure long, painful separations. . . . I was in the last three years of my nursing program in San Francisco determined to graduate. . . . It was a strained engagement, at times putting our relationship to the most severe tests of loyalty and faith. But we remained steadfast despite temptations and the turmoil around us. In fact, I believe that having to struggle through those years helped us mature and prepare for our life together."

Jackie's and Rachel's life as man and wife was not yet to begin, however. With time to fill between his discharge and spring training, Jackie sought out his former mentor from Los Angeles, Karl Downs, who was now the president of Samuel Huston College in Austin, Texas. The two had visited while Jackie was at Camp Hood, and Jackie later credited Downs's religious guidance for getting him through the ordeal of the court-martial. Now Downs offered Jackie a job as physical education instructor, and Jackie accepted, returning to Texas yet again.

Along with his religious and academic passions, Downs also was an activist for equal rights. His zeal influenced Jackie as well as his students. In an article in *The Crisis*, Downs criticized blacks for being "too timid" when confronting racial problems. He wrote, "The contemporary Negro students cannot hope to make any contributions to this cause unless they shake from their shoulders the shackles of timidity which have grown into their lives as a result of slavery's influence."

Samuel Huston College struggled with finances and a dwindling number of male students because of the war. However, assistance from the Methodist Church and Texas Congressman Lyndon B. Johnson, a segregationist who supported black colleges in order to keep the institutions segregated, kept the school's doors open.

Robinson organized physical education classes for all students and, despite the limited number of male students, fielded a basketball team in the all-black Southwestern Athletic Conference. In an *Austin American Statesman* article in 2014, former player Roland Harden recalled, "We were one of the few teams that ran all the time. He got out there with us and actually showed us what to do and was a better player than anybody on our team. Or anybody we played, really. And he was a gentleman. He required us to wear suits and ties when we got off the bus."

Jackie stood up for his team the same way he had stood up for his rights all his life. Harden remembered, "I saw him go after officials when we were playing. He didn't get ejected, but he would go to the breaking point."

Despite his previous athletic accomplishments, Jackie remained modest. When he announced to the team after the season ended that he was leaving to join the Monarchs, his trainer Harold Adanandus, according to a 1997 interview, recalled saying, "Well, Jackie, I didn't even know you played any baseball." Robinson had responded, "Yeah, I play a little."

Robinson got his chance to "play a little" immediately after joining the Monarchs in Houston. To his dismay, he found spring training not to be working on fundamentals but rather actually playing practice games. Three days after reporting to the team, Jackie was on a bus with the team for a game in San Antonio. On May 6, 1945, just as the war in Europe was coming to an end, the Monarchs opened their season in Kansas City.

The best part of playing with the Monarchs for Jackie was that he got to observe and learn from some of the finest players in the Negro Leagues. Jackie considered his monthly salary of $400 to be a "financial bonanza," but he wrote in his autobiography that his time with the Monarchs had "turned out to be a pretty miserable way to make a buck." There were also other aspects of being a Monarch that bothered Jackie. For one, a large part of the job was the travel that involved not only long bus rides but also Jim Crow laws that prevented the team's staying in white hotels and eating in white restaurants. Most of their meals were delivered in paper bags out the back door of eating establishments and consumed on the bus. Robinson also did not like the personal habits of many of his fellow players who stayed out late at night drinking and chasing women.

Jackie played well enough to earn a spot in the 1945 East-West All-Star Game, but he was becoming more and more dissatisfied with playing in the Negro Leagues. There were stories in the press about the possibility of ending the Jim Crow barriers in baseball, but, as Jackie later wrote, "I never expected the walls to come tumbling down in my lifetime." He added, "I began to wonder why I should dedicate my life to a career where the boundaries for progress were set by racial discrimination. Even more serious was my growing fear that I might lose Rae again. I began to sense in her letters that her patience was thinning. She had been hoping I'd settle down in California to work out our future. The way I was traveling we saw each other rarely. I felt unhappy and trapped. If I left baseball, where could I go, what could I do to earn enough money to help my mother and to marry Rachel?"

Robinson concluded, "The solution to my problem was only days away in the hands of a tough, shrewd, courageous man called Branch Rickey, the president of the Brooklyn Dodgers."

· *19* ·

Branch Rickey

$\mathcal{B}$aseball has been a part of American life almost since the country secured its independence with the first documented mention of baseball in Pittsfield, Massachusetts, in 1791. There is also a record that New Yorkers played "base ball" in 1823 on fields that is now Greenwich Village. Whether derived from the British games of rounders and cricket, as some people believe, or original to this country, as others claim, baseball became official on September 23, 1845, when a social club in New York City formed the Knickerbockers and published the game's first standardized rules—the Knickerbocker Rules.

The game evolved over the decades in somewhat predictable ways and in surprising twists in others. Idle soldiers during the Civil War, particularly on the Union side, increased the sport's popularity and helped standardize its regulations. In 1907, baseball officials declared "the first scheme for playing baseball, according to the best evidence obtainable to date, was devised by Abner Doubleday at Cooperstown, New York, in 1839." This was a claim that would have surprised the career army soldier who achieved the rank of general during the Civil War. Neither Doubleday himself nor his many papers made any mention of his "invention" of baseball. Nevertheless, the myth took sufficient root for the Baseball Hall of Fame to be founded in Doubleday's hometown of Cooperstown, New York.

The increase in railroad transportation during and after the Civil War allowed teams from distant cities to compete. Teams in the Northeastern United States formed the National League in 1876. Professional baseball expanded with teams in the Midwest and the formation of the American League in 1901. Neither league had any written policy concerning the inclusion of black players but there was a "gentleman's agreement" among Major League owners that players would be white only. Minor league owners voted in 1887 against signing contracts with black players. Baseball, which had become known as America's Pastime by the early twentieth century, would remain divided between white and black.

A few African Americans played in the white major and minor leagues before the agreements, but by the late nineteenth century only white players took the sanctioned baseball field. Being excluded from the official diamonds did not mean that blacks did not play and enjoy watching the game of baseball. In 1920, black team owners formed a professional baseball league of their own that evolved into the Negro National and American leagues in 1933 and 1937. The Negro League held its own All-Star game and championship playoff, just like the white Major Leagues and played by the same rules. Blacks, however, remained barred from Major League Baseball.

Negro League games often drew larger crowds than white baseball did, and many black players clearly displayed talents equal or superior to white players. Then World War II prompted the question for many Americans, and for some baseball owners, about why blacks could fight and die on the battlefield but could not play baseball on the fields at home. Some owners began to consider adding black players' talents to their teams. All owners could see that the Negro Leagues also drained admission dollars that, in their minds, could better be spent at Major League games.

While some owners talked, Branch Rickey, General Manager of the Brooklyn Dodgers, took action. The Ohio-born Rickey had played professional football and had been the president of the St. Louis Cardinals when he decided to volunteer for the army during World War I. Although thirty-six years old with a wife and four children, Rickey believed "War overshadows everything."

Rickey received a commission in the newly formed Chemical Warfare Service and sailed for Europe only to have influenza, known as the Spanish flu, sweep through his transport ship, killing more than one hundred servicemen. Rickey contacted the flu but recovered soon after reaching France. In the war's final weeks, his unit—which included future baseball Hall of Famers Ty Cobb and Christy Mathewson—participated in more than 150 operations supporting infantry and tank units.

After his discharge, Rickey rejoined the St. Louis Cardinals as field manager and then general manager to lead the club for more than twenty, mostly successful, years. In 1942, Rickey joined the Brooklyn Dodgers as part owner and general manager. His innovations included establishing the first full-time spring training facility and implementing the use of batting helmets, pitching machines, and batting cages.

Rickey was a man dedicated not only to baseball but to the God of his strict Methodist upbringing. He regularly attended church services and, for his entire career, did not play in or attend ball games on Sundays. He was bothered by the segregation of his sport. In early 1946, Rickey told *Look* magazine, "I cannot face my God much longer knowing that His black creatures are held separate and distinct from His white creatures in the game that has given me all that I can call my own."

With his religious convictions—and, no doubt, financial analysis— Branch Rickey decided to break Major League's color barrier.

Rickey's support of racial equality on the baseball diamond was reinforced by an incident that occurred while he was the coach for Ohio Wesleyan College in 1910. As Jackie related the story in his 1972 biography, "The team went to South Bend, Indiana, for a game. The hotel management registered the coach and team but refused to assign a room to a black player named Charley Thomas. In those days, college ball had a few black players. Mr. Rickey took the manager aside and said he would move the entire team to another hotel unless the black athlete was accepted. The threat was a bluff because he knew the other hotels also would have refused accommodations to a black man. While the hotel manager was thinking about the threat, Mr. Rickey came up with a compromise. He suggested a cot be put in his own room, which he would share with the unwanted guest. The hotel manager wasn't happy with the idea, but he gave in."

According to Robinson's version of the story, Thomas sat on the cot and wept and began "tearing at one hand with the other—just as if he were trying to scratch the skin off his hands with his fingernails."

An alarmed Rickey asked what he was trying to do. Thomas answered, "It's my hands. They're black. If only they were white, I'd be as good as everybody then, wouldn't I Mr. Rickey? If only they were white."

According to Robinson, Rickey replied, "Charley, the day will come when they won't have to be white."

Rickey often repeated the story and it appears in nearly every biography about or related to the baseball innovator. The veracity of the tale is somewhat debatable. Whatever the facts, this version makes a good story, and as they say in the newspaper business, "When the legend gets better than the facts, print the legend."

There is no doubt that Rickey had deep feelings about the mistreatment of African Americans from religious and moral standpoints. However, first and foremost, Rickey was a businessman, and, in business, profits prevail.

During the thirty-five years after the hotel incident, Rickey made only minimal efforts to assist blacks either in or outside the world of baseball. While with the St. Louis Cardinals, he did attempt to eliminate the Jim Crow segregated black spectator section and have general seating for all races. Confronted with the belief that, if blacks were allowed to sit with whites, attendance would decrease, he backed down.

When World War II finally concluded, Rickey determined that baseball and the country were ready to make baseball the national pastime for all Americans—black and white. Major League Baseball Commissioner Kenesaw Mountain Landis had opposed the acceptance of black players since he assumed the position in 1920. After his death in 1944, his replacement, Albert "Happy" Chandler, brought new ideas to the office. Shortly after he became commissioner, Chandler made it clear where he stood on the idea of integrating baseball. Referencing World War II battles, Chandler said, "If a black boy can make it at Okinawa and go to Guadalcanal, he can make it in baseball."

For several years Rickey had been circulating the idea of breaking the color line with other baseball owners and managers. Some showed interest, but most, some with extreme objections, did not. At one time, all fifteen of the other owners voted against the idea of breaking the color barrier. Undeterred, Rickey began his hunt for black ball players under the guise that he was forming a new Negro league. His primary prerequisite, of course, was that candidates play ball and play very well. He also insisted that they be moral, intelligent, and well spoken. He also hoped that they would be religious and, if at all possible, happily married. Although not spoken or recorded, this latter characteristic meant that he would not have to worry about his black ball players dating white women.

Rickey sent his scouts across the country to observe black players. They also went into Mexico, Cuba, and Venezuela to scout local black men as well as American Negroes playing in the foreign leagues who had become expatriates because of racism at home and opportunities abroad. Better known African American players—such as renowned pitcher Satchel Paige; Josh Gibson, known as "the black Babe Ruth"; and James "Cool Papa" Bell, perhaps the fastest base stealer to ever play the game—were considered too old, as they were nearing the end of their careers.

The name Jackie Robinson kept rising to the top of scouting reports. Rickey sent multiple scouts, each unaware of the other, to observe and talk with the ball player. By the end of the selection process Rickey's son, Branch, Jr., claimed the Dodger organization had spent $25,000 (more than $350,000 in today's money) in their scouting process.

Rickey thoroughly vetted Jackie. In addition to having his scouts evaluate his skills, Rickey personally investigated Jackie's early years growing up and attending schools in California. Jackie's play on the scholastic fields, his classroom attendance, and nearly complete degree from UCLA made a positive impression on the Dodger general manager. He was not deterred by Jackie's reputation of having a temper or by the incidents with the police in Pasadena and Los Angeles. Rickey saw that Jackie was a competitor who stood up for his rights and opposed racism. While Jackie had on occasion pushed his demands to the legal limits, he had remained within the system and emerged victoriously.

Rickey made no mention—at the time or in his later speeches or writings—about Robinson's court-martial by the U.S. Army. With the amount of money, time, and other assets dedicated to Jackie's investigation, Rickey doubtlessly knew about the trial, acquittal, and early-but-honorable discharge. To Rickey, it was likely just another example of Jackie's non-violence and successfully standing up for his rights. As a veteran, Rickey understood the military and understood the significance of Jackie's acquittal by a military court-martial.

There is no record of Rickey's knowledge of Jackie's ankle injury that granted him an honorable discharge from the army before the end of the war. Neither does Jackie mention the injury being treated nor bothering him once joining the Kansas City Monarchs. It is possible that it healed during his stay at Samuel Huston College where he was away from the rigors of army training.

The first face-to-face meeting between Robinson and Rickey occurred in the Dodger executive's Brooklyn office on August 28, 1945, just a week before Japan formally surrendered ending World War II. There have been many accounts of the conversation between the two, but Jackie offers a first-hand account in his 1972 autobiography. Jackie wrote, "Branch Rickey was an impressive looking man. He had a classic face, an air of command, a deep, booming voice, and a way of cutting through red tape and getting down to basics. He shook my hand vigorously and, after a brief conversation, sprang his first question. 'You got a girl?' he demanded."

Most likely Rickey already knew the answer, but he was, nevertheless, pleased with Jackie's response about Rachel and their hopes and plans. According to Jackie, the Dodger boss said, "When we get through today, you may want to call her up because there are times when a man needs a woman by his side."

Rickey then explained just why Jackie might need a strong woman "by his side" during the upcoming times. He told Jackie that he was not seeking players for a new Negro League but rather the club's all-white minor league team in Montreal.

"You think you can play for Montreal?" he asked.

Jackie wrote that he was thrilled, scared, excited, and incredulous and near speechless before he managed to reply, "Yes."

Rickey then briefly discussed with his scout if he thought Jackie could "make the grade" before abruptly pointing a finger and saying, "I know you're a good ball player. What I want to know is whether you have the guts."

Robinson replied, "I think I can play the game, Mr. Rickey."

Rickey then went into a lengthy prediction that Jackie would be called all kind of names, would have beanballs thrown at him, and would possibly be physically attacked.

Jackie recalled that he thought, writing, "The most luxurious possession, the richest treasure anybody has, is his personal dignity. I looked at Mr. Rickey guardedly, and in that second I was looking at him not as a partner in a great experiment, but as the enemy—a white man. I had a question and it was the age-old one about whether or not you sell your birthright. Mr. Rickey, I asked, 'Are you looking for a Negro who is afraid to fight back?'"

Rickey responded, "Robinson, I'm looking for a ball player with enough guts not to fight back."

He then said, according to Jackie, "'They'll taunt and goad you. They'll do anything to make you react. They'll try to provoke a race riot at the park. This is the way to prove to the public that a Negro should not be allowed in the major league. This is the way to frighten the fans and make them afraid to attend the games.'" He added, "They'll come in with spike high, cut you on the leg, and say 'How do you like that nigger boy?'"

Robinson wrote, "Could I turn the other cheek? I didn't know how I would do it. Yet I knew I must, I had to do it for so many reasons. For black youth, for my mother, for Rae, for myself. I had already begun to feel I had to do if for Branch Rickey."

Again, in this important conversation between Robinson and Rickey, there is no mention, or at least no record or writing, of the court-martial. If it was not mentioned, both parties were nevertheless aware of its importance in forming Jackie's abilities to react to and work within racism. It is also noteworthy that Jackie's recollections in 1972 of his 1945 conversation with Rickey are extremely detailed and marked with direct quotes. Very little of this conversation is in Jackie's 1948 biography and the passage of time and the desire to publish a best-selling book certainly must have played a role in Jackie's and his co-writer's memory. It is interesting that Jackie's use of the phrase "the great experiment" was not in use until several years after the cited conversation.

Whatever exactly occurred or was said, Rickey made a deep impression on Jackie. Rachel Robinson described the relationship between Ricky and her husband in her 2014 book. She wrote, "I believe they got along so well because temperamentally they were well matched. Rickey had the very traits that he sought in Jack. Both were religious. Both had unshakable integrity, and both possessed a hard-headed determination to compete at their best. There was no doubt about commitment to making integration work, which he tended to underplay in public. He and Jack were unequal in power and influence to be sure, but they were always interdependent in this social experiment. Neither could succeed without the other."

Rachel continued, "Baseball in the forties allowed players no salary negotiations—period. Jack accepted what was offered. He had no illusions about Rickey's business interest and never believed his motives to be simply altruistic. In fact, his vested interest in creating a winning team was reassuring to us. We could also see and appreciate Rickey's vision, meticulous planning, and sensitive anticipation of our needs as signs of an unwavering commitment to the social idea. He was accessible, though Jack didn't tend to call him, and willing to take charge when trouble surfaced. He gave us, young adults in our twenties, confidence, and we learned to mobilize our own strengths independently."

She concluded, "For me, Branch Rickey became a familiar source of comfort. I could count on him. I admired him and thought that he was too often caricatured by the press that the substance of the man was lost. When he crouched down by first base in spring training waving his hat shouting at Jack, 'Be daring, be daring' my spirit embraced them both with pride."

The non-negotiated salary mentioned by Rachel was $600 a month, more than $8,000 in today's dollars and a bonus of $3,500, more than $49,000 in today's dollars. On October 23, 1945, Branch, Jr., who headed the Brooklyn farm clubs, and Montreal Royals president Hector Racine held a press conference announcing Robinson's signing. Branch, Jr., said, "My father and Mr. Racine are not inviting trouble, but they won't avoid it if it comes. Jack Robinson is a fine type of young man, intelligent and college-bred, and I think he can make it too."

Branch, Jr., admitted that some of their International League opponents might resist playing against a black ball player and that some might even steer away from the Dodger organization with a Negro player on its roster. He added, "Some of them who are with us now may even quit, but they'll be back in baseball after they work a year or two in a cotton mill."

The news of Robinson's signing was met with mixed reactions. His breaking the color barrier in Minor League Baseball—with the possibility of his later doing so in the Major Leagues by joining the Dodgers—created a stir in the press; among club owners, managers, and players; and throughout the public. Active and retired players expressed doubts as to Jackie's being able to make it in Montreal, much less the Major Leagues. Controversy also swept through the Negro Leagues and the black community where many thought that other African American ball players were more deserving than Jackie to be the one to break the color barrier.

Whites—including club owners, officials and fans—expressed concerns over how the recruitment of the best black ball players would influence the future of the Negro Leagues. Some apprehension was sincere; other such speculation was just an excuse to keep Major League Baseball segregated. Negro League owners also opposed the move because they feared the loss of fans and revenue. The Kansas City Monarchs, with whom Jackie was still playing, threatened to sue the Dodgers on the basis that Jackie was their property. When the Monarch owners realized that African Americans overall were in enormous favor of the breaking of the color barrier, they withdrew their objections.

• 20 •

Spring Training

After his signing, Jackie followed Rickey's advice that he and Rachel make plans to finally marry. Rachel and her mother began preparations for a February wedding while Jackie fulfilled an earlier commitment to join an all-star black team on a barnstorming tour of Venezuela. Rachel, who had never been outside California, took the opportunity to briefly work in New York City, where, living in Harlem, she was for the first time in a community dominated by African Americans. Rachel initially found work in New York as a hostess in an upscale restaurant on Park Avenue but left when she observed the manner in which the establishment treated black patrons and employees. She quickly found another job, this time using her nursing education, at the city's Hospital for Joint Diseases.

After a twenty-four-game schedule in Venezuela, Jackie returned to the United States and spent several weeks in New York touring the city with Rachel as they discussed their upcoming marriage. In early 1946, the couple returned to Southern California where they were married on February 10th in the Independent Church of Christ, the largest black church in Los Angeles. The Reverend Karl Downs flew in from Texas to officiate the ceremony. The only reminder of the recent world war was Charles Williams, Rachel's older half-brother, who was still in uniform after recovering from his ordeal as a prisoner of war, as he escorted his sister down the aisle.

After a brief honeymoon, the Robinsons boarded an airplane in Los Angeles bound for the Dodger spring training camp at Daytona Beach, Florida. Mallie Robinson, knowing little about air travel but ever mindful of the difficulties in blacks' finding places to eat, sent them off with a shoebox full of fried chicken and boiled eggs.

The Robinson's journey to Daytona Beach was, unfortunately, typical of those of other black couples at the time. At their first stop in New Orleans, they were "bumped" from the flight for what an air attendant said was "military priorities." After having difficulties finding a restaurant that would serve blacks and a hotel not limited to whites, they boarded another plane the next morning. At the next stop in Pensacola, they were again bumped from the flight for a civilian white couple. They received no explanation.

After more difficulties in finding food and lodging, the Robinson's decided to take a bus for the remainder of their trip. Nearly fifteen years later, Jackie, in his autobiography, still vividly remembered getting on a nearly empty luxury bus, sitting in a middle row, pushing a button to recline the seat, and quickly falling asleep. At their first stop, a crowd of whites boarded. The bus driver, following the Florida Jim Crow law, motioned the Robinsons to move to the back of the bus. Robinson recalled, "The seats at the back were reserved seats—reserved for Negroes—and they were straight-backed. No little button to push. No reclining seats."

Jackie felt humiliation for himself and for Rae. He wrote, "I had been ready to explode with rage, but I knew that the result would mean newspaper headlines about an ugly racial incident and possible arrest not only for me but also for Rae. By giving in to my feelings then, I could have blown the whole major league bit. I had swallowed my pride and choked back my anger. Again, this time it would have been much easier to take a beating than to remain passive. But I remembered the things Rae and I had said to each other during the months we had tried to prepare ourselves for exactly this kind of ordeal. We had agreed that I had no right to lose my temper, and jeopardized the chances of all blacks who would follow me if I could help break down the barriers."

The Robinsons finally arrived in Daytona Beach late on the afternoon of March 2. Meeting them were two reporters from the black weekly *Pittsburgh Courier* whom Rickey had hired to be escorts, protectors, friends, and advisors to the Robinsons and to be their liaison to the local black community.

John Richard Wright, a New Orleans-born pitcher, who had starred with a Navy team during the war and more recently in the Negro Leagues with the Homestead Grays, also stood in the welcoming party. Rickey had signed Wright shortly after Robinson, and he conceivably could have been the first to break the Major League color barrier. Wright received little attention from the press because it was obvious to most that he was there more as a companion to Robinson rather than having any chance of making the Dodger roster. This proved true as Wright later played only a brief time with Montreal before returning to the Negro Leagues.

After several days in Daytona Beach, the team moved to "Rickey University," the Dodger baseball school, in nearby Sanford. The players, that is all but Robinson and Wright who stayed in the homes of local black residents, were put up in the segregated lake-front Mayfair Hotel.

The first person the two black players met at the practice field was in the club house. Babe Hamberger, the Dodgers's equipment manager told them, "Just go out there and do your best. Don't get tense. Just be yourselves." At 9:30 on the morning of March 4, 1946, the two black men stepped on the Sanford practice field and became the first African Americans to breach Major League Baseball's color barrier. Still a long way from Brooklyn, it was a start.

Robinson and Wright joined about two hundred white players on the field as they worked on their throwing, batting, and conditioning. The whites appeared mostly indifferent to the black pair as their interests lay more in preparing and competing for their own positions with the teams. Some had racial prejudices, but mostly they looked at the black players as completion for coveted positions on the minor and major league rosters. This low-key "welcome" may have also been the result of Rickey's warning a week earlier that he expected the whites to treat the blacks as just two more baseball players and to "be the gentlemen you have shown yourselves to be."

In Rickey's interviews with the press prior to the start of spring training, he downplayed any interest he might have in any kind of social experiment. He emphasized that his interests lay solely in winning ball games. He said that he did not intend to be a crusader and he never noticed the color of the skin of a ball player. Rickey added "If an elephant could play center field better than any man I have, I would play the elephant."

Rickey had no ball playing elephants but he did have two black athletes, one in particular, who had a chance to advance to the Major Leagues. It was the color of their skin that drew reporters to the Sanford playing fields. One of the first questions to Jackie was about how he thought he would get along with the white players. He said, "I've gotten along with white boys in high school, at Pasadena, at UCLA, and in the army. I don't see why these should be any different." Jackie made no mention of his difficulties with "whites" while in uniform or his court-martial. The reporters, likely unaware of the incident, did not question his claim.

Jackie showed confidence and ease in working with the reporters when one asked what he would do if a white pitcher threw at his head. He said, "I'd duck." His response drew a laugh from the reporters, but they probed further, asking if he intended to take the Montreal or even the Brooklyn shortstop job. Jackie replied, "I just mean to do the best I can." When asked if he thought he could make the Major Leagues, Jackie modestly said, "I can't worry about Brooklyn; I haven't made the Montreal team yet."

Reporters were important to Jackie's success and acceptance. In his 1948 autobiography, he wrote, "True there is still discrimination in America, and indignities are by no means limited to the world of baseball—as any Negro can testify. Some of us have to break the ice. And I have found that most players and fans are, if not actually pulling for me, at least neither hostile nor vicious. That fact I attribute largely to the ceaseless efforts by a whole army of outspoken sportswriters who have preached fair play and democracy."

On the field the two black ball players found their teammates made little effort to be friendly, speaking to them "only in the line of duty." Jackie later wrote that his Montreal manager, Clay Hopper, a Mississippi native, "never really accepted me, he was careful to be courteous, but prejudice against the Negro was deeply ingrained in him." Whatever his thoughts, Hopper extended his hand and shook Jackie's at their first meeting, something rare for Southerners.

Later Jackie learned that Rickey and Hopper, while observing practice, noticed him make "an unusually tricky play." Rickey was so impressed that he said to Hopper that the play was "superhuman." Hopper responded, "Do you really think a nigger's a human being?"

After the second day of practice at Sanford, a white man came to the home in the black neighborhood where Robinson, Wright, and the two Pittsburgh reporters were staying. He told them that he had just come from a meeting of dozens of local residents. The consensus was that if Robinson and the other blacks did not leave Sanford, their lives would be in danger. With an active Ku Klux Klan presence in the area, the threat had some validity. After a telephone call to Rickey, the group quickly left town for Daytona Beach.

Rickey had deliberately selected Daytona Beach as a site for his spring games for its general reputation as a liberal city that accepted blacks as well or better than other Florida cities. William Perry, mayor of Daytona Beach, approved of the integrated training, saying, "No one objects to Jackie Robinson and Johnny Wright training here with Montreal. The city officials and population simply regard them as two more ball players. We welcome them and wish them luck."

However, the forced move from Sanford and the Jim Crow laws that confronted Jackie and Rachel all across Florida made him question his decision to attempt to break the color line. He said, "What could I do? Quit? I wanted to; but just didn't have the nerve to walk out on all the people who were counting on me—my family and close friends, Mr. Rickey, the fourteen million Negroes from coast to coast, the legion of understanding white people. Dejected as I was, I just had to stick it out."

Jackie had difficulties finding anything to do when not on the practice field because of the segregation of local recreational facilities and movie houses until he found the local USO. Apparently, Jackie held no bad feelings about his time in uniform because he took advantage of the integrated facility to play table tennis and pinochle with other veterans and active duty military personnel.

While most of Jackie's fellow ball players remained mostly dismissive, several white players assisted him in his training as his coaches moved him from shortstop to first base and finally second base. The problems that arose came, instead, from other teams training in Florida and the towns in which they trained. In practice games the opposing players continued to taunt Jackie with racial epitaphs, and their owners and managers canceled games because they did not want to play against blacks. One town was a bit less than direct when it informed the Montreal Royals that they could not play because there was no lighting on the field—despite the fact that it was a daytime game. Another town reacted to an integrated game by having one of their policemen attempt to arrest Jackie for playing in an interracial contest on a public ball field.

Despite the bigotry, Jackie had few bad feelings toward the South. He let his playing on the field be his response to heckles and prejudices. In his final exposition game at Daytona Beach, the cheers for him drowned out the boos. In his 1948 biography, he wrote, "I discovered that afternoon in Daytona—and many times thereafter—that most of the people below the Mason-Dixon Line accept my presence on a baseball diamond along with white players. The American sports fan—North and South—is fundamentally the same. Above everything else, he admires and respects athletic prowess, guts, and good sportsmanship. And he demands a fair chance and fair play."

Robinson's 1948 biography, simply titled with his name, is somewhat supportive of his white owners, managers, players, and fans—particularly when compared to his 1972 biography titled *I Never Had It Made*. Regardless, by the time Jackie reached the end of spring training the fans were warming to him and him to them.

Robinson got his "fair chance and fair play" and at the end of spring training became a member of the Montreal Royals regular season team.

• 21 •

Montreal Royals

$\mathcal{S}$pring training was productive for the Robinsons—with Jackie's earning his place in the Montreal Royals' lineup and Rachel's becoming pregnant. Despite her condition, over the following season she attended all of Jackie's home games, offering moral and emotional support.

The Royals departed Daytona Beach on April 15 for games with the Jersey City Giants in route to their home in Montreal. On April 18, with clear skies and chilly weather, more than 25,000 fans filled the stands of Roosevelt Stadium in Jersey City to participate in the opening day pageantry of the season and to see the first black to play in the AAA Minor League. Jackie broke that barrier when he stepped to the plate as the second batter up in the top half of the first inning, smashing the color barrier in professional sports and changing the world of baseball forever.

Fans greeted Jackie mostly with cheers. He worked the count to full before hitting an easy grounder to the shortstop for an out. It would be the last time the Jersey City Giants got Jackie out for the remainder of the game. At day's end, he was four for five—a home run, four runs batted in, four runs scored, and two stolen bases. His activities on the baselines were so threatening that he caused the opposing pitcher to commit two balks.

After the game, the fans mobbed Jackie, patting him on the back and asking for his autograph. Jackie wrote, "Once again I was convinced that American sport fans are truly democratic. I was sure now that they would accept me—that they didn't care what color a player was. All I had to do was play good ball and never stop trying."

Montreal welcomed Jackie and Rachel. Despite the post-war housing shortage, they found a nice apartment in the French Canadian section. Food rationing coupons, another vestige of the war, were still required, and the Robinson's neighbors shared theirs with the young couple.

Jackie wrote, "The people of Montreal were warm and wonderful to us. After the rejections, unpleasantness, and uncertainties, it was encouraging to find an atmosphere of complete acceptance and something approaching adulation."

Most of Montreal's opponents in the International League treated Jackie fairly well on the field although there were frequent shouts and slurs from the stands, such as "Nigger, go home." Jackie ignored the taunts and responded by "going home" only when he rounded the bases. Being the object of more than the usual jabs from the opposing team bench, he let his play on the field be his response.

In one case, though, Jackie did react. The team from Syracuse rode him harder than any other in the league, and at one point, a player came out of their dugout holding a black cat, or perhaps, depending on the source, the cat just wandered onto the field. Whatever the origins of the cat, a Syracuse player shouted, "Hey Robinson, here's one of your relatives!"

Jackie said nothing. The umpire had the frightened animal removed. Then Jackie moved into the batter's box and gave his response by hitting a double. When the next batter singled to drive him home as the winning run, the usually non-vocal Jackie hollered as he ran by the Syracuse bench, "I guess that relative of mine is happy now, isn't he?"

As the season progressed, harassment decreased and attendance increased. Whites, as well as blacks, came out to see Jackie play. The greatest disappointment to Jackie was when the Royals cut Johnny Wright and sent him further down the minor leagues. Robinson was now the only black in the white man's world of AAA baseball.

The Royals easily won the International League pennant. Jackie led the league in batting with an average of .349 with 113 runs scored. His forty stolen bases ranked second in the league and his fielding percentage was at the top.

By winning their league title, the Montreal Royals went to the Little World Series against the Louisville Colonels of the American Association. The first three games were played in the rigidly segregated Louisville. Jackie wrote, "I had been booed pretty soundly before, but nothing like this. A torrent of mass hate burst from the stands with virtually every move I made."

As a result of the fan behavior, and good pitching, Jackie did not play well in Louisville, batting below .200 as the Royals dropped two of the three contests. He was dejected until the Royals returned to Montreal to a huge welcome by fans incensed by their team's treatment in Kentucky. The Royals won three of the four games at home with Jackie batting .400 and scoring the winning run in the final game to win the Series.

After the game, Manager Clay Hopper prepared to return to his Mississippi cotton farm for the off season. Before his departure, he approached Jackie, held out his hand, and said, "You're a great ballplayer and a fine gentleman. It's been wonderful having you on the team."

Although eight months pregnant, Rachel attended the final game in Montreal as she had all the home games. She later wrote, "At the end of the 1946 season, we left Montreal primed for the next steps. The stopover in Canada had prepared us to return to the ongoing struggle for equality in our own country with greater equanimity and a happy time to reflect on."

Rachel returned to Pasadena while Jackie went on a month-long exposition tour. He joined her in California for the birth of Jack Roosevelt Robinson, Jr., on November 18, 1946.

Near the end of the 1946 season, Jackie had thought he might be called up to help the Dodgers in their own pennant drive. Rickey, however, had decided that the time was not yet right, and in the spring of 1947, Jackie rejoined the Royals for joint spring training with the senior club in Havana, Cuba. He felt welcomed by Hopper and his teammates from the year before and felt that thoroughly integrated Havana saw the team members as just ball players rather than black or white ball players.

Rickey had deliberately selected the more tolerant Cuba over Florida for spring training. Three other black players, catcher Roy Campanella and pitchers Don Newcombe and Roy Partlow, joined the Royals/Dodgers, but, they along with Jackie, were lodged in a separate hotel despite no Jim Crow laws on the island. Rickey, ever looking forward rather than just at the present said, "I want this training session to be smooth. I can't afford to have any 'incidents.'"

When Jackie complained about the separate hotels, Rickey advised him to be patient because they were "on the threshold of success." He then told him, "I want you to hit that ball. I want you to get on base and run wild. Steal their pants off. Be the most conspicuous player on the field. The newspapermen from New York will send good stories back about you and help mold favorable public opinion."

Trouble was not as far into the future or as far away as the East Coast. In Cuba, Robinson and Rickey had more immediate concern about "public opinion" when several players on the Dodger roster started a petition to keep Robinson off the team. Dodger Manager Leo Durocher found out about the duplicitous activities and called a late-night meeting of his players. Following ample obscenities, he said, "I don't care if a guy is yellow or black, or if he has stripes like a fucking zebra. I'm the manager of this team and I say he plays. What's more, I say he can make us all rich. And if any of you cannot use the money, I will see that you are all traded." Rickey then met with the players who had signed the petition and reiterated that they would be traded if they refused to play with Robinson.

With no other major or minor league teams conducting spring training in Cuba, the Royals and Dodgers had only themselves, a Cuban all-star team, and a Panamanian team as competition. Robinson hit .625 and stole seven bases. Despite his play on the field and Rickey's promises, Jackie still remained with the Royals rather than the Dodgers when the two teams returned to New York for several exposition games before opening day.

The newspapers spent many headlines speculating about whether or not Jackie would be joining the big leagues. Rickey kept that decision to himself, announcing neither to the newspapers nor to Jackie his plans. On April 9, the debate over Jackie's elevation to the Major League was swept from the sports pages by manager Durocher's one-year suspension by league commissioner Albert "Happy" Chandler. Citing Durocher's "conduct detrimental to baseball," Chandler alluded to the manager's "associations with known gamblers." The primary reason, however—as in most cases—was the threat to overall revenues caused by Durocher's affair with Hollywood actress Laraine Day whose divorce was not yet final. The Catholic Youth Organization and others were threatening to boycott baseball if no action was taken. Chandler followed the money, and Durocher spent the next year as a spectator rather than as a manager.

Robinson had lost one of his biggest backers, but the coverage of Durocher's suspension opened the way for Rickey to do what he said was "the most important thing I ever did in my life." On the afternoon of April 10, during a game between Montreal and Brooklyn at Ebbets Field, just after Jackie bunted into an easy double play, each press box reporter received a typed note signed by Rickey. It simply stated, "The Brooklyn Dodgers today purchased the contract of Jackie Roosevelt Robinson from the Montreal Royals. He will report immediately."

Earlier in the day, Rickey had called him to his office and informed him about the upcoming announcement and sworn him to secrecy. Jackie kept the confidence and followed the instruction to "report immediately" as soon as the note was made public. Decades of efforts by his race fell behind him as he walked from the Royal's visitor's dressing room across the field to the Dodgers home facility. There he found his new locker complete with the Dodger blue 42 that would become the most famous number in baseball history.

Breaking the Color Barrier

$\mathcal{O}$n August 2, 1945, 2nd Lt. Jack R. Robinson, 0-1031586, assigned to a segregated tank battalion, appeared before an army court-martial that threatened to dismiss him from the army and place him in a military prison for his actions in refusing to go to the back of a bus. Less than two years later, on April 15, 1947, Jackie Robinson, wearing Brooklyn Dodger number 42, stepped out on Ebbets Field to start a Major League Baseball game against the Boston Braves. In the stands were 26,623 fans, about 14,000 of whom where African Americans. Jackie not only broke the color barrier, he shattered the bigoted traditions of Major League Baseball that dated back to its early organization. The sport, and even race relations, would never be the same.

Times were good for all Americans. Servicemen and women were home from World War II, rationing had ended, the United States was working to rebuild Europe with the Marshall Plan, and American military superiority with the atomic bomb promised at least some period of peace. Baseball had survived as America's pastime and its popularity became even larger in the post-war years with the increase in prosperity and the introduction of television that brought games to the living rooms of fans. African Americans continued their quest for equality and Jackie's step on the diamond was symbolic as well as solid progress. Rachel wrote, "Jack and I began to realize how important we were to black America and how much we symbolized its hunger for opportunity and its determination to make dreams long deferred possible."

The crowd greeted Jackie and the team mostly with cheers. Brooklyn was a close community within a large city and its citizens heartily supported their "bums." A few boos were directed at Jackie at first base but overall he was welcomed as a Dodger rather than being rejected as a black man.

Boston pitcher Johnny Sain took the mound, and Jackie ground out in his first Major League at bat. Sain—a naval air cadet in 1943—had been the last pitcher to face an all-star team featuring the aging Babe Ruth. Sain said, "Then in 1947, I was the first pitcher to face Jackie Robinson, so I made history again, the first to face Jackie and the last to face the Babe." Sain added, "I don't remember any commotion that first day. It was like any other opener."

In a newspaper interview, Jackie said, "I was nervous in the first play of my first game at Ebbets Field, but nothing has bothered me since."

After the series with the Braves, the Dodgers moved to the Polo Grounds to face their rival Giants. More than 90,000 fans filled the stands for the two-game series—the largest in their history. The Dodger radio announcer, Red Barber, said, "They came to see Jackie Robinson. He became the biggest attraction in baseball since Babe Ruth."

After the games, hundreds of fans gathered in hopes of getting Jackie's autograph. Thousands of letters arrived at Dodger headquarters. A few notes made negative racial comments, but most writers congratulated and encouraged Jackie. He also received many invitations to speak and to appear at all kinds of events. Rickey, ever vigilant, acted as he always did with Jackie: he carefully determined just when and to whom Jackie would speak.

Jackie did not face extraordinary racism until they returned to Ebbets Field on April 22 for a three-game series with the Philadelphia Phillies who were revved up on "bench jockeying"—a baseball practice of taunting opposing players to "take them off their game" and to entertain themselves to pass the time. No subject—appearance, ethnicity, personal problems, or any other distinction small or large—was off limits. Dugout shouts called players Dagos, Wops, and Jew boys. Bald or bullet heads were noted as were large ears, noses, and lips. Bad plays or wide strikes received laughter as well as jokes. With Jackie on the field, the Phillies' bench added "nigger" to their individual list of insults and "nigger lovers" as their taunt to the entire Dodger team.

Manager Ben Chapman, who had grown up in Birmingham, Alabama, not only encouraged his Philadelphia players to shout at Jackie, but he also joined in their racial taunts. What followed came from racism as well as personal insecurities on the part of the players who knew that Jackie was only the first of many African Americans who would soon be challenging them for their positions on the roster.

Jackie wrote, "Starting to the plate in the first inning, I could scarcely believe my ears. Almost as if it had been synchronized by some master conductor, hate poured forth from the Phillies dugout."

"Hey, nigger, why don't you go back to the cotton field where you belong?"

"They're waiting for you in the jungles, black boy."

"Hey, snowflake, which one of those white boys' wives are you dating tonight."

"We don't want you here, nigger."

"Go back to the bushes."

Chapman and the Phillies players also shouted insults at Jackie's Dodger teammates. "Carpetbaggers" and "nigger lovers" were just a few of their epithets.

To the public and press, Jackie said that the shouts did not bother him. A column in the *Pittsburgh Courier* quoted him as saying, "The things the Phillies shouted at me from their bench have been shouted at me from other benches and I am not worried about it. They sound just the same in the big league as they did in the minor league."

Outside the public eye, Jackie felt differently. He held most of his emotions until much later when he wrote his autobiography in 1972. He wrote, "I felt tortured and I tried to play ball and ignore the insults. But it was really getting to me. What did the Phillies want from me? What, indeed, did Mr. Rickey expect from me? I was, after all, a human being. What was I doing here turning the other cheek as though I weren't a man? In college days I had the reputation as a black man who never tolerated affronts to his dignity. I had defied prejudice in the Army. How could I have thought that barriers would fall, that, indeed, my talent could triumph over bigotry?"

Jackie continued, "For one wild rage-crazed minute I thought, to hell with Mr. Rickey's 'Great Experiment.' It's clear it won't succeed. I have made every effort to work hard, to get myself into shape. My best is not enough for them. I thought what glorious, cleansing thing it would be to let go. To hell with the image of the patient black freak I was supposed to create. I could throw down my bat, stride over to the Phillies dugout, grab one of those white sons of bitches and smash his teeth in with my despised black fist. Then I could walk away from it all. I'd never become a sports star. But my son could tell his son someday what his daddy could have been if he hadn't been too much a man."

Jackie did not physically retaliate. He continued in his story, "Then I thought of Mr. Rickey—how his family and friends had begged him not to fight for me and my people. I thought of all his predictions, which had come true. Mr. Rickey had come to a crossroads and made a lonely decision. I was at a crossroads. I would make mine. I would stay."

Early in the game, the torment from the Phillies bench bothered Jackie into making easy outs. However, in the bottom of the eighth inning, he singled, stole second, went to third on wide throw, and scored the winning run on a teammate's single.

The Phillies manager and players continued their verbal abuse for the remainder of the three-game series. By the time the final game wound to an end, both the Dodgers and the press were tiring of—if not angry about—the Philadelphia team's behavior. Some of the Dodgers began to shout back, defending Jackie. One called the Phillies "yellow-bellied cowards."

Dan Parker, sports editor at the *New York Mirror* also disliked the treatment of the hometown ball player. He wrote, "During the recent series between the Phils and the Dodgers, Chapman and three of his players poured a stream of abuse at Jackie Robinson. Jackie, with admirable restraint, ignored the guttersnipe language coming from the Phils dugout, thus stamping himself as the only gentleman among those involved in the incident."

Branch Rickey said, "Chapman did more than anybody to unite the Dodgers. When he poured out that string of unconscionable abuse, he solidified and united thirty men, not one of whom was willing to sit by and see anyone kick around a man who had his hands tied behind his back—Chapman made Jackie a real member of the Dodgers."

Things were a bit easier for Jackie after the Philadelphia series but occasional taunts from the opponent's dugout and from the stands, especially on the road, continued. In May, the St. Louis Cardinals threatened to strike if Jackie played. National League President Ford Frick took immediate action. He said, "If you do this you will be suspended from the league. You will find that the friends you think you have in the press box will not support you, that you will be outcasts. I do not care if half the league strikes. Those who do it will encounter quick retribution. They will be suspended and I don't care if it wrecks the National League for five years. This is the United States of America, and one citizen has as much right to play as another. The National League will go down the line with Robinson whatever the consequence. You will find if you go through with your intention that you have been guilty of complete madness."

The St. Louis protestors backed down. Although Jackie's treatment by the players and fans continued to improve, some conditions and incidents did not change. Hotels on the road refused to admit Jackie and restaurants would not serve him. Along with fan mail came hate letters and death threats against Jackie and his family. On the field, opponent runners spiked him on the base lines and pitchers threw at his head when he was at the plate.

Good things happened as well. In Boston when spectators heckled Pee Wee Reese for playing ball with a black man, Jackie later wrote, "Pee Wee didn't answer them. Without a glance he left his position and walked over to me. He put his hand on my shoulder and began talking to me. His words weren't important. I don't even remember what he said. It was the gesture of comradeship and support that counted. As he stood talking with me with a friendly arm around my shoulder, he was saying loud and clear, 'Yell. Heckle.

Do anything you want. We came here to play baseball.' The jeering stopped, and a close lasting friendship began between Reese and me."

Although this is Jackie's recollection, there is no television film or video tape to confirm the story. Other accounts say that the incident occurred in Cincinnati, and Jackie, at times, remembered the story happening in 1948 rather than 1947. Whenever and wherever the gesture occurred, it has become a major part of the Robinson, as well as the Reese, legacy.

Jackie earned that legacy as much by controlling his temper as he did by making astounding plays on the field. One example involved Phillies manager Ben Chapman. The man had received so much bad publicity after his racial tantrum in their first meeting that he and the Philadelphia club owner attempted to revive his reputation. They approached Rickey with their request. According to Jackie, Rickey thought "it would be gracious and generous if I posed for a picture shaking hands with Chapman. The idea was also promoted by the baseball commissioner. I was somewhat sold—but not altogether—on the concept that a display of such harmony would be 'good for the game.' I have to admit, though, that having my picture taken with this man was one of the most difficult things I had to make myself do."

The consolatory Chapman told the press, "Jackie has been accepted in baseball and we of the Philadelphia organization have no objections to his playing and wish him all the luck we can."

Even in quieter times awkward moments arose with teammates with whom he had a good relationship. Atlanta native Hugh Casey was one of the earliest Dodgers to befriend Jackie. He spent hours hitting balls to him to improve his fielding and gave him tips from a pitcher's point of view. Casey, like many of his teammates, was insensitive—or perhaps just ignorant—about what they said to Jackie. During a poker game on the road, Casey, who had been having bad luck at the table as well as on the mound as a relief pitcher, said, "You know what I used to do down in Georgia when I ran into bad luck? I used to go out and find me the biggest, blackest nigger woman I could find and rub her teats to change my luck."

Jackie wrote, "I don't believe that there was a man in that game, including me, who thought that I could take that. I had to force back my anger. I had the memory of Mr. Rickey's words about looking for a man 'with guts not to fight back.' Finally, I made myself turn to the dealer and told him to deal the cards."

Jackie's success and acceptance opened the way for other black players to ease through the now broken barrier of segregated Major League Baseball. On July 3, the Cleveland Indians signed Larry Doby from the Newark Eagles in the Negro Leagues to become the first black player in the American League.

Later in the season, the Boston Braves, also in the American League, signed two more African American players.

Near the end of the year, Jackie later wrote, "I had started the season as a lonely man, often feeling like a black Don Quixote tilting at a lot of white windmills. I ended it feeling like a member of a solid team."

Some owners and players had only reluctantly or superficially accepted Jackie, but they were more than happy with the results. Whenever Jackie and the Dodgers came to town, they could be sure of their grandstands being full of whites as well as blacks. At home Brooklyn drew 1,828,215 paying fans for the season—a club record. Wendell Smith, sports editor for the *Pittsburgh Courier*, best summed the profits brought in by Robinson, "Jackie's nimble, Jackie's quick, Jackie's making the turnstiles click."

On September 23, a day after the Dodgers had secured the National League Pennant, Brooklyn held "Jackie Robinson Day" at Ebbets Field. In addition to a Tiffany's gold watch, a television set, and other gifts, a grateful Brooklyn presented Jackie a new Cadillac. Both Jackie and Rachel later commented that they were so happy that they would now no longer have to ride buses and the subway. They were also extremely pleased that Jackie's mother Mallie had taken her first airplane ride in order to attend the festivities.

Three days later the *Sporting News* awarded Jackie "Rookie of the Year" honors. The editor of the *News* wrote, "In selecting the outstanding rookie of 1947, the *Sporting News* sifted and weighed only stark baseball values. That Jackie Robinson might have had more obstacles than his first-year competitors, and that he perhaps had a harder fight to gain even Major League recognition, was no concern of this publication. The sociological experiment that Robinson represented, the trail-blazing that he did, the barriers he broke down, did not enter into the decision. He was rated and examined solely as a freshman player in the Big Leagues—on the basis of his hitting, his running, his defensive play, his team value."

Jackie's stats certainly merited the award. He led the National League in stolen bases, batted .297 while appearing in 151 of the 154 games, and scored 125 runs.

The Dodgers took the New York Yankees to seven games before losing the 1947 World Series. Jackie played well, hitting .296 and playing error-free in the field. Baseball's great experiment had come to an end—or to a beginning. Jackie, the sport, and the country were changed forever.

• 23 •

Federal Bureau of Investigation

$\mathcal{B}$y the end of the 1947 Major League Baseball season, Jackie Robinson stood as the best known and most respected African American in the country. Within the black community his popularity exceeded that of boxer Jack Johnson, rivaled that of Joe Louis who still reigned as heavy-weight champion, and eclipsed that of entertainers like Cab Calloway and Count Basie. In a national-wide poll, Jackie's popularity topped that of President Harry Truman, generals Dwight Eisenhower and Douglas MacArthur, and comedian/actor Bob Hope. According to the poll, the only person in America, white or black, whose popularity was greater than Jackie's was the country's first multimedia star, Bing Crosby, who led record sales, radio ratings, and motion picture grosses from 1931 to 1954. In addition to dozens of front-page photos on sports publications, Jackie appeared on the cover of *Time* magazine on September 22, 1947.

The post-season of his first year in Major League baseball also presented the opportunity for Jackie to make some money. Jackie had signed with Rickey for the Major League minimum salary of $5,000—more than $58,000 in today's dollars. There had been no bonuses during or at the end of the season. During the year, he, Rachel and Jackie, Jr., had lived in a single room in a hotel, and before the gift of the Cadillac had used public transportation. Rickey had prevented Jackie from making outside appearances or endorsing any products during the season.

Once the World Series concluded, it was time for Jackie to start making some real cash. He signed with the General Artists Corporation of Manhattan and soon appeared on billboards, in magazines, and on radio and television praising products such as bread, milk, and cigarettes as the first black representative of products aimed at both white and black consumers. His endorsement of Old Gold cigarettes drew some criticism. Jackie did not smoke, but in the early post-war years seemingly every other American did.

Jackie's first autobiography, written with Wendell Smith of the *Pittsburgh Courier,* came out in early 1948. The thin paperback, with the cover price of only $1 made Jackie's story affordable to everyone. Unfortunately, in the rush to write and publish the book, Jackie apparently did not have time to proof the final version as written by Smith. In addition to other errors, it has Jack's name as John and his mother's name as Mollie rather than Mallie.

There were also preliminary talks and even contracts for the production of a motion picture about Jackie's life, but it would be several more years before his story came to the screen. Although it added little or nothing to his reputation, it did increase his bank account and Jackie went on a four-week vaudeville tour across the country. After the performance by various singers, dancers, and comedians, Jackie took the stage to answer a series of scripted questions.

Jackie also spoke at testimonial dinners, civic club meetings, charity events, and National Association for the Advancement of Colored People (NAACP) gatherings. The Alameda County NAACP chapter in California presented him their Annual Merit Award as "the first man in the history of your country to grip the handle of a baseball bat and knock prejudice clear out of a Big League Ball Park."

Jackie's many appearances were nearly always accompanied by huge amounts of excellent food. He admitted, "We ate like pigs, and for me it was disastrous." At twenty-five pounds overweight, Jackie had to play himself back into shape when he reported to spring training in the Dominican Republic in 1948. Rickey had selected another "racial neutral" setting to get the Dodgers prepared for the regular season. Other than losing weight, Jackie moved from first base to his more natural position of second after a trade left the position open.

Jackie was not aware, but another event was taking place that would closely document much of the rest of his life. J. Edgar Hoover, the director of the Federal Bureau of Investigation, focused much of his organization's investigative powers on the threat, or at least his perceived threat, of communism in the United States. Of particular concern to him was the possibility of communist influence on African American organizations, such as the NAACP, and on black leaders, including Jackie Robinson.

The FBI claims it never began an investigation or opened an official file on Jackie. Just exactly when the FBI began their "unofficial file" on Jackie is unclear, but a summary of the first documents acquired about Robinson include, "The June 1, 1946, issue of 'People's Voice' reported that Jackie Robinson, the first Negro to break into organized baseball, has accepted chairmanship of the New York State Organizing Committee for United Negro and

Allied Veterans of America (UNAVA). The 'People's Voice' has been cited by the California Committee on Un-American Activities as being communist initiated and controlled. The UNAVA has been cited as a communist front by the Internal Security Subcommittee of the Senate Judicial Committee."

The report continued, "The November, 1946, issue of 'Fraternal Outlook' contained an article concerning the opening of the Solidarity Center of the International Workers Order (IWO) in Harlem, New York. The name, Jackie Robinson, baseball player, was listed as one of the persons on the Advisory Board of this Center."

The person's name and organization who requested the information is redacted. Concluding the report is the statement, "The foregoing information is furnished to you as a result of your request for an FBI file check and is not to be construed as a clearance or a nonclearance of the individual involved. This information is loaned for your use and is not to be disseminated outside of your agency."

There is no evidence that Jackie had any hint of the FBI's "non-investigation investigation" of him nor did he knowingly have any interaction with communists. His interests lay in playing baseball. Jackie began the 1948 season slowly with a typical sophomore slump at the plate but improved as the months passed. In what even Rachel noted as "a so-so" campaign, Jackie nevertheless finished the season batting in 85 runs with an average of .296 and led the National League as a second baseman with a fielding average of .983.

Robinson also led the league with what he called "a dubious distinction" of being hit by a pitch seven times. He and other black players entering the Major Leagues and those in the minors were frequent victims of brush back pitches or deliberate beanballs aimed at the player's head or body. Some of this was "just baseball," but beanballs were also an expression by white pitchers still not accepting black players.

Despite the beanballs, the continuing hate mail, and racial taunts from the stands, Jackie felt he truly belonged in the Major Leagues. He wrote, "The most important thing that happened to me in 1948, as far as I am concerned, is that I got thrown out of a game for heckling an umpire." In a game against Pittsburgh, a teammate received a bad call from umpire Butch Henline. When the Dodger bench got on Henline, the umpire gave them a warning. Jackie continued to berate Henline until the umpire tore off his mask, pointed at the dugout, and shouted, "You! Robinson. Yer out of the game."

Robinson wrote, "He didn't pick on me because I was black. He was treating me exactly as he would any ballplayer who got on his nerves. That made me feel great, even though I couldn't play anymore that day. One of the newspapers said it in the best headline that I ever got: *Jackie Just Another Guy.*"

House Un-American
Activities Committee

$\mathcal{B}$y 1949, Jackie Robinson was so popular that four songs about him were copyrighted by the Library of Congress. Woodrow "Buddy" Johnson's recording of "Did You See Jackie Robinson Hit That Ball?" became an instant classic as it advanced to Number 13 on the national charts. Count Basie's version later in the year became a baseball standard.

Fan mail by the sack full arrived at the Dodgers headquarters in Brooklyn. Efforts were made to separate the hate mail before the letters were forwarded to Jackie. There was so much mail that Rachel and Jackie hired a neighbor to prepare responses. He reviewed every response before he signed each letter.

In addition to his popularity on the baseball field, Jackie had become a representative figure for all of black America. In July 1949, the House Un-American Activities Committee (HUAC) invited Jackie, along with prominent black attorneys, educators, and civil leaders, to appear before the Congressional group. The purpose of the committee's meeting was to receive the opinion from black leaders on the recent statement by singer, actor, and activist Paul Robeson on what had been interpreted as his claiming that African Americans would not fight against the communist Soviet Union if the Cold War became hot.

Although twenty years his senior, Robeson's life resembled that of Jackie's. He had been a star athlete at Rutgers College before going on to national fame as a singer and actor. By the time Jackie joined the Major Leagues, Robeson was one of the most famous black Americans at home as well as overseas. Robeson traveled widely, including to Africa and to the Soviet Union where he expressed appreciation for the equal treatment he received.

In April 1949, at a peace conference in Paris, Robeson said about the United States and the Soviet Union, "It is unthinkable that American Negroes would go to war on behalf of those who have oppressed us for generations against a country which in one generation has raised our people to the full dignity of mankind."

The invitation to speak to HUAC was not a subpoena. Jackie's attendance would be voluntary. Jackie had no desire, as he later wrote, "to fall prey to the white man's game and allow myself to be pitted against another black man." Rachel and Jackie had long talks and also received much advice from members of the black press on whether or not he should testify. Rickey, a staunch anti-communist, encouraged him to appear before the committee. Jackie, who preferred to be a ballplayer rather than a politician, finally relented.

In his 1972 biography, Jackie wrote that ultimately his decision came from not believing anyone, including Robeson, had the right to supposedly speak for all black people. He also referenced his own military service when he wrote, "I wasn't about to knock him for being a Communist or a Communist sympathizer. That was his right. But I was afraid that Robeson's statement might discredit blacks in the eyes of whites. I was black and he wasn't speaking for me. I had served in the Armed Forces and had been badly mistreated. When [sic] I couldn't defend my country for the injustice I suffered, I was still proud to have been in uniform."

In the days before his appearance, Jackie made it clear to reporters about what would be the basics of his testimony. He told them that black Americans would defend the United States—just as they had in World War II when he served as a second lieutenant—against any and all enemies.

On July 18, 1949, Jackie, with Rachel seated behind, appeared before the HUAC in the capitol building in Washington, D.C. After commenting that he had no experience in politics, but a lifetime living as a black man, he began his testimony talking, not about Robeson, but rather Jim Crow. He said, "The white public should start toward real understanding by appreciating that every Negro who is worth his salt is going to resent any kind of slurs and discrimination because of his race, and he is going to use every bit of intelligence such as he has to stop it. This has got absolutely nothing to do with what Communists may or may not be trying to do. And white people must realize that the more a Negro hates Communism because it opposes democracy, the more he is going to hate any other influence that kills off democracy in this country—and that goes for racial discrimination in the Army, and segregation on trains and buses, and job discrimination because of religious beliefs or color or place of birth.

"And one other thing the American public ought to understand, if we are to make progress in this matter: The fact that it is a Communist who denounces injustice in the courts, police brutality, and lynching when it happens doesn't change the truth of his charges. Just because Communists kick up a big fuss over racial discrimination when it suits their purposes, a lot of people try to pretend that the whole issue is a creation of Communist imagination.

"But they are not fooling anyone with this kind of pretense, and talk about Communists stirring up Negroes to protest only makes present misunderstanding worse than ever. Negroes were stirred up long before there was a Communist Party, and they'll stay stirred up long after the party has disappeared—unless Jim Crow has disappeared by then as well."

Robinson then responded directly on the questions about Paul Robeson. "I've been asked to express my views on Paul Robeson's statement that American Negroes would refuse to fight in any war against Russia because we love Russia so much. I haven't any comment to make on that statement except that if Mr. Robeson actually made it, it sounds very silly to me. But he has a right to his personal views, that is his business and not mine. He's still a famous ex-athlete and a great singer and actor."

Jackie concluded with more remarks about the loyalty of black Americans and their continued fight for equality. "I understand that there are some few Negroes who are members of the Communist Party, and in the event of war with Russia they'd probably act just as any other communist would. So would members of other minority and majority groups. There are some colored pacifists, and they'd act just like a pacifist of any color. And most Negroes—and Italians and Irish and Jews and Swedes and Slavs and other Americans—would act just as all groups did in the last war. They'd do their best to help their country win the war—against Russia or any other enemy that threatened us. This isn't said as any defense of the Negro's loyalty, because any loyalty that needs defense can't amount to much in the long run. And no one has ever questioned my race's loyalty except a few people who don't amount to much.

"What I'm trying to get across is that the American public is off on the wrong feet when it begins to think of radicalism in terms of any special minority group. It is the thinking of this sort that gets people scared because one Negro, speaking to a communist group in Paris, threatens an organized boycott of 15,000,000 members of his race.

"I can't speak for any 15,000,000 people any more than any other one person can, but I know that I've got too much invested for my wife and child and myself in the future of this country, and I and other Americans of many races and faiths have too much invested in our country's welfare, for any of us to throw it away because of a siren song sung in base (a reference to Robeson's singing). I am a religious man. Therefore I cherish America where I am free to worship as I please, a privilege which some countries do not give. And I suspect that 999 out of almost any thousand colored Americans you meet will tell you the same thing.

"But that doesn't mean that we're going to stop fighting race discrimination in this country until we've got it licked. It means that we're going to fight it all the harder because our stake in the future is so big. We can win our fight without the communists and we don't want their help."

After his testimony, the Robinsons hurried to the airport to catch a plane back to New York where the couple arrived in time for Jackie to contribute to the 3–0 remarks over the Chicago Cubs at Ebbets Field. Newspapers praised Jackie's comments about Robeson but said little about his comments on the battle against Jim Crow. Jackie's testimony with a brief analysis also made it into his FBI file. Even though his comments were made publicly and reproduced in their entirety, the FBI classified the document "Confidential" and did not declassify it until after Jackie's death.

Jackie's game on the field continued to improve. By the end of the 1949 season, he led the league with a .349 batting average and in stolen bases with 37. He was not only selected for the All-Star Game but also as the league's Most Valuable Player as well. The Dodgers won the National League but once again fell to the Yankees in the World Series.

• 25 •

Fame, Death Threats, and Retirement

The year 1950 brought even more good fortune and fame to Jackie and his family. On January 13, in New York's Flower Fifth Avenue Hospital, Rachel gave birth to their daughter Sharon. Three weeks later Jackie flew to Los Angeles to begin filming the Eagle Lion Studio production of *The Jackie Robinson Story.*

Production began in February with Jackie playing himself and the popular actress Ruby Dee appearing as Rachel. By shooting scenes day and night, the movie wrapped in time for Jackie to report to spring training. The motion picture opened at a New York Broadway theater on May 16—with the Robinsons, the Cab Calloways, Adam Clayton Powell, and many other celebrities in attendance—to positive reviews despite the film's cheap production values. Audiences enjoyed its theme of Jackie's overcoming obstacles to the soundtrack of patriotic background music that included the repeated use of "America the Beautiful." Even the critics wrote positively about the film, including Bosley Crowther of the *New York Times* who wrote, "Here the simple story of Mr. Robinson's trail blazing career is reenacted with manifest fidelity and conspicuous dramatic restraint. And Mr. Robinson, commandeering that rare thing of playing himself in the picture's leading role, displays a calm assurance and composure that might be envied by many a Hollywood star."

Neither Jackie nor Rachel were completely happy with the film. Rachel wrote, "*The Jackie Robinson Story* was a scantily researched low-budget film completed between seasons. However, the very fact that Jack played himself made it a classic of sorts."

Jackie wrote, "It was exciting to participate in it. But later I realized it had been made too quickly, that it was budgeted too low, and that, if it had been made later in my career, it could have been done much better."

Jackie's growing fame expanded to other media. The May 8, 1950 edition of *Life* magazine featured him on its cover, and in that same month Fawcett Publishers released the first of a series of six comic books by sportswriter Charles Dexter about Jackie's life and career, each costing a mere ten cents to reach adults as well as children.

Despite the Hollywood and the other star treatment, Jackie eased back into his full-time job as a baseball player. Once again he made the All-Star team and finished the year with a batting average of .328.

At the end of the 1950 season, moves within the ownership of the Dodger organization forced Branch Rickey to sell his part of the team and step down as president. According to Rachel, "I believe Jackie missed Branch Rickey, not in the old role of defender, but as mentor and friend. He and Walter O'Malley, Rickey's successor as president, were never able to develop a comfortable relationship. O'Malley called Jack a 'Rickeyman' and a prima donna. Tensions between them surfaced frequently."

With the opening of the 1951 season, Jackie allowed his emotions to surface on the field, perhaps because Rickey was no longer there to influence him or perhaps because he was simply feeling more confident about his standing. He questioned calls and stood up to umpires as well as to opposing players. He no longer held back the quick temper that he had exhibited since a child. As Rachel wrote, "Jackie began to speak out more forcefully." Some sportswriters, as well as fans, labeled Jackie temperamental but most recognized that he was standing up for his rights—no differently than any ball player white or black. He finished the year with his batting average ten points above the previous at .338.

The FBI continued to keep their file on Jackie. Not all the efforts of the Bureau focused on following his association with organizations that had communist ties. They also investigated death threats against Jackie that came through the U.S. mail, which made them federal crimes. Of the 131 pages in his FBI file, almost a third are dedicated to the investigations of death threats against Jackie during the 1951 season. The FBI's "Synopsis of Facts" about the first incident stated, "Letters addressed to the 'Cincinnati Enquirer,' Cincinnati Police Station, and the 'Cincinnati Reds' baseball club, all apparently written on same type stationery with block-type printing, containing threats to shoot and kill JACKIE ROBINSON, New York Brooklyn Dodgers baseball player. Victim and Manager of Brooklyn Dodger ball club advised of letters prior to games without incident. Laboratory examination made of one letter, with negative results. No suspects developed."

Forensic results on the letters, FBI interoffice memos and transfer documents, and newspaper articles about the threats make up the majority of the file. The threats and investigations were of sufficient importance to merit

Director Hoover personally acknowledging several of the documents with his signature.

Despite the death threats, beanballs, and racist taunts from opponents, by 1951 Jackie was well accepted by his teammates, and he enjoyed the respect, if not idolization, by most fans in Brooklyn and many across the country. He remained, however, one of the few blacks in the Major Leagues. In 1951, African Americans numbered fewer than 3 percent of Major League rosters. Some teams, like the Boston Red Sox, remained all white until 1959 when the number of Negro players rose to nearly 9 percent.

Jackie continued to bat over .300 during the next three seasons as the Dodgers won the National League Pennant in 1952 by four and a half games and again in 1953 by a whopping thirteen games. They finished second in 1954, led the National League in 1955, and then beat the New York Yankees in the World Series in seven games.

By the time the Dodgers won the World Series, Jackie was confronting even more issues. His injuries and age—Jackie was twenty-eight years old his rookie season, meaning that he had missed several of his prime years—were taking their toll, and he was having recurring conflicts with the Dodger owners and managers. His having never developed strong relationships with them after Rickey left, Jackie found himself plagued with internal fights he did not need.

Jackie began considering retirement a year before the World Series win. He wrote, "By the end of the 1954 season I was getting fed up and I began to make preparations to leave baseball. I loved the game but my experience had not been typical—I was tired of fighting the press, the front office—and I knew I was reaching the end of my peak years as an athlete."

Several events ultimately hastened his decision. Friends let William Black, president of Chock Full o' Nuts, know that Jackie was contemplating retirement. Having taken his company from a single stand selling nuts in 1922 to a chain of successful Manhattan coffee shops, Black was eager to recruit Jackie to join his team when the time came. Although white, Black staffed his company headquarters and his shop workers with a large number of African Americans while offering generous salaries and health benefits to his employees.

In early December 1956, Black and Jackie met at a Manhattan Chock Full o' Nuts restaurant. According to Jackie, "We took to each other and negotiations began for me to become a vice president in the company when I retired from baseball."

Black later told the press that after the lunch, "I was convinced he is the man for us."

Black and Jackie agreed to meet again on December 12th at the Chock Full o' Nuts headquarters in Manhattan to sign a contract. In the meantime,

Jackie contacted *Look* magazine, with whom he had signed an agreement two years preciously for the huge sum of $50,000 for exclusive rights to his retirement story. Simultaneously, he was delaying a meeting with Dodger General Manager Buzzie Bavasi, requested by his staff on the 11th.

Late on the 12th, after he had signed the contract with Black and had informed *Look* to go forward with their retirement story planned for January 8, Jackie called Bavasi. Before Jackie could tell him about his retirement, Bavasi informed Jackie the Dodgers had traded him to the New York Giants. Bavasi rationalized his decision by explaining that the trade would benefit both parties: the Dodgers could bring up younger players from the minor leagues and Jackie could stay in New York.

There is no evidence that the Dodgers knew about Jackie's recent decision to leave baseball; the trade apparently was strictly business and "part of the game." "Surprised and stunned" at the news, according to his own accounts, Jackie was tempted to tell Bavasi that he was retired and was no longer Dodger property to be traded. In accordance with his agreement with *Look* to make the announcement, however, he said nothing. He received nice notes from Bavasi and O'Malley expressing their "regrets" on having to trade him. The Giants were pleased to acquire the ball player. Jackie avoided interviews and, with *Look* paying the bills, flew to California "to visit family and to keep the press off our backs."

The article in *Look* leaked to the press on January 8, 1957, three days before its official release. Jackie rushed back to New York to face reporters. The Giants raised their salary offer for Jackie to reconsider and join their team. Not only were his skills on the diamond in demand, but also his appeal that filled the stands—perhaps the more important motivation. In his autobiography, Jackie admitted to having second thoughts about retiring, but, when Bavasi told the press he was talking about leaving baseball only to get a higher salary from the Giants, he made his final decision.

Jackie wrote, "Some of the writers damned me for having held out on the story. Others felt it was my right. Personally, I felt that Bavasi and some of the writers resented the fact that I had outsmarted baseball, before baseball outsmarted me. The way I figured it, I was even with baseball and baseball with me. The game had done much for me, and I had done much for it."

Late on a cold night in January, Jackie returned to the Dodger clubhouse to clean out his locker. As he left for the last time, an Associated Press photographer snapped a picture of the graying, slightly overweight icon dressed in a heavy overcoat with a bat and bag over his shoulder. A clubhouse cat appeared in the background as one of the few witnesses to the departure from baseball of the man who had broken the Major League color barrier and went on to become one of baseball's all-time greats.

· 26 ·

Life after Baseball

$\mathcal{T}$o his friend Hank Aaron, Jackie once said, "The game of baseball is great, but the greatest thing is what you do after your career is over." Jackie was more than ready for his post-baseball life.

By the time Jackie retired from baseball, he was financially secure from savings from his baseball salary, the *Look* article, and his various endorsements. The Robinsons completed their family with the birth of David on May 14, 1952; they built their dream home in North Stamford, Connecticut, in 1955. Jack commuted daily, driving his own car to the Chock Full o' Nuts offices in Manhattan where he got along well with founder Bill Black and enjoyed working with the employees and settling worker conflicts. Jackie also appreciated Black's support for civil rights in the form of his being allowed to use company time to travel the country to speak for the NAACP.

Early in his employment at Chock Full o' Nuts, Roy Wilkins, the executive secretary of the NAACP, asked Jackie to chair a major nation-wide funding drive for the association's activities. Jackie agreed but only on the condition that he would be an active participant and not just a figurehead. Wilkins concurred, and Jackie soon took to the road as he changed from a famous baseball player into a noted civil rights spokesman.

Rachel and Jackie both strongly supported the Civil Rights Movement, admiring the protests of blacks in the South but recognizing that prejudices and bigotry were not limited to any area of the United States. Rachel wrote, "In the South, the dimensions of the fight were clear, legislated, and up for challenge. In the North, racism was disguised, denied, and pernicious."

Jackie hosted a weekly radio show on WNBC and WNBT as well as writing a column three times a week for the *New York Post*. He addressed politics, international affairs, baseball, and civil rights. He noted that the num-

128

ber of black players in the Major Leagues was still small and that there were no African Americans in baseball's front offices or in the dugouts as managers.

Jackie had always been in exemplary health. Shortly after his retirement, however, he began to lose weight for no apparent reason and to experience excessive thirst. A doctor's visit revealed a diagnosis of diabetes that called for a program of exercise, proper diet, and insulin therapy. The exercise part was easy. Jackie was a scratch golfer and even broke 70 on one round. Rachel eliminated the baked goods and sweets from their home, and Jackie conducted his tests and injected his insulin. Diabetes would at times slow Jackie, but for the next decade and a half, he never let it stop his efforts to gain equality for all.

Jackie continued his efforts to support and advance the black community. He led the fund-raising efforts in 1962 to rebuild two African American churches that had been burned by anti-black factions. Jackie and Rachel stood side-by-side with hundreds of thousands before the Lincoln Memorial in Washington, D.C. on August 28, 1963 to hear King's "I Have a Dream" speech. In 1964, he helped found the Freedom National Bank, a black-owned-and-operated commercial bank in Harlem. Jackie also sought to directly assist black families when he formed a construction company in 1970 to build low-income housing.

Jackie also became involved in politics. In the 1960 Democratic Presidential Primary, Jackie supported Hubert Humphrey because he admired the Minnesota Senator's support for civil rights. When Humphrey was defeated by John F. Kennedy, Jackie met with the Massachusetts senator but was disappointed that he knew little of the problems in the black community. More importantly, Jackie had difficulty with Kennedy's failure to look him in the eye during their dialogue.

As a part of his radio show, Jackie said, "I have always felt that blacks must be represented in both parties." With that said, he began discussions with Vice President Richard Nixon, the Republican nominee. Jackie determined that Nixon rather than Kennedy would do more to help African Americans. However, as the campaign progressed, Jackie became disillusioned with Nixon, especially after he failed to assist in the release of Dr. Martin Luther King, Jr., from a Georgia jail.

In 1962, Jackie met Nelson Rockefeller and was impressed with the New York Governor's stances on civil rights. He resigned from Chock Full o' Nuts in 1964 to join the governor's presidential nomination campaign as one of his six national directors. After Barry Goldwater won the nomination, a disappointed Jackie briefly left the Republican Party before rejoining Rockefeller in 1966 as a special assistant for community affairs when Rockefeller was reelected governor of New York. Jackie left that position as well as the

Republican Party in 1968 when he switched his allegiance to Humphrey against Nixon.

Over the years Jackie attended occasional "old timers" baseball events, including throwing out first pitches at the World Series, but he had mostly put baseball behind him as he struggled to support the Civil Rights Movement. When he did speak at baseball functions, he emphasized the need for black managers and administrative positions. In 1965, Jackie broke another barrier in becoming the first black analyst on the ABC Television telecast of the Major League Baseball Game of the Week.

• 27 •

More FBI

$\mathcal{J}$ackie's work with and fundraising for the NAACP and other black or-
ganizations—as well as his later interactions with Dr. King, Malcolm X, the
Black Panther Party, and other African American leaders—brought him under
more scrutiny by the FBI. On June 30, 1958, a bureau agent in the New
York office, whose name is redacted, prepared an eight-page classified memorandum for the Washington headquarters on Jackie's activities supporting the
International Workers Order to end racial discrimination in Levittown, New
York, and his chairmanship of the New York State Organizing Committee
for United Negro and Allied Veterans of America (UNAVA). Ten articles
about Jackie's activism that had appeared in the Communist Party-sponsored
New York newspaper the *Daily Worker* and other related periodicals were
cited. The memo also provided balance by including Jackie's testimony before
HUAC and a July 9, 1949, article in the *New York Times* that quoted Jackie as
saying, "he would fight for the United States against Russia or any aggressor
because 'I want my kids to have the same things that I have.'"

While the FBI never, in their words, officially investigated Jackie, they
certainly kept a close watch and an updated file on his activities. In a two-
page response on September 2, 1958, subject line "Jack R. Robinson," to and
from redacted names, the Bureau said, "No investigation pertinent to your
inquiry has been conducted by the FBI concerning the captioned individual.
However, the files of this Bureau reflect the following information which may
relate to the subject of your name check request."

The response, classified as Confidential, then referenced some of the articles from the June 30 memo, adding that several of the publications had been
found "to be Communist initiated and controlled, or so strongly influenced

as to be in the Stalin solar system." Another paragraph said that the UNAVA was a communist front "to provoke racial friction."

The New Haven branch of the FBI began its own investigation of Jackie after the Robinsons moved to Connecticut. On October 16, 1963, the New Haven office submitted a report to the Director of the FBI with the subject, "Re: Jackie Robinson, Board of Directors and Co-chairman National Life Membership Committee, National Association for the Advancement of Colored People."

The report, with the exception of being on United States Department of Justice, Federal Bureau of Investigation, New Haven, Connecticut, letterhead is nearly identical to the Office Memorandum of June 30, 1958. It is likely that someone or some agency requested a more official looking report.

Over the following years, the FBI kept files on Jackie but did not make a summary of their findings until June 29, 1965. On that date, an analyst, name redacted, submitted a thirty-six-page report—the largest in Robinson's file—titled "Correlation Summary"—to a coordinator whose name and position are also redacted. Classified as "Secret" and divided in two parts, the report contains summaries of Jackie's activities dating back to 1945 with Rickey's initial consideration for signing him to break the Major League color barrier. It then followed his associations with various organizations that the FBI deemed subversive over the next two decades. Some of his information came from the press clippings and other from "this informant," "a highly confidential source," "a delicate confidential source," "a confidential informant," or redacted "advised." About a fourth of the first part of the summary is so redacted that it is confusing at best and limiting in understanding at worst.

The second part of the summary is a list of nearly one hundred newspaper articles from major U.S. cities about Jackie's participation or appearance with the NAACP and his speaking out on baseball, school, and housing integration and civil rights in general. All of these citations include reference numbers to the source of the entire articles located in the FBI files.

There are no findings in any of these reports that provide any direct accusations of Jackie's having anything to do with the Communist Party except his being written about in their publications and being a member of organizations engaged in promoting civil rights. Some of these organizations were, in fact, targeted by communist agents to increase racial unrest, but Jackie, as he had in the army, pursued peaceful means in his efforts to gain equality for African Americans.

Jackie made no attempt to back down in his beliefs or to the director of the FBI. An article in the *Detroit Free Press* on December 12, 1964, included Jackie's thoughts on J. Edgar Hoover. The Director's fears and beliefs that communists had infiltrated the Civil Rights Movement were well known.

Hoover had also recently called Dr King a liar. Jackie said, "I always thought J. Edgar Hoover should be down on his hands and knees blessing Martin Luther King, for if it had not been for King, there would have been bloody race riots. King in a way was doing the FBI job."

The article continued by saying that Hoover was "out of step" and basically a "states righter." This latter accusation was a thinly veiled belief that Hoover harbored prejudices and bigotry. Whether or not Jackie had any idea at the time of the size of his "unofficial" FBI file is not known.

On June 15, 1966, the New York FBI office submitted a report that a source "reliable in past" advised that Jackie Robinson would be leading a group from Memphis, Tennessee, to Jackson, Mississippi, to protest the shooting of James Meredith and the racial oppression in the Mississippi Delta. The source then claimed the group would join the march on to Jackson. Nearly half of the report is redacted.

The final report of significance is dated July 24, 1969 and is headed by a letter from Director Hoover to John D. Ehrlichman, Counsel to President Richard Nixon. It states, "Reference is made to your name check request concerning [redacted] and a number of other individuals." After nearly two pages of redacted names is a paragraph that states, "Attached are separate memoranda regarding the following individuals" followed by more redactions and the name Jackie Robinson.

The memorandum contains some of the same articles from 1946 linking Jackie with several suspected communist organizations. At the end of the memo is the only current information that states, "According to a news release on September 13, 1968, Jackie Robinson, former baseball star, while speaking at a news conference minutes before leaving to address a Black Panther meeting in Brooklyn, New York, was reported as having stated, 'The Black Panther organization is one with an interest in seeking peace and reports otherwise are due to misinformed newsmen. Improper reporting has determined that they (the Black Panthers) are a militant group while the fact is they are seeking peace.'"

Following a redacted paragraph, the memo disagreed with Jackie's assessment of the Black Panthers, "The Black Panther Party has been described as a black extremist, militant, violent prone organization whose members have been involved in confrontations with law enforcement officers."

The memo concluded, "The fingerprint files of the Identification Division of the FBI contain no arrest data identifiable with captioned individual based upon the background information submitted in connection with this name check request."

The reasons for Ehrlichman's interest in Jackie are unknown. It may have been because of his defense of the Black Panthers or possibly because of Jackie's support of Humphrey in the recent presidential election. It may have also been research for the preparation of Nixon's infamous enemy list. Whatever the reason, there was no further requests from the White House about Jackie. Ehrlichman soon had his own problems and would be jailed for eighteen months for his part in the Watergate break-in.

Despite the many hours obviously spent by FBI investigators and those who maintained the records, there is no information in Jackie Robinson's file about his time in the army beyond his serial number and dates of service that are included on a page about his family and work history. There is no mention of his court-martial or of his early discharge—all facts that would have been easily discovered by minimal research.

Ironically, the final document in Jackie's FBI file is neither a memo of investigation nor a report from a "reliable source." Rather it is a letter from Jackie dated June 14, 1972, to Pat Gray, the Acting FBI Director, who had assumed the Bureau's leadership after the death of Hoover the previous May 2. The letter, written on "Jackie Robinson Development Company" letterhead, says, "This note brings you my personal and deep appreciation of your efforts on my behalf regarding the matter that Jack Anderson had in his column."

No other information is in the file explaining what Anderson had written about Jackie or what the FBI had done on his "behalf." It is likely, however, that this had to do with accusations of Jackie's relationship with communist organizations and the militant Black Panthers. It is also further evidence that Jackie had no idea that the FBI had been keeping a file on him since the late 1940s.

· 28 ·

Final Days

$\mathcal{J}$ackie continued his active schedule of work and public appearances during the early 1970s despite a mild heart attack in 1968 and another in 1970. His advancing diabetes deteriorated his eyesight and caused extreme pain in his legs. In early 1972, his vision became so poor he could no longer drive; he hired a chauffeur and continued his busy schedule.

On June 4, 1972, in a ceremony at Dodger Stadium, Jackie's number 42—along with Roy Campanella's number 39 and Sandy Koufax's number 32—were retired by the Dodgers. Sportswriters noted that Jackie could hardly see and had difficulty walking. They made no mention that the two African Americans and one Jewish American were the honorees.

Despite his physical impairments, it was a happy day for Jackie. He said, "This is truly one of the greatest moments in my life."

Before the second game of the World Series between Oakland and Cincinnati on October 15, Major League baseball honored Jackie on the 25th anniversary of his entering the Major Leagues. Jackie threw out the first pitch and said, "I am extremely proud and pleased. I'm going to be tremendously more pleased and proud when I look at that third base coaching line one day and see a black face managing in baseball."

At the time of the ceremony, Jackie was very nearly blind, and he was having trouble moving his legs. As the family gathered for a family portrait a few days before the World Series honors, just before a photographer snapped their picture, Rachel heard Jackie whisper, "the last hurrah."

Jackie was prophetical. On the morning of October 23, he worked at his development company office and in the afternoon had his chauffer take him to various wholesalers to gather and deliver food baskets to the Brooklyn Nazarene Baptist Church's needy. Early the next morning Rachel was in the kitchen preparing breakfast when Jackie rushed in from their bedroom, hugged her, and said, "I love you." He then dropped to the floor from a massive heart attack. Jackie died on the way to the Stanford hospital. He was only fifty-three years old.

Rachel later wrote, "My dearest Jackie, my giant, had been struck down, striving to live and loving to the very end."

Jackie's funeral was held on October 29 at New York's Riverside Church. Dignitaries from baseball, other sports, civil rights leaders, and politicians attended. Jesse Jackson, an emerging leader in the equal rights movement, said, "For a fleeting moment, America tried democracy and it worked. For a fleeting moment, America became one nation under God. This man turned the stumbling block into a stepping stone."

He concluded, "No grave can hold this body down. It belongs to the ages, and all of us are better off because the temple of God, the man with convictions, the man with a mission, passed this way."

· 29 ·

Legacy

$\mathcal{J}$ackie secured his legacy when he stepped out on Ebbets Field on April 15, 1947, as the first African American to play in the Major Leagues. He added to his reputation not only by his breaking the baseball's color barrier and opening the door for future African Americans, but also he filled the daily game box scores as well. Jackie was not just a black ball player, he was superior athlete in all aspects of the game—a great baseball player, period.

In 1962, in his first year of eligibility, Jackie was inducted into Baseball's Hall of Fame. Prior to the voting for the award, Jackie told baseball writers that, when considering his candidacy for the Hall, they should look only at his playing ability and not the fact that he had broken the Major League race barrier. When he first met Branch Rickey, Jackie said, "It's the box score that really counts." Reflecting his request, his Hall of Fame plaque makes no mention of race and states:

Jack Roosevelt Robinson
Brooklyn, N. L. 1947–1956

"Leading N.L. batter in 1949. Holds fielding mark for second baseman play in 150 or more games with .992. Led N. L. in stolen bases in 1947 and 1949. Most Valuable Player in 1949. Lifetime batting average .311. Joint record holder for most double plays by second baseman, 137 in 1951. Led Second basemen in double plays 1949–50–51–52."

On June 25, 2008, with the approval of Rachel and Sharon Robinson, the Hall of Fame retired the old plaque and dedicated a new one. Hall of Fame Board Chairman Jane Forbes Clark said at the unveiling ceremony, "At his induction in 1962, his plaque reflected his wishes—it only recounted his magnificent playing career. But as we all know, there's no person more central or more important to the history of baseball for his pioneering ways. His impact on our game is not fully defined without the mention of his extreme courage in crossing the color line."

The second plaque states:

Jack Roosevelt Robinson
"Jackie"
Brooklyn, N. L., 1947–1956

"A player of extraordinary ability renowned for his electrifying style of play. Over 10 seasons hit .311, scored more than 100 runs six times, named to six All-Star teams and led Brooklyn to six pennants and its only World Series title, in 1955. The 1947 Rookie of the Year, and the 1949 N. L. MVP when he hit a league-best .342 with 37 steals. Led second basemen in double plays four times and stole home 19 times. Displayed tremendous courage and poise in 1947 when he integrated the modern Major Leagues in the face of intense adversity."

On April 15, 1997, Major League Baseball retired Jackie's number 42 throughout the league. In 2009, all Major League Baseball players, managers, coaches, and umpires wore number 42 on April 15 in what has now become an annual event.

Ball fields, buildings, and other facilities across the country are named in honor of Jackie. The UCLA Bruins baseball team plays in Jackie Robinson Stadium. A statue of Jackie stands at the stadium as do similar monuments in front of Pasadena City Hall and the Jackie Robinson Ballpark in Daytona Beach. California inducted him into their state Hall of Fame and, on March 2, 2005, President George Bush presented Rachel, on Jackie's behalf, the Congressional Gold Medal, the highest civilian award in the United States. It is presented to those "who have performed an achievement that has an impact on American history and culture that is likely to be recognized as a major achievement in the recipient's field long after the achievement." The U.S. Postal Service honored Jackie on three separate postage stamps in 1982, 1999, and 2000.

Hall of Fame New York Yankee catcher Yogi Berra best summarized Jackie's baseball career when he said, "He could beat you in a lot of ways."

Others have lauded Jackie's contributions to the African American community and to race relations in the United States. Hank Aaron noted, "Jackie Robinson gave all of us—not only black athletes but every black person in this country—a sense of our own strength."

National columnist George Will wrote that Jackie's life represented, "One of the great achievements not only in the annals of sports, but of the human drama anywhere, anytime."

Teacher and historian Professor Henry Louis Gates, Jr., observed, "It is so easy for us to underestimate the enormous significance, both symbolically and politically, of Jackie Robinson's integration of the Major Leagues. His courage and bravery played a major role in the history of integration, both on the field and throughout American society, and no history of the Civil Rights Movement would be complete without noting Robinson's major role, and according him a place of honor and immortality in African-American history because of it."

Philosopher, political activist, and social critic Cornel West wrote, "More even than either Abraham Lincoln and the Civil War, or Martin Luther King, Jr. and the Civil Rights Movement, Jackie Robinson graphically symbolized and personified the challenge to a vicious legacy and ideology of white supremacy in American history."

Jackie so greatly earned the respect and adoration of the American public—both white and black—on the diamond and in the fight for equality for all Americans that it would seem that only he could damage his legacy to any degree. Unfortunately, in his final days, he made statements that contradict his long-expressed pride in being an army officer and belief that he and all African Americans had a responsibility to fight for their country.

In the Foreword to his 1972 autobiography, *I Never Had It Made,* he wrote, "I must tell you that it was Mr. Rickey's drama and that I was only a principal actor. As I write this twenty years later, I cannot stand and sing the anthem. I cannot salute the flag; I know that I am a black man in a white world. In 1972, in 1947, and at my birth in 1919, I know that I never had it made."

Those bitter words came in a time of national turmoil—protests against the Vietnam War, controversy over civil rights, threats from the Black Power Movement, all of which were at their height that year. Perhaps Jackie was disillusioned by the disorder and division; maybe he had re-evaluated his life and found his influence and impact not what he had thought; possibly Jackie's conclusions came in a fit of anger prompted by old humiliations. Or conceivably, they may not have been his reflections at all.

While Forewords are generally written by authors after they have finished the bulk of their books, in this case, this preface may not be Jackie's words because his last autobiography was actually an "as told to" book. The interpreter of Jackie's story was Alfred Duckett, who worked with Martin Luther King, Jr., as a speech writer, including on "I Have a Dream." Yet, even if Duckett did write the words, Jackie approved them because, according to Rachel, she read the final galleys to her nearly blind husband shortly before he died.

Whatever the reason for the quote, it does not reflect the attitudes he professed throughout his life or his evaluations of his contributions to baseball and America. Throughout his career, he stated his appreciation for the opportunity to play ball, his gratitude to the sports writers for their support, and his thanks for his white fans who were supportive. Jackie may have written "I never had it made," but all evidence points to the fact that he had opportunities beyond even his own wildest dreams, and, in the end, he had it made because he made having it happen.

• *30* •

Conclusion

The court-martial of Jackie Robinson was a pivotal event—in Jackie's life, in the development of Major League Baseball, and in the Civil Rights Movement. Had he not been put on trial, Jackie might very well have become a footnote rather than a headline to history.

If Jackie had not been ordered to the back of the bus that night at Camp Hood, he would have returned to McCloskey Hospital without incident. Because of the encouragement and support of his battalion commander, it is likely that he would have had his medical evaluation change to "fit for duty and overseas assignment." Within weeks he would have deployed with the 761st Tank Battalion to the East Coast and then to England before joining the Allied offensive on October 10 to liberate France, fight in the Battle of the Bulge, penetrate the Siegfried Line, and meet the Russians on the Enns River in Austria at war's end.

The 761st Tank Battalion deployed with thirty-six officers—six white and thirty black—and 676 African American enlisted men. Three officers and thirty-one enlisted men died in action, another twenty-two officers and 180 enlisted men were wounded. This meant that, if Jackie had not been court-martialed and had gone to the European Theater, there was nearly a 70 percent chance he would have been killed or wounded. Death would have ended everything for him, of course, and being seriously wounded would have erased all possibility of his ever playing ball again.

Also, the 761st did not deactivate and send its soldiers home until June 1, 1946. If Jackie had survived the war, he would not have joined the Kansas City Monarchs in March 1945, come to the attention of Branch Rickey the following August, signed with the Montreal Royals in December, or made his Major League debut on April 15, 1947.

Major League Baseball history would not have been the same. Rickey certainly would have selected another black ball player to break the Major League color barrier. If that substitute had not had Jackie's grit, talent, and self-discipline, the great experiment might have failed because any lesser man would have caved to the harassment and quit or physically fought back thereby setting back race relations and the integration of the Major Leagues even further.

If Jackie had survived the war and ultimately been able to make his way to the Major Leagues, it would have likely been several years after his actual debut in 1947, thus shortening his already abbreviated career even more. He might not have had sufficient time and accomplishments to be selected to the Hall of Fame or to have earned America's respect and admiration that led to his success in the Civil Rights Movement.

The court-martial itself was significant in that it showed Jackie that, if he followed the rules, he could stand up to racism and prevail. If he had been convicted, he might well have faced stockade time or been dismissed from the service—or both. Such a dismissal as an officer in the time of war would have equaled an enlisted man's dishonorable discharge, thereby diminishing his chances of signing with any ball club at any level as well as impacting his civilian job opportunities. His conduct in standing up for what was right and then successfully—and peacefully—navigating his way through a flawed but basically fair military system likely played an important role in Branch Rickey's selecting him for his noble experiment.

Epilogue

People, Places, Things—Today

$\mathcal{A}$**rticles of War:** The Uniform Code of Military Justice replaced the Articles of War when approved by the U.S. Congress on May 5, 1950. The word *uniform* in the Code's title refers to its consistent application to all the armed services and is applicable to all military members worldwide. Except for the changing of many of the articles' numbers—for example, the investigation standards under Article 70 were renamed Article 32. Essentially, the UCMJ of today differs little from the Articles of War under which Jackie was tried.

Bates, Lt. Col. Paul L.: Paul Bates refused promotion to full colonel so he could stay with the 761st Tank Battalion as it joined Patton's Third Army in the European Theater. Ironically, Bates was the first soldier in the battalion to be wounded in action. He later received his promotion to colonel and served in Korea and Vietnam before his retirement in 1963. For the remainder of his life, Bates remained in close contact with veterans of the 761st and their families. Bates died in 1995 at age eighty-six in Dunedin, Florida; he is buried in Arlington National Cemetery. His obituary, as well as nearly every biography in print and online, inaccurately states that he refused to sign Jackie Robinson's court-martial charges during World War II.

Brooke General Hospital: Renamed the Brooke Army Medical Center in 1946, the hospital today serves active duty and veteran service members. In addition to training army and air force medical personnel, the facility is the military's preeminent injury rehabilitation center.

Brooklyn Dodgers: The Dodgers played their final game in Ebbets Field on September 24, 1957, before moving to Los Angeles.

Camp Breckinridge, Kentucky: Camp Breckinridge deactivated in 1949 and later reopened for infantry training during the Korean War from 1950–1954. It then served as a National Guard training center until its final closure in 1963.

Fort Clark, Texas: Fort Clark inactivated in 1946 and its land and facilities were sold. The area was later used as a guest ranch.

Camp Hood, Texas: Camp Hood continued as a training center and home to several divisions returning from Europe at the close of World War II. Unlike most of the temporary camps established in the war's expansion years, the camp did not close with the end of the war. On April 15, 1950, it was officially made a permanent installation and renamed Fort Hood. Over the years, the post has expanded to become one of the army's largest with 212,000 acres and more than 45 thousand troops. One of every ten U.S. Army soldiers is currently assigned to Fort Hood. The temporary wooden barracks and administrative buildings have been replaced with permanent structures. Elvis Presley, the only soldier serving at Fort Hood who rivaled Jackie's fame, trained with the 3rd Armored Division from March to September 1958 at the post before his transfer to Germany. He was an exemplary soldier and faced no disciplinary measures during his time at Fort Hood.

Chapman, Ben: The Philadelphia Phillies fired Chapman midway through the 1948 season. He coached for a year with the Cincinnati Reds in 1952. In an interview in the 1990s, Chapman expressed regrets about his racial taunts toward Jackie, saying, "A man learns about things and mellows as he grows older. I think maybe I've changed a bit. . . . The world changes." Chapman died at age eighty-four in 1993 at his home in Hoover, Alabama. He is buried in Birmingham's Elmwood Cemetery.

Casey, Hugh Thomas: Casey left the Major Leagues in 1949 as one of the most successful relief pitchers of his time. He briefly returned to the Minor Leagues before opening a steak house in New York City. Separated from his wife, facing a paternity suit from another woman, and owing a huge fine to the Internal Revenue Service, he committed suicide in an Atlanta, Georgia, hotel room by shooting himself in the neck with a shotgun on July 3, 1951.

Cline, William A.: After his discharge at the end of the war, "Billy" Cline returned to Wharton, Texas, and rejoined his family law practice. He served two terms as the director of the State Bar of Texas and was a long-time member of the Wharton Chamber of Commerce, Lions Club, Red Cross Chapter, and Historical Society as well as the American Legion.

Cline lived to the age of 101 before his death on June 12, 2012. As the oldest living participant in the trial of Jackie Robinson, his recollections often take precedence over that of his fellow officers. In his later interviews he gave no indication that anyone other than himself had performed the duties of defense attorney in the trial. Cline is buried in the Wharton City Cemetery. His obituary in the Wharton newspaper said, "His philosophy as a lawyer was to serve his clients in the most honest, efficient and proper way and to treat all peoples with respect and dignity."

Fort Riley, Kansas: Fort Riley has been in continuous use by the U.S. Army since its establishment in 1853. Today it is the home of the 1st Infantry Division and has a day-time population of more than 25,000.

Johnson, Robert H.: After the war, Johnson returned to his native Bay City, Michigan, where, in 1948, he established a law firm that is today Birchler, Fitzhugh, Purtell, & Brissett PLC. Johnson died in 1951.

Major League Baseball: When Jackie broke the color barrier there were sixteen Major League teams; today there are thirty. The number of African Americans in the league slowly, but steadily, increased over the years, reaching its apex in 1981 when they accounted for 18.7 percent of the total number of players and 22 percent of the All-Star Roster. Today their numbers have decreased to 8.4 percent of the total and 5 percent of the All-Stars. This decrease is apparently due to athletically superior black athletes being drawn more to the National Football League, about 70 percent black, and the National Basketball Association, about 80 percent. Also, there is a lack of youth baseball programs in the inner cities for the development of young black baseball players.

McCloskey General Hospital: McCloskey General Hospital closed on March 31, 1946, and, after considerable downsizing, converted to a Veterans Administration facility that is still in operation. Today it is known as the Olin E. Teague Veterans Center and serves veterans throughout Central Texas.

Montreal Royals: In 1960, two years after their move to Los Angeles, the Dodgers ended their affiliation with the Royals. The Royals then affiliated with the Minnesota Twins and in 1961 moved to New York where they became the Syracuse Chiefs. Montreal secured a Major League franchise in 1969. With the name Royals already taken by Kansas City, they became the Montreal Expos.

Rickey, Branch: Rickey retired from baseball in 1964. On November 13, 1965, he collapsed while giving an acceptance speech in Columbia, Missouri, after his election to the Missouri Sports Hall of Fame. His final words before saying he could not continue were, "Now I'm going to tell you a story from the Bible about spiritual courage." He died on December 9 of heart failure at the Boone County Memorial Hospital in Columbia without ever regaining consciousness. Elected to the Baseball Hall of Fame in 1967, the final line on his plaque states, "Brought Jackie Robinson to Brooklyn in 1947." Rickey is buried near his boyhood home of Stockdale, Ohio.

Robinson, David: The youngest of the Robinson's three children attended Stanford University for a year and then worked in community development in Harlem. In 1983, he moved to Tanzania in East Africa where he grows coffee and heads a coffee co-op.

Robinson, Edgar: Jackie's oldest brother dropped out of school after the sixth grade, never married, and spent most of his life studying the Bible. Edgar lived to be eighty-four years old and died alone surrounded by shelves of books, recordings, and other media dedicated to religion.

Robinson, Jack Roosevelt, Jr.: Jackie, Jr., experienced learning difficulties in his early formal education and his parents enrolled him in several schools to assist his development. At eighteen years of age in 1964, Jackie joined the U.S. Army for "learning and discipline." A picture of Jackie in uniform is in Rachel's book as well as another of him standing with his proud parents. After training, Jackie, Jr., served in Vietnam where he received a Purple Heart for being wounded in action. After his return home with an honorable discharge, he became addicted to drugs, was arrested several times, and eventually spent two years in Connecticut's Daytop, Inc. Rehabilitation Center. After his recovery, he remained on the Daytop staff for a year. On June 17, 1971, Jackie, Jr., fatally crashed his car into a fence and then a concrete abutment on Route 123 near his parents' home in Stamford, Connecticut. He is buried in the Brooklyn Cypress Hill Cemetery.

Robinson, Mallie McGriff: Mallie Robinson died in Pasadena, California, on May 21, 1968 at age seventy-eight. She is buried in the nearby Rose Hills Cemetery in Whittier. Mallie had no desire to be returned to her native Georgia for interment.

Robinson, Rachel Isum: After Jackie retired from baseball, Rachel returned to her nursing career and earned a master's degree in psychiatric nursing from New York University. She later became an assistant professor at the Yale School of Nursing and then the Director of Nursing at the Connecticut Mental Health Center. From 1972 to 1982 she acted as president of the Jackie Robinson Development Corporation that continued to provide low-income housing and in 1973 founded the Jackie Robinson Foundation that provides educational and leadership opportunities for minority students. At this writing in 2019, she, at age ninety-seven, still heads the Foundation. According to her staff, she is "holding on" and intends to live to be 100.

Robinson, Sharon: Sharon Robinson earned her bachelor's degree from Howard University and her master's from Columbia. She had a twenty-year career as a nurse midwife and educator before joining Major League Baseball as an educational consultant. At this writing she is the vice chairperson of the Jackie Robinson Foundation. She resides in New York City and Sarasota, Florida.

Samuel Huston College: The Southern Association of Colleges and Schools approved Samuel Huston College as a four-year senior college on December 14, 1951. The following October 24, it merged with Tillotson College to form Huston-Tillotson College. Over the following years, the college expanded to cover twenty-three acres on Austin's east side. It was renamed Huston-Tillotson University on February 28, 2005. Jackie Robinson was elected to the school's Board of Regents in 1968 and served in that capacity until his death.

Southern California: Pasadena and its surrounding towns remain one of the country's most progressive regions. However, poverty and police brutality, particularly in Southern Los Angeles continues and, over recent decades, incidents have led to rioting and looting. Pasadena Junior College, now Pasadena Community College, has about 26,000 students. Approximately 4 percent are African Americans. The University of Southern California currently has a student population of about 45,000 undergraduates and graduate students. Only about 3 percent are African Americans. Blacks, however, compose the majority of their major athletic teams.

United States Army: On July 26, 1948, President Harry Truman signed Executive Order 9981 ending segregation in the Armed Forces. The order said, "It is hereby declared to be the policy of the President that there shall be equality of treatment and opportunity for all persons in the armed services without regard to race, color, religion or national origin. This policy shall be put into effect as rapidly as possible, having due regard to the time required to effectuate any necessary changes without impairing efficiency or morale."

Army officials paid more attention to the last sentence than the first. Using the excuse of having due time to make the necessary changes without impacting efficiency or morale, army leaders initially made little effort to integrate the ranks. It was not until the need for replacement soldiers in the Korean War that black soldiers were thoroughly integrated into formerly all-white units.

By the time of the Vietnam War, black enlisted men and officers were integral parts of every unit. The turmoil of the race difficulties certainly impacted the army, but over the years, racial justice in the army exceeded that of the civilian world. In his autobiography, *My American Journey*, General Colin Powell, former Chairman of the Joint Chiefs of Staff and the 65th U.S. Secretary of State, wrote, "The Army was living the democratic idea ahead of the rest of America. Beginning in the fifties, less discrimination, a truer merit system, and leveler playing fields existed inside the gates of our military posts than in any Southern city hall or Northern corporation. The Army, therefore, made it easier for me to love my country, with all its flaws, and to serve her with all my heart."

Wright, John Richard: The New Orleans-born Wright, although considered by both black and white scouts to be a superior pitcher, only appeared for the Montreal Royals in two relief appearances before being demoted to the Class C Three Rivers team in Quebec. He departed there after the season closed and played two years in the Negro Leagues and then two more in Mexico before leaving baseball for good. Wright never seemed comfortable around white people, having experienced the bigotry of Jim Crow all his life. He returned to New Orleans where he worked at the National Gypsum Company until his retirement. He died in Jackson, Mississippi on May 4, 1990. Wright rarely talked about his baseball career with his co-workers and friends. No reporter did an in-depth interview on his part in breaking the baseball color barrier.

Historical Perspectives

$\mathcal{O}$ne cannot wholly apply the standards held today to the times of Jackie Robinson's life. To totally understand the racial climate and conditions in which he lived, it is necessary to consider the historical perspectives that surrounded his early years and time as a soldier in the U.S. Army.

Historical Perspective 1

Slavery and Racism

*C*heap labor, though, was not the only justification for slavery. Most whites looked upon blacks as an inferior race. Virginia attorney George Fitzhugh wrote several articles and books in the 1850s on what he called "the universal law of slavery." He postulated that there is a natural inequality of men and that both whites and blacks benefited from slavery. Fitzhugh declared,

> *He, the Negro is but a grown child, and must be governed as a child, not as a lunatic or criminal. The master occupies toward him the place of parent or guardian. . . . The Negro is improvident; will not lay up in summer for the wants of winter; will not accumulate in youth for the exigencies of age. He would become an insufferable burden to society. Society has the right to prevent this, and can only do so by subjecting him to domestic slavery. In the last place, the Negro is inferior to the white race, and living in their midst, they would be far outstripped or outwitted in the chaos of free competition.*

Doctor John H. Van Evie, a prominent Washington, D.C. physician and publisher, supported the Fitzhugh thesis. In 1853 he published his "plurality" theory that claimed the brains of Negroes were significantly smaller than those of whites, which explained why the black race had "never of its own volition passed beyond the hunter condition." Van Evie elaborated,

> *The Negro is a man, but a different and inferior species of man, who could no more originate from the same source as ourselves than the owl could from the eagle, or the shad from the salmon, or the cat from the tiger; and who can no more be forced by human power to manifest the facilities, or perform the purposes assigned by the Almighty Creator to the Caucasian man, than can either of these forms of life be made to manifest faculties other than those inherent, specific, and eventually impressed upon their organization.*

Thus, in the pre Civil War period, many Americans believed that slavery was not only good economics, but also that it was beneficial for the enslaved. James Henry Hammond, a wealthy South Carolina plantation owner, addressed the U.S. Congress to claim that bondage actually improved the conditions of Negroes as compared to their brothers remaining in Africa. He described slaves in the South as "happy, content, unaspiring, and utterly incapable, from intellectual weakness" of giving their owners any trouble.

Hammond then outlined his "mud-sill" theory that said in any viable society there must be two groups, one superior and one inferior. He continued,

In all social systems, there must be a class to do the menial duties, to perform the drudgery of life. That is, a class requiring but a low order of intellect and but little skill. Its requisites are vigor, docility, fidelity. Such a class you must have, or you would not have the other class which leads progress, civilization, and refinement. It constitutes the very mud-sill of society and of political government; and you might as well attempt to build a house in the air, as to build either the one or the other, except on this mud-sill. Fortunately for the South, she found a race inferior to her own, but eminently qualified in temper, in vigor, in docility, in capacity to stand the climate, to answer all her purposes.

By the mid-nineteenth century, the United States had divided themselves into "slave states" in the South and "free states" in the North. Although there was a legitimate abolitionist movement in the Northern states, the overall support for banning slavery was more economically driven than morality based. The small farms and dairies of New England could easily operate without the assistance of slaves. The number of white European immigrants willing to work for low wages were more cost efficient to hire than housing, feeding, clothing, and otherwise supporting the necessities required for owned individuals. In the Southern states, however, the staple plantation crops of cotton, tobacco, and rice relied on slave labor. In general, the owners were not troubled by the concept of slavery but rather built their lifestyle around it.

Inevitably, the North and South went to war with one of their main contentions being the fate of slavery in the country. The North's victory over the South in 1865, and the subsequent legislation that followed, legally ended slavery in the United States. It secured freedom for African Americans in theory but could not mandate equality and opportunity in practice for the blacks in either the South or the North. The agricultural South still needed cheap labor and former owners found ways to exploit former slaves into continuing the manual labor in little-changed circumstances; the North embraced the concept of freedom for blacks but few northerners wished to actually live side-by-side with their black brothers and sisters.

With slavery now illegal, the Southern states turned to their courts and legislatures to keep the newly freed African Americans in their "place"—their "place" being anywhere the white majority was not. Even then, whites closely governed just what blacks could own and what they could do. During the immediate years after the Civil War, Southern states adopted what became known as the Black Codes limiting the rights of blacks, that differed little from the Slave Codes dating back more than a century. In some cases, states merely changed the word Slave to Black.

Provisions of the initial Black Codes in the former Confederate States, including the Robinson's home state of Georgia, denied blacks the right to vote, the right to public education (some of the earlier Slave Codes made it a crime to teach a slave how to read and write), and equal treatment under the law. The Codes denied blacks the right to own property, conduct business, buy or lease land, and move freely through public places. Some of the Northern states adopted similar measures. In addition to racism, these codes were specifically concerned with keeping blacks in their primary "place" of being available as a cheap labor source.

The 13th Amendment of the U.S. Constitution abolished slavery and involuntary servitude in 1865; the 14th Amendment defined citizenship and equal protection in 1868; and the 15th Amendment guaranteed the right to vote for all men in 1870. Yet, the Black Codes negated much of this legislation. What efforts that were made to enforce the Constitutional amendments in the South basically concluded with the end of Reconstruction in 1877.

However, reconstruction had failed by every measure even before it officially ended. Even the primary agency for assisting newly freed slaves did more to support economic issues than human rights. Instead of providing "forty acres and a mule" to each freed slave, Federal authorities supported the governments of various Southern states in maintaining a cheap labor source. One of the first Black Codes was to require blacks each January to acquire written proof of employment for the following year. If they left their job before the end of the year, they had to forfeit previous earnings and be subject to arrest.

An unemployed black was considered a vagrant—and vagrancy was a crime. Vagrant blacks were arrested, sentenced to labor details, and even returned to the farms on which they had been previously working as unpaid prisoners. The farmers paid the local government for convict workers, filling the coffers of local governments (and often government officials) as they turned the low-price labor into larger profits. This, in turn, lowered property taxes, making everyone happy except for the former slaves, now prisoners, who had little or no say so about their own lives.

The enactment of Jim Crow legislation further enforced racial segregation. Origins of the term Jim Crow dated back to a popular song and dance caricature of Negroes performed by white actors in black face titled *Jump Jim Crow*. As a result, Jim Crow became a pejorative term meaning Negro and lent its name to the segregation laws. Jim Crow laws mandated segregation in housing and in all facilities, including public schools, transportation, restrooms, drinking fountains, and other public places.

The passage of years did not diminish the number of Jim Crow laws or their enforcement. In some places, such as the U.S. government, segregation actually increased. After the Civil War, the U.S. government became one of the most integrated workplaces in America. This changed in 1912 with the election of Woodrow Wilson, a president who was the son of a Virginia slave owner. Early in his administration Wilson re-segregated all government facilities, defending his polices by writing that segregation removed "friction" between the races. Ironically, Wilson, a huge baseball fan, who had played center field on his college team was the first sitting president to throw out the first ball and attend a World Series game. Wilson died in 1924 and did not live to see Jackie Robinson break the Major League racial barrier.

The U.S. Supreme Court supported Wilson's segregation policy, as well as the Jim Crow laws, in the landmark decision of *Plessy v. Ferguson* issued in 1896. By a vote of 7–1, the court upheld racial segregation laws for public facilities as long as they were equal in equality. This decision became known as "separate but equal" and it would not be until the 1954 case *Brown v. Board of Education* determined that the "separate but equal" doctrine for public education was unconstitutional. Other court cases further eroded *Plessy v. Ferguson*, but the decision itself has never been explicitly overturned.

To further keep black Americans in their "place," whites in both the South and North organized chapters of the Ku Klux Klan to intimidate, punish, or even torture and kill Negroes. Originally formed shortly after the close of the Civil War, the KKK ceased operations in the 1870s because of Federal opposition and the end of Reconstruction. It re-emerged in 1915 during a ceremony held on Stone Mountain in North Georgia. Chapters all over the South, and many in the North, burned crosses in yards of blacks as warnings and whipped and beat those who did not cower to their threats or who violated the Jim Crow laws.

When intimidation and physical violence failed to keep blacks in their place, the KKK saw to it that the place for a Negro was at the end of a hangman's rope. From 1877–1950 the KKK and other white mobs lynched more than 4,000 African Americans. A report by the Equal Justice Initiative in a report titled "Lynching in America: Confronting the Legacy of Racial Terror," stated, "Indeed, some public-spectacle lynchings were attended by the entire white community and conducted as celebratory acts of racial control and domination."

In the summer and fall of 1919—a time that became known as the Red Summer—racial riots broke out all over the United States. In some places, blacks fought back as whites lynched or beat random African Americans and burned their residences and businesses. Many in the white government and press claimed that the black activism and standing up for equality was rooted in Soviet Bolshevism brought back by African Americans who fought in Europe. By the end of the Red Summer, thirty-two riots had occurred, including one in Chicago that left twenty-three blacks dead, another 500 injured, and 1,000 homeless. Riots were not restricted to the cities. In rural Elaine, Arkansas, and its surrounding county of Phillips, whites attacked blacks for their efforts to form an organization of sharecroppers. For two days a white mob swept across the county, killing an estimated 100–240 black men and women, and destroyed their homes and possessions.

Although the number of race riots diminished over the next few years, they did not cease. On May 31–June 1, 1921, whites attacked blacks and looted their homes and businesses in the Greenwood section of Tulsa, Oklahoma, killing more than 100 and destroying more than thirty-five blocks of black homes and businesses. By the end of the riot, what had been the wealthiest black community in the United States lay in ashes.

Lynching of blacks was so common that the deadly act even made its way into popular song lyrics. In 1939, Billie Holiday sang about the "strange fruit" of black bodies swinging from trees in the southern breeze. Mississippi led the nation in the number of lynchings, but Georgia was a close second. Although Robinson's Georgia home county was not on the list, five nearby Southwestern Florida counties were among the leaders in the number of lynchings. As late as 1946, a Georgia mob executed two married black couples because one of the men was accused of stabbing a white man. No one was ever brought to trial for the killing of the four.

In 1937 Patsy Mitchner, a former slave in North Carolina, recalled in an interview for the *Slave Narrative Collection* of the *Federal Writers' Project,* "Slavery was a bad thing and freedom, of the kind we got with nothing to live on was bad. Two snakes full of poison. One lying with his head pointing north, the other with his head pointing south. Their names were slavery and freedom. The snake called slavery lay with his head pointed south and the snake called freedom lay with his head pointed north. Both bit the nigger, and they were both bad."

Historical Perspective 2

Grady County, Georgia

$\mathcal{G}$rady County, formed in 1905 from the neighboring counties of Decatur and Thomas, had a population of around 20,000 in 1919 with a black population percentage similar to that of Cairo. It received its name from Henry Woodfin Grady, the editor of the *Atlantic Journal* who worked to have the former rebel states readmitted to the Union. He originated the term "New South" when he wrote that the "Old South" rested everything on slavery and agriculture while a "New South" that was "thrilling with consciousness of growing power and prosperity."

Grady's "New South," however, was not good for the Robinsons or other Georgia African Americans. Grady also wrote and spoke out about white supremacy and emphasized the necessity for whites to remain in social control over newly freed blacks. To African Americans, the New South looked little different than the Old South.

Spanish Flu Epidemic

Segregation and racial bias were not the only influences that greeted the birth of Jackie Robinson in 1919. The influenza pandemic was its second year in what became known as the greatest medical holocaust in history. More than 50 million died around the world over a two-year period of what was called the Spanish flu. About one in four Americans were infected and an estimated 675,000 died—more than ten times the number of American soldiers killed in World War I. The flu was one of the few things in early twentieth-century America that had no racial bias—both whites and blacks were affected at the same rate.

Historical Perspective 4

Pasadena, California

$\mathcal{A}$ group from Indiana, wanting to flee the bitter winters of the midwest, established the city of Pasadena in 1873. They named their town Pasadena, derived from a Chippewa Indian word for "valley" or "of the valley." The founders were not interested in establishing a center of industry and manufacturing but rather in developing education, tourism, and the arts. They were successful as they attracted luxury hotels, the California Technical Institute, the Huntington Museum, and the Busch Gardens. Its Orange Grove Boulevard became known as Millionaire's Row for its mansions that still today mark one of the richest streets in America. In 1922 the city built the Rose Bowl and sponsored the annual Rose Bowl Parade that brought national and international attention to the city.

Many of the Indiana founders of Pasadena shared an abolitionist background. Soon after its establishment, Pasadena welcomed Jason and Owen Brown, sons of John Brown who had been hanged for attempting to start a slave rebellion when he attacked Harpers Ferry, Virginia, in 1859. Owen had participated in the raid.

African Americans in the Military

$\mathcal{B}$y the late 1930s, African Americans, through organizing labor unions and developing a diligent black press in major cities, were able to make some inroads on gaining a degree of equality. Steps, however, were small and hard-fought. The only real acceptance by the white majority that assisted the black minority resulted from the "two needs"—number one was that whites needed blacks in time of war to work in the defense industry and to fill the ranks of the military during time of war and number two they needed blacks during election years to vote Democrat.

Although it had been a Republican administration that won the Civil War and freed the slaves, by the 1930s, 90 percent of blacks sided with the Democrats. They had been among the Americans who elected and reelected Franklin Roosevelt whose Executive Order 8802 which banned discriminatory employment practices by Federal agencies and all unions and companies engaged in war-related work, was as much a political move as one to offer equality. In fact, it would not have been issued at all if the Brotherhood of Sleeping Car Porters, the most powerful black union in the country, had not threatened to march on Washington to protest the exclusion of African Americans "from the defense industries and their humiliation in the Armed Forces."

As the U.S. Armed Forces approached World War II, military officials advocated and enforced strict segregation between whites and blacks. This included units, housing, mess halls, recreation, clubs, hospitals, and all other facilities. Post chapels held separate worship hours for Protestants, Catholics, Jews, and Negros. Segregation was even a part of the extremely speedy construction—seventeen months—of the U.S. military headquarters at the Pentagon in Northern Virginia across the Potomac River from Washington, D.C. Included in its 3.7-million square feet of floor space were twice as many bathrooms as the normal facility would have had because strict Virginia laws demanded separate white and colored restrooms.

Train cars, as well as eating places along their routes, were strictly segregated, generally the oldest and most poorly maintained for blacks. When white German prisoners were moved from ports to prisoner of war facilities inland, they rode in the white cars and ate in the white section of cafés.

A large number of army posts were in the South where black soldiers faced Jim Crow laws and lingering prejudices in the local community. Black officers and non-commissioned officers were never assigned where they would be superior to white soldiers. The level of separation was so great that the Red Cross refused to take blood from black doners because white soldiers would refuse plasma that came from black veins despite the fact that a black doctor, Charles Drew of Howard University Medical School, had made the major scientific developments of blood banks.

In 1940, Secretary of War Henry L. Stimson issued a memorandum outlining the army's official position. Stimson, a native New Yorker who attended Yale University and graduated from Harvard Law School, wrote that blacks had not performed well during World War I and said that segregation "has been proven satisfactory over a long period of years and to make changes would produce situations destructive to morale and detrimental to the preparations for national defense."

African Americans were also not welcomed in the navy or Marine Corps. The only job open to black sailors was as mess boys who served officers aboard ship. Only at the height of the American Revolution had the Marine Corps ever enlisted a single African American prior to World War II when both services relaxed their entrance criteria and accepted blacks—albeit on strict segregated terms. As casualties increased with more American involvement, many whites expressed their opinion of military desegregation by commenting on "Sambo's right to die"—meaning all the better if a black man died instead of a white.

On October 25, a week before the 1940 election, President Roosevelt had appointed one of the surviving black officers, Col. Benjamin O. Davis, Sr., to the temporary rank of brigadier general—the first African American to wear stars in the U.S. military.

On November 1, Roosevelt announced the appointment of Judge William H. Hastie, dean of the Howard University Law School, as an assistant secretary in the War Department to advise on black military issues. He also added a black to the staff of the National Selective Service System to advise and assist in matters about the draft.

The black press readily recognized the purpose of Roosevelt's efforts, especially the promotion of Davis. The *Guild Lawyer* stated, "The promotion of Davis . . . is another incident of our traditional practice to single out an individual for honors, at the same time to keep the mass of Negroes in inferior status or suppressed." The *Baltimore Afro-American* more concisely labeled Roosevelt's action as "appeasement."

Secretary of War Stimson noted in his personal diary that Davis's promotion was of political rather than substantive value. Stimson sarcastically wrote, "I had a good deal of fun with [Frank] Knox (Secretary of the Navy) over the necessity that he was facing appointing a colored admiral and a battle fleet full of colored sailors . . . and I told him that when I called next time at the Navy Department with my colored brigadier general, I expected to be met with the colored admiral."

Neither Stimson nor Knox took the promotion seriously. In fact, the navy would not have a black admiral until 1971 and the Marine Corps first general would not be promoted until 1979. Davis, however, approached his promotion and duties with enthusiasm. He began a series of visits to army posts across the country to evaluate the treatment and assimilation of black soldiers. His findings were not positive. After an inspection tour in 1943 he wrote in a memorandum, "There is still great dissatisfaction on the part of colored people and soldiers. They feel that, regardless of how much they strive to meet War Department requirements; there is no change in the attitude of the War Department. The colored officers and soldiers feel that they are denied the protection and awards that ordinarily result from good behavior and proper performance of duty. . . . The colored man in uniform receives nothing but hostility from the community officials. . . . The colored man in uniform is expected by the War Department to develop a high morale in a community that offers him nothing but humiliation and mistreatment. . . . Officers of the War Department General Staff have refused to attempt any remedial action to eliminate Jim Crow. In fact, the army, by its directions and actions of commanding officers, has introduced Jim Crow practices in areas, both at home and abroad, where they have been hitherto not practiced."

Historical Perspective 6

Max Schmeling

$\mathscr{M}$ax Schmeling was accompanied by a Nazi party publicist who issued statements that a black man could not defeat Schmeling and that when Schmeling won, his prize money would be used to build tanks in Germany. On the night of June 22, 1938, Louis and Schmeling met for the second time in the boxing ring.

Historical Perspective 7

Joe Louis

$\mathcal{I}$n an era when white men managed most black fighters, Louis instead selected African American John Roxborough to manage his career. Louis later said in his autobiography that Roxborough convinced him that white managers would have no real interest in seeing a black boxer work his way up to title contention. He wrote that Roxborough "told me about the fate of most black fighters, ones with white managers, who wound up burned-out and broke before they reached their prime. The white managers were not interested in the men they were handling but in the money they could make from them. They didn't take the proper time to see that their fighters had a proper training, that they lived comfortably, or ate well, or had some pocket change. Mr. Roxborough was talking about Black Power before it became popular."

Roxborough managed Louis's personal conduct as well as his actions in the ring. In a deliberate effort to shape the media's and public's opinion of the boxer, Roxborough encouraged Louis never to have his picture taken with a white woman, never to gloat over a fallen opponent, never to engage in fixed fights, and to live and fight clean. As a result, in the mid-1930s Louis advanced up the rankings of heavy weights.

Langston Hughes, the noted author, poet, and member of the Harlem Renaissance said of Louis's impact on African Americans, "Each time Joe Louis won a fight in those depression years, even before he became champion, thousands of black Americans on relief or W.P.A. and poor, would throng out into the streets all across the land to march and cheer and yell and cry because of Joe's one-man triumphs. No one else in the United States has ever had such an effect on Negro emotions—or on mine. I marched and cheered and yelled and cried, too."

Historical Perspective 8

1st and 2nd U.S. Cavalry Divisions

With the use of horse cavalry no longer practical on the modern, mechanized battlefield, the 1st Cavalry Division began converting to infantry in February 1943 and trained to deploy to the Pacific Theater over the following months. The 2nd Cavalry Division also dismounted and turned in their horses to begin training as infantry for transfer to North Africa. Officials in the War Department did not favor committing another black infantry division claiming that African Americans did not perform well in battle. After protests from black leaders and the black press, the War Department deployed the 2nd Cavalry to Oran in North Africa on March 9, 1944. It was deactivated the next day and its soldiers reassigned to construct airfields for the Tuskegee Airmen and perform garrison and supply duties in North Africa. The division also provided replacement troops for the all-black 92nd Infantry Division that was fighting in Italy.

Historical Perspective 9

Texas and Race Relations

$\mathscr{T}$exans had lingering animosity for Indians. Comanche and Kiowa warriors raided, tortured, and killed from the Texas Panhandle all the way to the Gulf Coast in the years after the Civil War. By the turn of the twentieth century, Indians were no longer a problem in Texas because the U.S. cavalry, including regiments of black "Buffalo Soldiers," had neutralized their ability to defend their lands. Except for one very small reservation in East Texas, most of the state's Indians were dead. Survivors had been removed from Texas and re-settled in Oklahoma.

Mexicans had fought both for and against the independence of Texas and, at the outbreak of World War II, still played an important role in the economy of the Rio Grande Valley and San Antonio. Despite their integration into the World War II army, Mexicans still suffered from many of the Jim Crow laws that governed blacks. Several early Texas gunfighters as well as lawmen, particularly Texas Rangers, boasted about the number of men, "not including Mexicans," they had killed.

African Americans in Texas celebrated Juneteenth (June 19) as the day in 1865 that the Union Army in Galveston issued General Order No. 3 announcing the freedom of all slaves. Texans did not take well to blacks being free. The racism, forced segregation of all facilities, poll taxes, and literacy tests to prevent their voting, kept black Texans in what the whites thought of as "their place." If these restrictions did not achieve desired behavior, Texans readily turned to local law officials, Texas Rangers, and the Ku Klux Klan to further impede the safety and prosperity of African Americans. Many businesses in Texas, including in Killeen, had signs posted on their doors that read, "No niggers, Meskins, or dogs allowed." Some went so far in their prejudices to add "soldiers" to their restricted list—especially if they did not need their business.

164

Overall, black soldiers in earlier years in Texas had done their best to master their jobs as soldiers in preparation to defend their country that often neither recognized nor appreciated their efforts. At times the racism and bigotry they experienced became too much and they fought back. In 1906 the War Department announced the transfer of the black 25th Infantry Regiment to Fort Brown at Brownsville on the Texas-Mexico border. Local officials wrote Secretary of War, and future president William Howard Taft, requesting that black soldiers not be assigned to their town.

Taft refused to change the orders and wrote back, "The fact that a certain amount of race prejudice between white and black seems to have become almost universal throughout the country; and no matter where colored troops are sent there are always some who make objections to their coming. It is a fact, however, as shown by our records, that colored troops are quite as well disciplined and behaved as the average of other troops, and it does not seem logical to anticipate any greater trouble from them than from the rest."

The citizens of Brownville cared little about what Taft thought of black soldiers. They barred blacks from their saloons, cafés, and other public facilities including the local park. Signs stating "No niggers or dogs allowed" abounded. The only place in Brownsville that welcomed the troops was a bar run by two African American ex-soldiers. Soldiers of the 25th Regiment also often crossed the bridge into Mexico where they and their dollars were well received.

On August 5, a white customs agent severely beat two black soldiers for not getting off the sidewalk and standing in the gutter when approached by several white women. A week later another custom official beat a black soldier returning across the border from Mexico. The Fort Brown commander imposed a curfew of 8:00 pm until tempers cooled on post and in town. This measure was not sufficient. A few minutes after midnight on August 14, a group of six to twenty men allegedly gathered on the road across from the B Company barracks. For ten minutes the men fired into Brownsville breaking streetlights and business windows. Random bullets also killed a local bartender and wounded a police lieutenant and a newspaper editor.

Before the shooting had concluded, Fort Brown officials had held a roll call that accounted for all men present. The only evidence that the shooters were black soldiers was used military bullet cases left on the ground. This was not positive evidence of soldier participation because expended shells were not kept secured on the post and could have been picked up by anyone. Despite little evidence, Brownsville officials blamed black soldiers for the incident and telegraphed President Theodore Roosevelt asking for the transfer of the 25th Regiment from Fort Brown. Roosevelt sent an investigation officer, but before he could finish his report, more pressure from Brownsville and other officials pressured the president to order the transfer of the regiment to Fort Reno in the Oklahoma Territory. Twelve soldiers were left behind in custody as the possible shooters. A grand jury could find no evidence to send them to trial and they rejoined their regiment at Fort Reno.

Even after the unit's departure, Brownsville officials and residents as well as several congressmen continued to demand punishment for the regiment. Roosevelt, Jackie's namesake and previous supporter of black causes, put politics ahead of truth and what was right and approved the discharge of members of the regiment. He also delayed the announcement until after the election on November 9, "for fear of its effect on the colored vote."

Between November 16 and November 19, 1906, all 167 soldiers of the 25th Infantry Regiment who were present for duty on the night of August 13 at Fort Brown were discharged without honor, denied all back pay and pension benefits, and barred from reenlistment in any branch of the U.S. armed forces. Several of the black soldiers wept as they turned in their uniforms and other equipment. Of the 167 soldiers dismissed from the service, one had loyally served for more than twenty-seven years; twenty-five had been on active duty for more than a decade; fully half had been in uniform for more than five years, and fifteen had earned medals or certificates of merit for combat in Cuba or the Philippines. The dismissal of the 25th Regiment's soldiers is the only example of mass punishment without the benefit of formal trial in U.S. military history.

Brownsville citizens and whites across the country welcomed the dismissal. The *New Orleans Picayune* reported, "Whatever may be the value of Negro troops in time of war, the fact remains they are a curse to the country in time of peace." Newspapers in the south and north supported the action, sharing the opinion of the *New York Times* that said the black soldiers had only themselves to blame.

The black press reacted with outrage. Booker T. Washington best summed up the general mood of African Americans saying, "The race feels hurt and abandoned."

Neither the army nor the government took further action until the time of elections in the fall of 1908. A board of officers announced that fourteen of the 167 soldiers would be allowed to reenlist in what many saw as tokenism and politics. Eleven of the fourteen chose to do so. The remaining 153 black soldiers lived out their lives without any veteran's benefits. Only one remained alive when President Richard Nixon ordered the Change of Records of all the men to reflect "honorable discharge" in 1972.

A decade after the Brownsville incident, African American soldiers in Houston rioted against the bigotry of and mistreatment by the Houston Police Department. In July 1917, the 3rd Battalion of the 24th Infantry Regiment received orders to report to Houston to guard and assist construction workers building Camp Logan where white troops were to train before transferring overseas. The black soldiers of the 24th Regiment resented doing mostly manual labor while not being deployed to the European front.

Houston, a city at the time with African Americans numbering nearly a quarter of its residents, welcomed the income from additional troops at Camp Logan, but its white population were not happy with the inclusion of a battalion of armed black men in their midst. The Houston Police Department was so poorly trained and led that it had little respect from the locals as well as soldiers of both races at Camp Logan, The *Houston Chronicle* went so far as to print that the city seemed to be without a police force at all.

Although the Houston police were inefficient in all aspects of law enforcement, they did manage to focus their efforts on policing the black soldiers. From their arrival, the soldiers of the 24th Regiment suffered harassment, beatings, and arrest for not honoring local Jim Crow laws, including segregated seating on city streetcars. Their treatment at the camp was no better with white civilian construction workers calling the soldiers "niggers" and "coons."

The black soldiers finally had enough. On August 23, 1917, a black civilian housewife with five children complained about two patrolmen shooting into her neighborhood while attempting to apprehend two young crapshooters. One of the policemen told the woman, "You all God damn nigger bitches, since those God damn sons of bitches nigger soldiers came here, you are trying to take the town."

One of the policemen grabbed the woman and dragged her to a call box from where he requested a patrol wagon to transport her to jail. A group of black citizens gathered to complain about the mistreatment of the woman. Alonzo Edwards, a private in uniform from the 24th Regiment stepped forward offering to pay the woman's fine if they would release her. Policeman Lee Sparks responded by drawing his revolver and striking the soldier several times on the head. Although the soldier had made no physical move against him, Sparks later said, "I wasn't going to wrestle with a big nigger, like that. I hit him until he got his heart right."

Sparks then took the woman and Edwards to the city jail. When the senior member, Cpl. Charles W. Baltimore, of the battalion provost guard went to the jail to check on the welfare of Edwards, Sparks, apparently with no provocation other than bigotry, again drew his gun. He struck Baltimore in the head and then fired three shots at the corporal as he ran away. Sparks chased down Baltimore, pistol whipped him some more, and then placed him in a cell with Edwards.

Although Camp Logan officials secured the release of the two black soldiers, rumors swept the camp that Houston police had killed Baltimore. In the early evening, soldiers gathered and murmurs and then shouts for wanting vengeance filled the air. At approximately 8:40 p.m., about a hundred soldiers armed with their military rifles, including Cpl. Baltimore, poured out of Camp Logan into the streets of Houston. More a mob than a military formation, Sgt. Vida Henry had what little control there was of the group.

The black soldiers made no efforts to destroy public or private property but deliberately sought out members of the Houston police force. Over the next two hours the soldiers killed four policemen. Their bullets also killed two uniformed Illinois National Guardsmen mistaken as police as well as nine civilians. They shot twelve more, including a policeman who later died from his wounds. Three black soldiers died in the fight against the police in what became known as the Houston Munity. Sgt. Henry died from an apparent self-inflicted wound after the riot concluded. Later some would claim he planned the entire munity while others say he participated only out of responsibility to his men. Whatever his motivation, he obviously did not want to face the consequences of his actions and took his true motivation to the grave.

Roll calls at Camp Logan noted the absence of 156 men during the riot. Fewer than forty-eight hours after the incident, the entire 3rd Battalion, 24th Infantry Regiment boarded trains for transfer to remote Fort Furlong in Columbus, New Mexico. Upon arrival, the 156 men who had missed roll call were placed in the stockade. Unlike the Fort Brown incident, this time the army did not do a mass discharge of the participants but rather conducted a thorough investigation into the actions of each soldier.

The investigation was fair, but its results were brutal. On November 1, a court-martial convened at Fort Sam Houston in San Antonio to try sixty-three soldiers charged with munity and premediated murder. It was the largest military trial in U.S. history and the examination of its 196 witnesses resulted in 2,100 pages of typewritten pages. On November 12 the court martial board found fifty-four of the defendants guilty of all charges and sentenced thirteen to be executed and forty-one to life in prison. Four received lesser sentences and five went free.

In the dark hours just before dawn on December 11, 1917, army executioners hanged Baltimore and twelve other black soldiers on newly erected scaffolding on the banks of Salado Creek on the outskirts of San Antonio. They were buried where they died.

Over the next several months additional courts-martial sentenced six more black soldiers to the gallows and others to long prison sentences. The 3rd Battalion, 24th Infantry Regiment received replacements and continued to serve in New Mexico before being disbanded in 1921. Other battalions of the regiment remained in isolated assignments until "need" called upon their service in World War II.

The white press applauded the trial results. On December 13, 1917, the *Atlanta Constitution* reported, "Justice has been done in Houston, not summary, hair trigger, hasty justice, but deliberate, mature, carefully weighed.

Opinions among the black press expressed regret and anger. The December 15, 1917, edition of the *Chicago Broad Ax* expressed regret that the 24th Infantry Regiment had "blown their past splendid record to the winds." The *Houston Observer* expressed regrets over the incident, but also noted that "the chances of it occurring would have been remote" if the policeman had not overstepped his bounds in dealing with Sgt. Baltimore.

After the first trial and executions, perhaps W. E. B. Du Bois expressed the most widely felt belief of the black community about the Houston Mutiny. In the January 1918 edition of *The Crisis* he said, "They have gone to their death, 13 young, strong men; soldiers who have fought for a country which never was wholly theirs, men born to suffer ridicule, injustice, and at last, death itself. They broke the law. Against their punishment, if it was legal, we cannot protest . . . the shameful treatment of which these men, and which we, their brothers, receive all our lives, and which our fathers received, and our children await; and above all we raise our clenched hands against the hundreds of thousands of white murders, rapists, and scoundrels."

For twenty years the bodies of the executed nineteen 24th Regiment soldiers lay in graves near where they died. It was not until 1938 that seventeen were removed and reinterred in the Fort Sam Houston National Cemetery. Their Department of Veterans headstones contain only their names and date of death. There is no mention of their unit, the riot, or their execution. The other two soldiers were reinterred in family plots.

Racial tensions did not ease with the passage of time. In Sherman, near the Oklahoma border north of Camp Hood, a black man was on trial for the rape of a white woman. On May 9, 1930, despite the defense efforts of Texas Rangers and National Guardsmen, a white mob stormed the courthouse. When they could not secure the black defendant, they burned the courthouse down on him, then took his corpse, drug it behind a car, and set the remains on fire. The rioters then destroyed Sherman's black business section.

After the Sherman Riot, mob violence and lynchings in pre-World War II Texas decreased to "only" about one incident a year. Shortly before Jackie reported to Camp Hood, a mob in Texarkana on July 13, 1942, dragged a black man, accused of assaulting a white woman, behind a car through the streets of the town before lynching him on a cotton gin winch. On June 15, 1943, a mob of 4,000 whites in Beaumont on the Texas Gulf Coast rioted against blacks who they thought were taking away high paying jobs in the shipyards. By the end of the violence, one black man lay dead, fifty were injured, and move than a hundred homes in the city's African American district were in ashes.

Historical Perspective 10

McCloskey General Hospital

$\mathcal{M}$cCloskey General Hospital was built on land donated by the people of Temple and named in honor of Maj. James A. McCloskey who was killed on Bataan on March 26, 1942—the first regular U.S. Army doctor to lose his life in World War II.

Historical Perspective 11

Camp Hood, Texas, MP Station

The statements supporting the charges had been taken at the Camp Hood MP Station that stood in row after row of recently constructed buildings, structures so new they still smelled of pine and sawdust. World War II camps across the United States were virtually the same with two-story barracks with open bays for the troops and single rooms at their ends for NCOs. Additional two-story buildings with cubical-like rooms were for officers. A chapel and a gymnasium, identical at each camp stood in each brigade-size barracks area. Command, supply and other administrative functions were conducted from single-story buildings generally located in the center of the battalion and brigade areas.

The MP Station in question contained a room with a high desk where a senior NCO met visitors and determined where to place those alleged offenders brought in by the MP patrols. An adjoining duty room for MPs and offices for officers and senior NCOs occupied the remainder of the building. None of the barracks or administrative buildings contained air conditioning. A few fans likely stirred the humid air that had gone down to about seventy-six degrees after daytime temperatures in the high nineties.

Appendixes

The documents in the following appendixes are reproduced with only minor corrections to spelling and punctuation. The narrative as well as abbreviations, acronyms, and designations of rank are as they appear in the original papers.

Appendix A

Sworn Statement of
2nd Lt. Jack R. Robinson,
Company B, 761st Tank Battalion,
Camp Hood, Texas, 7 July 1944

I left McCloskey General Hospital, Temple, Texas, about 1730, 6 July 1944, and went to Temple, Texas on the city bus. I got on another bus and came out to the Officers Club, Camp Hood, Texas, the colored officers club located on 172nd Street. I arrived there at approximately 1930. I was in the club for some time. While in the club I saw Captain McHenry, Lt. Long, Captain Woodruff, and Captain Wales.

I remained at the Officers Club until approximately two and one-half hours later. At approximately 2200 I got on the bus at the 172nd street and Battalion, I believe just outside the colored officers club. I got on the Camp Hood bus. I entered at the front of the bus and moved toward the rear and saw a colored girl sitting in a seat at the middle of the bus. I sat down beside the girl. I knew this girl before. Her name is Mrs. Jones. I don't know her first name. She's an officer's wife here on the post. I sat down there and we rode approximately five or six blocks on the bus and the bus driver turns around and tells me to move to the rear which I did not do. He tells me that if I don't move to the rear he will make trouble for me when we get to the bus station, and I told him that was up to him. When he got to the bus station a lady got off the bus before I got off, and she tells me that she is going to prefer charges against me. That was a white lady. And I said that's all right, too, I don't care if she prefers charges against me. The bus driver asked me for my identification card. I refused to give it to him. He then went to the dispatcher and told him something. What he told him I don't know. He then comes back and tells the people that this nigger is making trouble. I told the bus driver to stop fucking with me, so he gets the rest of the men around there and starts blowing his top and someone calls the MP's. Outside of telling this lady that I didn't care if she preferred charges against me or not, I don't know if they were around or not, sir, I was speaking directly to that bus driver, and just as I told the captain (indicating Captain Wigginton, Camp Officer of the Day) if any one of you called me a nigger I would do the same thing, especially from a civilian, a general or anybody else. I mean I would tell them the same thing. I told him, I'm using a "general," and general, if anybody calls me a nigger, I don't know the definition of it. That's just like anyone going around calling you something you don't know what is. The colored girl was going to Belton, her home, and she got off the same time that I got off. The only time I made any statement was when this fellow called me a nigger. I didn't have any loud or boisterous conversation. That's the only profane language I used if you call it profane. (When told by Captain Bear that that was vulgar and vile language Lt. Robinson said: "That's vulgar is it, that's vile is it?") I want to tell you right now sir, this private you got out there, he made a statement. The private over there in that room, I told him that if he, a private, ever called me that name (a nigger) again I would break him in two. (The private referred to was later called to the MP orderly room and identified as being PFC Ben W. Mucklerath, 37061068, Company B, 149th Tng Bn, 90th Regt, IRTC, Camp Hood, Texas.)

Appendix B

Original Charge Sheet
Camp Hood, Texas, 17 July 1944

Name of accused: Robinson, Jack R. 0-1031586 Second Lieutenant, Cavalry
Company C 758th
Tank Battalion

Charge I: Violation of the 63rd Article of War
Specification 1: In that Second Lieutenant Jack R. Robinson, Cavalry, Company C, 758th Tank Battalion, did, at Camp Hood, Texas, on or about 6 July 1944, behave himself with disrespect toward Captain Peeler L. Wigginton, Quartermaster Corps, 1848th Unit, Eighth Service Command, Army Service Forces, his superior officer, by saying to him, "Captain, any Private, you, are any General calls me a nigger and I'll break them in two, I don't know the definition of the word," or words to that effect, and by speaking to the said Captain Peeler L. Wigginton in an insolent, impertinent and rude manner.

Specification 2: In that Second Lieutenant Jack R. Robinson Cavalry, Company C, 758th Tank Battalion, did, at Camp Hood, Texas, on or about 6 July 1944, behave himself with disrespect toward Captain Gerald M. Bear, Corps Military Police, 1848th Unit, Eighth Service Command, Army Services Forces, his superior officer, by contemptuously bowing to him and giving him several sloppy salutes repeating several times "OK Sir," "OK Sir" or words to that effect, and by acting in an insolent, impertinent, and rude manner toward the said captain Gerald M. Bear.

Charge II: Violation of the 64th Article of War
Specification: In that Second Lieutenant Jack R. Robinson, Cavalry, Company C, 758th Tank Battalion, having received a lawful order from Captain Gerald M. Bear, Corps Military Police, 1848th Unit, Eighth Service Com-

mand, Army Service Forces, his superior officer, to remain in a receiving room and be seated in a chair on the far side of the receiving room, did, at Camp Hood, Texas, on or about 6 July 1944 willfully disobey the same.

Charge III: Violation of the 95th Article of War
Specification 1: In that Second Lieutenant Jack R. Robinson, Cavalry, Company C, 758th Tank Battalion, did, at Camp Hood, Texas on or about 6 July 1944, wrongfully use the following abusive and vulgar language toward Milton N. Renegar, a civilian, Hood Village, Texas, "I'm not going to move a God damn bit" or words to that effect, and called the said Milton N. Renegar a "son of a bitch," in the presence of ladies.

Specification 2: In that Second Lieutenant Jack R. Robinson, Cavalry, Company C, 758th Tank Battalion, did, at Camp Hood, Texas on or about 6 July 1944, wrongfully say the following vile and obscene language toward Elizabeth Poitevint, a civilian, Killeen, Texas, "You better quit fuckin with me" or words to that effect.

Specification 3: In that Second Lieutenant Jack R. Robinson, Cavalry, Company C, 758th Tank Battalion, did, at Camp Hood, Texas on or about 6 July 1944, wrongfully use vile, obscene, and abusive language in a public place in the presence of ladies, to wit, on a public bus and at the Central Bus Station, Camp Hood, Texas.

Appendix C

Sworn Statement of
Capt. Peelor L. Wigginton,
QMC, Camp Laundry Officer,
Camp Hood, Texas,
7 July 1944

*D*uring my tour of duty as Camp Officer of the Day, Camp Hood, Texas, 6 July 1944 at approximately 2230 I was summoned to the Military Police Guard House by the Sergeant of the Guard, Sergeant Painter, to interview a colored 2nd Lt., Jack R. Robinson of the 761st Tank Battalion. When I entered the Guard Room Lt. Robinson was talking in an insolent manner and directing his words to the Sergeant of the Guard, and a Pfc. Ben W. Mucklerath. I inquired of Sgt. Painter as to the nature of the trouble, and he inferred to me that Lt. Robinson had been picked up at the Central Bus Station upon the request of the dispatcher there, for creating a disturbance. I then asked the Lt. to give me a resume of the incident, and he gave me the following story: that he had boarded camp shuttle outside the colored officer's club, and saw a colored girl, a Mrs. Jones, wife of an officer on this post, sitting about half-way down the isle of the bus; he sat down with her and before arriving at the next bus stop the bus driver asked him to move to the rear of the bus. Lt. Robinson then told the bus driver that he was the equal of anyone, and would not move; the bus driver then told the Lt. that if he did not move he would make plenty of trouble for him when they arrived at the Central Bus Station. When they arrived at the Bus Station the driver asked the dispatcher to call the MPs, and Lt. Robinson told me that he then told the bus driver that "If you don't quit fuckin' with me I'll cause you plenty of trouble." He further said that the bus driver then asked him for his name, rank, and serial number, and organization, and that he refused to give the information to the driver, and said that he would not give his name to a "damn civilian. He said that the white soldier, PFC Mucklerath, and some others were standing there and that they called him a nigger, and then some white lady said she was going to report him to the MPs, and that he told them he didn't care what they did,

178

that he didn't know what "nigger" meant, and that anyone who called him that was going to get into plenty of trouble.

I then asked Pfc. Mucklerath for his statement regarding the incident, and he gave me the following story: he was standing outside the bus station waiting for a bus when the bus on which the colored Lt. was riding pulled into the station, and that there was quite a lot of loud and vulgar talk going on. That he saw the colored Lt., Lt. Robinson, got off the bus and was following a white lady toward the bus station, and that he heard the colored Lieutenant say to the lady:

"I don't care if you do report me, and if you don't quit fuckin with me you'll get into trouble." At this point in Pfc. Mucklerath's story, Lt. Robinson interrupted and said that he was not addressing the white lady, but was addressing Pfc. Mucklerath because he had heard Mucklerath say something about a nigger. Pfc. Mucklerath then told me that he had not called the Lt. a nigger, and up until that time he had not said one word either to nor about the Lt. Lt. Robinson then said to me, "Captain, and Private, you, or any General, calls me a nigger, and I'll break him in two. I don't know the definition of the word." He repeated that he would break anybody in two and he didn't care who it was if they called him a nigger. Pfc. Mucklerath then told me that the Lt. had told him in the presence of several MPs that he would break him (Pfc. Mucklerath) in two if he ever saw him again. Lt. Robinson interrupted again and said that what he told Pfc. Mucklerath was that he would "break anyone in two if they called him a nigger," and he then asked all the MPs present if that wasn't what he had said, but the MPs present all said, "No," that Pfc. Mucklerath had repeated the incident correctly and used exactly the words that Lt. Robinson had used. At that time the Lt. interrupted again and began saying that he didn't have a chance. I then asked Lt. Robinson to be silent until I had heard Pfc. Mucklerath's story, and Lt. Robinson said sneeringly, "So this is democracy, I don't have a chance, shh-." While he was talking to me and while I was talking to him, Lt. Robinson was leaning on the high desk in the interior Sgt. of the Guard Room, in a very disrespectful manner. His attitude was in general was very insolent, disrespectful, and smart-elec, and certainly his actions were unbecoming to an officer and a gentleman, particularly in the presence of the enlisted men together with other officers.

Shortly after that I called for Captain Bear, Assistant Provost Marshal, and Miss Wilson, stenographer in Provost Marshal's Branch to come to the Guard Room to take statements regarding the incident.

Lt. Robinson told me that he was from McCloskey General Hospital, Temple, Texas, but he did not tell me that he was there for purely administrative purposes, and led me to believe that he was a patient.

When Captain Bear arrived I was relating the incident to him as I had heard it from Lt. Robinson and Pfc. Mucklerath, and Lt. Robinson continually interrupted us, and it was impossible to carry on an intelligent conversation with his interruptions. Captain Bear finally ordered the Lt. to stay in the outer room of the Guard Room and wait until he was called. He directly disobeyed this order and returned to the swinging door between the two rooms and attempted to start another argument with Captain Bear. Captain Bear ordered him back to the room and told him to sit down in a chair and wait until he was called. Lt. Robinson walked back into the room but did not stay there. He walked outside the Guard Room and was talking to the driver of a jeep belonging to the 761st Tank Battalion, OD, whom I had called. Captain Bear again ordered him to wait in the outer Guard Room until he was called.

Later Lt. Robinson was called to the MP Orderly Room, advised of his rights under the 24th Article of War by Captain Bear, and asked if he wished to make a statement under oath regarding the incident. Lt. Robinson stated in the presence of Captain Bear, Captain Hamilton, Camp Prison Officer, and Miss Wilson that he would like to make a statement. He was then duly sworn by Captain Bear and proceeded to make his statement. From time to time, Captain Bear, who was conducting the investigation, asked Lt. Robinson material questions which covered the issue. Lt. Robinson's attitude during this time was very disrespectful, and insolent. At one time during the questioning Captain Bear asked the Lt. about when and where he used profane language in the presence of ladies, and the Lt. stated that the only time he used profane language was when he told the bus driver to "stop fuckin with me," and asked, "if you'd call that profane" in a very sneeringly manner. At that point Captain Bear said, Lt. that wasn't profanity, that is vulgar and vile." Then Lt. Robinson said in the same sneering, half-laughing manner, "So that's vulgar, is it, that's vile, is it?" That is only one example of his superior, and at other times, facetious manner during the questioning.

Before the statement was taken Captain Bear had contacted Major Wingo, Commanding Officer, 761st Tank Battalion, and talked to him over the telephone regarding the Lt. At that time it was understood between Captain Bear and Major Wingo that the Lt. could return to McCloskey General Hospital. Major Wingo indicated that it would be sometime before he could arrange for transportation and necessary guards to return Lt. Robinson to the hospital. After the questioning was completed, Lt. Robinson was informed that he would be returned to McCloskey under guard. He objected to the arrangements that had been made, not only for his convenience but for his own safety, and for protection of all concerned. He continually argued with Captain Bear, attempted to force Captain Bear to contradict himself, was belligerent, and even after Captain Bear explained that the arrangements had been made in accordance with the wishes of his Commanding Officer, Lt. Robinson demanded to talk to Major Wingo, and took the attitude that

Captain Bear was preventing him from seeing his Commanding Officer. He was continually arguing with Captain Bear about whether he was under arrest or not, and the argument had lasted sometime, with Captain Bear trying to reason with the insolent officer. At that point I, as Camp Officer of the Day, stepped in and stated that if there was any more argument at all I would place the Lt. under arrest for insubordination and disrespect to superior officers. At one time during the questioning, Captain Bear asked the Lt. for the name of the colored girl he was sitting with so that he could contact the girl to take a statement regarding the incident. Captain Bear then asked him what her first name was, and in a very insolent manner he told the Captain, rather reminded him, that he had been sworn to tell the truth, the whole truth, and nothing but the truth. His manner was very insolent and he seemed to think it funny that he could tell Captain Bear the name "Miss Jones." He finally said that she was the wife of an officer on the Post, but gave no details.

Generally, the conduct and actions of this officer were very disrespectful to his superior officers. His conduct was rude, insolent, and very unbecoming to an officer and a gentleman. His conduct toward superior officers in the presence of enlisted men was very bad, and highly detrimental as an example.

Appendix D

Sworn Statement of Capt. Gerald M. Bear, Assistant Provost Marshal, Camp Hood, Texas, 7 July 1944

Arriving at the MP Guard Room 2305 on 6 July 1944, I found 2nd Lt. Jack R. Robinson in the MP Guard Room. I asked the Lt. to step outside the MP Guard Room to wait in the receiving room. Captain Wigginton, Camp OD, was relating and explaining to me what had just occurred as to the incident at the Central Bus Station, Camp Hood, Texas. Lt. Robinson kept continually interrupting Captain Wigginton and myself and kept coming to the Guard House door-gate. I cautioned and requested Lt. Robinson on several occasions to remain at ease and remain in the receiving room that I would talk to him later. In an effort to try to be facetious, Lt. Robinson bowed with several sloppy salutes, repeating several times, "OK, sir, OK, sir," on each occasion. I then gave Lt. Robinson another direct order to remain in the receiving room and be seated on a chair, on the far side of the receiving room. Later on I found Lt. Robinson on the outside of the building talking to the driver of the 761st OD's jeep. I then directed Lt. Robinson to go inside the building and remain in the receiving room.

Lt. Robinson's attitude in general was disrespectful and impertinent to his superior officers, and very unbecoming to an officer in the presence of enlisted men.

Appendix E

Sworn Statement of Mr. Milton N. Renegar, Bus Driver, Southwestern Bus Company, Camp Hood, Texas, 7 July 1944

I drive a bus for the Southwestern Bus Company. At approximately 10:15, 6 July 1944, I was driving my bus and stopped at bus stop #23, on 172nd Street, Camp Hood, Texas. Some white ladies, maybe a soldier or so, and a colored girl and a colored Second Lieutenant got on the bus. The colored girl and the colored Lt., whom I later learned to be 2nd Lt. Jack R. Robinson of the 761st Tank Battalion, sat down together about middle ways of the bus. On that particular run I have quite a few of the white ladies who work in the PX's and ride the bus at that hour almost every night. I did not say anything to the colored Lt. when he first sat down, until I got around to bus stop #18, and then I asked him, I said, "Lt., if you don't mind, I have got several ladies to pick up at the stop and will have a load of them before I get back to the Central Bus Station, and would like for you to move back to the rear of the bus if you don't mind." When I asked him to move to the rear he just sat there, and I asked him to move back there the second time. When I asked him the second time he started cursing and the first thing he said was, "I'm not going to move a God damned bit." I told him that I had a load of ladies to pick up and that I was sure they wouldn't want to ride mixed up like that, and told him I'd rather he would either move back to the rear or get off the bus, one of the two. He kept on cursing and saying that he wasn't going to get back, and I told him that he could either get back or he'd be sorry of it when I got to the Bus Station, or words to that effect. He kept saying something about it after I started up the bus, but I could not understand what he was saying. He continued to sit there with the colored girl and the girl did not say anything. When we arrived at the Bus Station I had "Pinky" Younger, the Dispatcher, call the MP's. Everybody on the bus was mad about it. I had asked the Lt. in a nice way to move and he had refused. One of the ladies who was riding said,

"I don't mind waiting on them all day, but when I get on the bus at night to go home, I'm not about to ride all mixed up with them." This lady works at PX #10 and I believe her daughter works with her and was with her last night. The colored Lt. kept on doing a lot of cursing and the feeling on the bus was pretty bad. All the people were very much upset about the situation and wanted something done about the lieutenant's attitude. When I told the Dispatcher to call the MP's I told him I was having some trouble with a negro Lieutenant. This White lady asked me if I was going to report the Lieutenant and I told her "yes," and she said, "well if you don't I am." At that time the colored Lieutenant said to the lady, "you better quit fuckin'" with me," and he meant everybody that was trying to do something about the trouble he was causing. There were white women and children and soldiers present, it looked to me like forty or fifty people within hearing distance, and when the Lt. said that it was outside the Bus Station but could have been heard plainly inside the station. After the MP's arrived and the Lt. went to get in the patrol wagon he called me a "son-of-a-bitch," and walked around to get in the wagon, he said, "I don't know why that son-of-a-bitch wanted to give me all this trouble," and the women were all still there at that time. The MP's just asked the Lt. a few questions and he kept cursing and so the MP told him he was using a lot of bad language in the presence of ladies and told him he was going to take him over to the Provost Marshal Office and let him talk to the Provost Marshal about it. I had told the lieutenant to hush once and he just kept on waving and cursing. What the Lieutenant said to the lady in the presence of other ladies as I have stated it above, he said three or four other times, and said it to everyone there. He also said something about this white lady as he went around to get in the patrol wagon and I know he was cursing the lady, but I could not tell what he said. I heard him say something to the MP about wanting his name and organization, but I don't know what that was. The only time I heard the colored girl who was with him say anything was when he started to leave with the MP's and she just asked him what the trouble was.

Appendix F

Sworn Statement of PFC Ben W. Mucklerath, Company D, 149th Tng Bn, 90th Regt, IRTC, Camp Hood, Texas, 7 July 1944

*O*n 6 July 1944, I went over the 162nd Street Service Club, Camp Hood, Texas, and was there a short while and started on my way to my barracks on the bus. I rode the bus and got off at the Central Bus Station, and sat down on a seat to wait for my bus to go to the barracks. It was approximately ten minutes after ten when I arrived at the Bus Station. About ten minutes later a bus pulled into the Bus Station and I was there on the outside, sitting down on a seat along side of the Bus Station building. I saw a white lady step off the bus and start into the bus station. A colored Lt. also got off the bus and was directing obscene language at her, he said, "You better quit fuckin' with me." That's all I heard him say at that time. He said this in the presence of a large number of ladies and children, and it was plainly heard by those present. I then heard the white lady say to the colored Lt. whom I later learned to be 2nd Lt. Jack R. Robinson, "I'm going to report you," and the Lt. repeated a second time, what he had just said to her. I then went into the Bus Station and called the MP headquarters. When I went outside again the MP patrol car had already arrived. I asked the driver of the patrol car if he had a colored Lt., and the Lt. turned to me and said, "You better quit fuckin' with me." He also said to the MP driver, "There's no God-damned son-of-a-bitch going to tell me where to sit. The driver told me that he wanted me to go along, with him to MP headquarters with him as a witness, and ordered me to get in back of the truck. When the white lady had first stepped of the bus and started toward the Bus Station Lt. Robinson was approximately three paces behind her, following her, and he turned around and went back into the bus driver, and at that time I went into the Bus Station to call the MP's, but I heard him using some very obscene and vulgar language; I distinctly heard him say "son-of-a-bitch," and some other words which I could not hear plainly. He was talking in a course, rough and harsh tone of voice and could be heard plainly by all the women and children and soldiers present. His conduct, generally, was very unbecoming to an officer and a gentleman. I got in the MP truck and came to the MP Headquarters, and upon arrival there I was telling the Sergeant of the Guard that I was present, and what I had seen and heard at that time the colored Lt. turned to me and said, "If I ever see you again, I'll break you in two." I turned to the Sergeant of the Guard and said, "Sergeant, I would like that to be a matter of record, that the Lt. threatened me and I would have the names of all the men present who heard that." About that time Captain Wigginton, the Camp Officer of the Day, entered the Guard Room and I reported my story of what I had seen and heard and this colored Lt. interrupted me two times and had to be called down by Captain Wigginton. I was interrupted when he threatened me, and he accused me of calling him a damn nigger. Captain Wigginton called him down that time and told him that he would talk to him later and not to interrupt me. I had not at any time called the Lt. a "nigger," and had not at any time spoken to nor said anything to the Lt. I was talking to the Sergeant of the Guard, and the Lt. was just jumping on me because I was telling him what I had heard. I had told the Sergeant of the Guard what I had seen and heard, and Lt. Robinson said, "I have my rights, this is a democracy, shh_," and I understood him to say, "shit," but not in a very audible tone, however there were other witnesses present in the Guard Room at that time.

Appendix G

Sworn Statement of Mr. Bevlia B. Younger, Dispatcher, Southwestern Bus Company, Central Bus Station, Camp Hood, Texas, 7 July 1944

I am the dispatcher for the Southwestern Bus Company, on duty at the Central Bus Station, Camp Hood, Texas. I was on duty last night, 6 July 1944, at approximately 10:00 or 10:15 when a bus driven by Mr. M. N. Renegar pulled into the Bus Station. The first thing I knew of any trouble on the bus was when Mr. Renegar called and asked me to call for the MP's. Before calling I walked out the north entrance of the bus station to see exactly what the trouble was. On my exit from the bus station I heard a colored Lieutenant, whom I later learned to be 2nd Lt. Jack R. Robinson, in a loud and boisterous voice make the remark: "what is the matter with you fuckin' people around here, you can't fuck me in this manner." Upon hearing these remarks I said nothing to the lieutenant, but immediately returned to the telephone and called for assistance from the MP's. Upon the arrival of the MP, Corporal Elwood whom I knew, he asked me what the trouble was. I told him that the trouble was with a nigger Lt.; the nigger Lt. hearing the remark, resented being called so—and informed Cpl. Elwood that, 'No God-damned sorry son-of-a-bitch could call him a nigger and get away with it.'" These remarks by the colored Lt. were made in the presence of perhaps 100 to 200 ladies and other passengers on the buses, some of which informed us that they would be glad to make statements as to what he had said. Immediately after the arrival of Cpl. Elwood, he carried the Lt. to MP headquarters. Before this, and immediately after calling the MP's I went back outside the Bus Station to watch the colored Lt., to see if he tried to leave because I felt that he should be delivered to the Military Police after making such remarks which were very unbecoming to an officer and a disgrace to the uniform he wears. When Cpl. Elwood arrived the colored Lt. tried to get Cpl. Elwood to take his name and let him go on, but Cpl. Elwood told him that he would have to take him over to talk to the Provost Marshal about it. There was a great deal of nervous tension shown among the ladies and the white soldiers present. The feeling was very high, and the people were demanding that something be done about the colored lieutenant talking in such a manner.

Appendix H

Sworn Statement of Mrs. Elizabeth Poitevint, Employee PX#10, Camp Hood, Texas, 8 July 1944

On the 6th of July 1944, at approximately 10:00 p.m. I left PX # 10 where I work and got the bus at Bus Stop #23, to go to the Central Bus Station. When we got on the bus a colored girl was there and got on the bus and sat down about middle ways of the bus. I was sitting about five seats back on the other side of the bus. A colored Second Lieutenant got on the bus there and sat down beside the colored girl. We were going up Battalion Avenue and stopped at another Bus Stop and some white women, most of them with their babies, got on the bus. The driver came back to the colored Lt. and said, "Lieutenant, will you move to the back of the bus so these people can sit down?" The colored Lt. said I certainly will not. I paid my fare and I don't intend to move out of this seat," and he said, "I'm going to sit right here, and driver, you go right back up to the front of this bus and sit down and drive this bus to wherever you're going, because I don't intend to move." Then the driver said, "You will either have to get off the bus or move to the back," and he told the Lieutenant to make up his mind what he was going to do, and the Lt. said, "I am going to stay right where I am," and the bus driver said, "Well, if you're on this bus sitting in that same seat when we get to the Central Bus Station you are going to cause yourself some trouble." Then the Lieutenant said, "Well, I don't care, I'm going to be sitting right in the same seat when you get wherever you're going." When we got to the Central Bus Station we all got off, and the driver asked the Lieutenant for his identification card, and the Lt. said "I haven't done anything and I'm not going to show you my identification card, I'm going to get on another bus and go." The driver said, "I want your identification card, I'm going to turn you in," then I said to the driver, "If you want any witnesses as to what he has done to you, you can call on me, because I've heard everything he has said." Then the Lt. turned to me and said, "Listen here you damned old woman, you have nothing to say about what's going on. I didn't want to get into this, they drafted me into this, and my money is just as good as a white man's." And I told him, I said, "Well, listen buddy, you got to know where you should sit on the bus." I started on to the Bus Station and asked the bus driver if he was going to report him, and I told him that if he didn't report the colored Lieutenant that I was going to report him to the MP's. I had to wait on them during the day, but I didn't have to sit with them on the bus. At no time on the bus did the Lt. get up and offer his seat to any of the women with children. After the MP's came to the bus station, and the Lt. went to get in the MP wagon, the colored girl went up to him and said, "What are we going to do now, honey?" and he told her not to worry and said he'd be back in a couple of minutes and for her to wait right there. He said the worst they could do to him was take his bars. Once I heard the colored Lieutenant say, "No sorry son-of-a-bitch can tell me where to sit." He was very hateful to the bus driver, and the bus driver was very polite to him. I did not at any time hear anyone call the Lt. a nigger. I am sure that no one called him a nigger because I was there all the time. I was the only woman who took any hand in the argument and all the Lt's. remarks were pointed to me because I had told the bus driver that he could call on me for a witness. When I got off the bus and started into the Bus Station the Lt. was following me, and was shaking his hand at me in a threatening manner. While we were still on the bus, and the white women kept getting on and pushing to the back with their children, the bus driver asked the Lt. three times if he wouldn't give some of the ladies a seat, and he said "No, I'm not going to move a God damned bit," and he didn't move either. The driver was very nice to him and I asked him to "please" move to the rear on one occasion. When he went to get off the bus at Central Station we all stood up and said that is the colored Lt. had to ride in the middle of the bus, he could've just wait until all of us got off. I stood up and put my hand out on his seat and he waited until we all got off. He was the last one to get off, and then he said something about "We're all in this together and my money is as good as a white man's." When I got off the bus and asked the bus driver if he was going to report him, the Lt. said to me, "You better quit fuckin' with me." He said that three or four times, after we got off the bus, and all that profane and obscene language used could have been heard by anyone around there, and there was a big crowd there too. The colored Lieutenant thought that he could go on around the Bus Station and get another bus before the MP's got there and he walked around to the other side of the Bus Station, to catch the bus, but when the MP truck came, the first one came up on that side of the building and one came up the other was, from the opposite direction, and the MP's called the Lieutenant over to where they were and talk to him.

Sworn Statement of Mrs. Ruby Johnson, Employee PX #10, Camp Hood, Texas, 7 July 1944

I am employed at PX #10, Camp Hood, Texas, and last night, 6 July 1944, when I got off from work at approximately 10:00, I left the PX and caught a bus at bus stop #23. I was with Mrs. Elizabeth Poitevint and her daughter, Mary LeConey. A colored girl was standing at the Bus Stop when we walked up and we got on at the same time as the colored girl did. At the same stop a colored Second Lieutenant whom I later learned to be Second Lieutenant Jack R. Robinson, got on the bus. I don't know whether he was with the colored girl or not but he sat down with her. Mrs. Poitevint, Mary and I all sat at the same seat, over the left rear wheel, and we saw the colored Lieutenant and colored girl set two or three seats in front of us on the right side of the bus. No one said anything about the colored people sitting there at the time. The bus wasn't crowded then. When we got to about Bus Stop #18, the driver stopped and there were a lot of soldiers' wives and children got on the bus. At that time the bus driver asked the colored Lieutenant if he would move to the back of the bus. The Lt. said, "No, I'm going to sit here, I'm not going to move to the back of the bus," he said that in a very forceful voice, and then he told the driver, "You had better sit down and drive the bus wherever you're going." He told the bus driver that twice, and the bus driver told the Lt. that he would wish he had gone to the back of the bus when they got to the Central Bus Station. The women and children pushed onto the back, and some of them stood up as we rode on to Central Station. When we first arrived the Belton bus hadn't arrived and I went around to the front of the bus station to the line for the Belton bus. Just as I went past him I heard the colored Lieutenant tell the bus driver that he could call all the damned MP's he want to, that it didn't make a difference to him. After that I got on another bus and left.

Appendix J

Sworn Statement of Acting Cpl. George A. Elwood, MP Section, Enl Det, 1848 U, Camp Hood, Texas

I was on duty as driver of MP Motor Patrol 6 July 1944 when the Sgt of the Guard sent me to the Central Bus Station, Camp Hood, Texas, at approximately 2220 to investigate a disturbance caused by a colored Lieutenant. When I arrived at the Central Bus Station I found a colored Lt. whom I learned to be 2d Lt. Jack R. Robinson of the 761st Tank Battalion. When I drove up to the Bus Station the Dispatcher, Mr. Younger, came over and told me that this colored Lt. had been giving a lot of trouble and using a lot of profane and vulgar language. Then the Lt. came over to the patrol car and said that he was tired of the "God-dammed sons-of-bitches trying to push me around," and said that, by God he wasn't going to stand for it anymore. There were several ladies present there, and I told the Lt. to watch his language. The Dispatcher told me of the incident that had happened and I told the Lt. to get in the patrol car, that I was going to take him to the Guard Room and contact one of my officers or the OD. He wanted to give me his name but I told him he would give that to one of the officers and for him to get in the pick-up. Then he got in the pick-up with me, and a white soldier whom I learned to be Pfc Mucklerath, came over to the pick-up and asked me if I got that nigger Lieutenant. Right then the lieutenant said, "Look here, you son-of-a-bitch, don't you call me no nigger. I'm an officer and God damn you, you better address me as one," or words to that effect. I again cautioned the Lt. about his language, that there were ladies present. There was one white lady who was right by the patrol car with the dispatcher, and she told me that she wanted the Lt. taken care of, and said she had never heard such profane and vulgar language, and had never been cussed out by a nigger. The lady left and I had the Lt. and wanted to get him away from those bus drivers and the Dispatcher before something happened. I was patrolling alone at the time, and I took the colored Lt. into the MP Guard Room. I also told Pfc. Mucklerath to get in the back of the truck and go along as a witness. I heard the colored Lt. say that "No God damned son-of-a-bitch is going to tell me where to ride." He said that when he were still there at the Bus Station. After we arrived at the MP Guard Room I reported to the Sgt of the Guard and told him what I had seen and heard at the Bus Station, and told him who I had brought in and that I had brought them in for the OD or one of our officers to question. I turned the colored Lt. over to the Sgt. of the Guard who began trying to locate the OD or one of our MP officers. Lt. Robinson and Pfc. Mucklerath were in the MP Guard Room and Mucklerath was talking to the Sgt of the Guard and I heard the Lt tell Pfc Mucklerath that if he ever saw him again he was going to break him in two. I left then and went after Captain Bear and later when I returned to the Guard Room Captain Wigginton the Camp OD was trying to explain the situation to Captain Bear and the colored Lt. interfered and he wouldn't be quiet, and I distinctly heard Captain Bear tell the Lt. to be at ease and wait outside the Sergeant's of the Guard Room. This Lt. interrupted continually and when Captain Bear would speak to him he would bow from the hips and give him a very sloppy salute, and had sort of a smart smile on his face all the time, and he said, 'OK, sir,' two or three times, and this was very disrespectful considering his manner. Finally, Captain Bear told him to go sit down on a chair in the corner back away from him and had Sgt. Painter stay out there and see that he stayed down in the chair. The colored Lt. had a smart attitude and was very disrespectful toward the officers and the MP's present. Shortly after that I left and went after some of the witnesses.

Appendix K

Sworn Statement of Sgt. William L. Painter, MP Section, Enl Det 1848 U, Camp Hood, Texas, 7 July 1944

I was on duty as Sgt. for the Guard, Camp Hood, Texas, on the night of 6 July 1944 at approximately 2215 when I received a call from the central bus station to send an MP because of a disturbance caused by a colored Lieutenant. Add approximately 2235 Acting Corporal George A. Elwood, MP, whom I had dispatched to the scene returned to the Guard Room with a colored Lieutenant who I later learned to be Second Lt. Jack R. Robinson, and a soldier, Pfc Ben W. Mucklerath. I asked them what the trouble was and Pfc Mucklerath started to tell me what it was all about, and Lt. Robinson interrupted him and told him, "If I ever see you again I'll break you in two." Then the soldier, Pfc Mucklerath told me he wanted that to be a matter of record and that he wanted me to get the name of all the witnesses who heard Lt. Robinson threaten his life, and I told him OK. I was present when both Lt. Robinson and Pfc Mucklerath entered the Guard Room and the only reason I know of why Lt. Robinson threatened Pfc Mucklerath it was because he was trying to tell me what had happened and the Lieutenant didn't want him to tell me. Pfc. Mucklerath did not at any time, in my presence, call the Lieutenant a nigger, nor address the Lieutenant in any manner. Pfc. Mucklerath was talking to me and did not say anything at all to the lieutenant. Every time Pfc Mucklerath tried to talk the Lieutenant kept interrupting and refused to remain quiet. The camp O.D., Captain P. L. Wigginton, arrived shortly after that and he asked what had happened. Both Pfc Mucklerath and the Lieutenant started talking, and as Pfc Mucklerath was talking the Lieutenant was saying, "That's not so," and he started in trying to tell about it. Captain Wigginton told the Lieutenant to be at ease and let the soldier do the talking, that he would have a chance to talk later. The Lt. told Captain Wigginton to let the soldier talk at first, and then when the soldier tried to talk the Lt. again interrupted, and Captain

194

Wigginton had to remind the Lt. that he had asked the soldier to talk first. His attitude, generally, was very insolent and disrespectful toward Captain Wigginton and the MP's present. Captain Bear, Assistant Provost Marshal, arrived and asked what the trouble was, and Captain Wigginton started to tell him and the Lt. interrupted Captain Wigginton. Captain Bear asked the Lt. to be at ease and step away from the Guard Room door and not interrupt them. Lieutenant Robinson would salute Captain Bear in a bowed manner, and exaggerate the salute as though he were making fun of Captain Bear. His attitude was very smart-alec, and he paid no attention to Captain Bear and Captain Wigginton's orders and continually interrupted them. Captain Bear told Lt. Robinson to stay in the outer office of the Guard Room, and instead Lt. Robinson went outside of the guard room and talked to the driver of a jeep belonging to the OD, 761st Tank Battalion. Captain Bear had called this OD because the 761st Tank Battalion was Lt. Robinson's organization. I witnessed Lt. Robinson refuse to obey the direct orders of Captain Bear and Captain Wigginton, to be quiet and to stay in the outer office of the Guard Room. At one time when Pfc Mucklerath was telling Captain Wigginton about the incident, Lt. Robinson interrupted and said, "I have my rights, and if this is a democracy, shh–" and his last word was obscenity. This was said in the presence of others who were in the Guard Room.

Appendix L

Sworn Statement of
Acting Cpl. Eugene J. Henrie,
MP Sec, Enl Det, 1848 U, Camp Hood,
Texas, 8 July 1944

$\mathscr{I}$ was on duty as Corporal of the Guard, MP Guard Room, Camp Hood, Texas, on the night of 6 July 1944, at approximately 2235 or 2245 when we received a call to send an MP to the Central Bus Station. Corporal Elwood was dispatched to go investigate trouble. When he came back to the Guard Room he brought a colored Second Lieutenant whom I learned to be 2nd Lt. Jack R. Robinson of the 761st Tank Battalion, and he also brought a Pfc Ben Mucklerath from the IRTC, as a witness. Sgt. Painter, Sgt. of the Guard asked what the trouble was and this soldier, Pfc. Mucklerath, started to tell him and the Lt. interrupted and wouldn't let him talk. Every time Mucklerath started to talk the Lt. butted in. I had to leave the Guard Room for a few minutes and when I returned I heard Lt. Robinson say to Pfc. Mucklerath, "If I ever see you again, I'll break you in two." I did not at any time hear Pfc. Mucklerath speak to Lt., talk to him, nor talk back to him. He was talking to the Sergeant of the Guard when he was talking. Shortly after that Captain Wigginton arrived. Pfc. Mucklerath was trying to tell him what had happened, and Captain Bear, Assistant Provost Marshal, had arrived, and they were all talking to the Sgt. of the Guard, and Lt. Robinson continually interrupted them and acted insolent toward them. At one time Captain Bear told the Lt. to remain at ease and that he would talk to him later or words to that effect. He also told the Lt. to stay in the outer room of the Guard Room and instead, the Lt. left the guard room and went outside and talked to the colored driver of the jeep. The jeep belonged to the OD of the 761st Tank Battalion, same Battalion which Lt. Robinson belonged to. I did not at any time here Pfc Mucklerath say anything disrespectful to the Lt. nor call him a nigger. In fact, he did not even speak to the LT. in my presence. The lieutenant was threatening Pfc Mucklerath because Mucklerath was trying to relate what had occurred. At one time

196

Captain Bear and Lt. Robinson were in the outer room of the Guard Room and Captain Bear started through the swinging door between that room and the Sergeant's of the Guard private room the Lt. started to try to go through the door with Captain Bear and Captain Bear told him to wait in the outer room, that we would call him when he wanted him, and Lt. Robinson bowed from the hips and gave Captain Bear a sloppy salute in a mocking manner, and said, "Ok, sir," "Ok, sir," and kept bowing. Captain Bear saluted him back and ignored his mocking manner. His attitude and actions toward the Commissioned Officers present was very bad. He was insolent, impertinent and acted smart, continually interrupting the officers. I had to leave shortly after that to Post Guards, and don't know what else happened after I left.

Appendix M

Sworn Statement of
Acting Cpl. Elmer S. Feris,
MP Sec Enl Det. 1848 U, Camp Hood, Texas,
8 July 1944

$\mathcal{I}$ was in the MP guard room, 6 July 1944, when Cpl. Elwood, MP, brought in a colored Second Lieutenant whom I later learned to be 2nd Lt. Jack R. Robinson, and a white soldier, Pfc Ben W Mucklerath, and I stood there and listened to the conversation. The first I heard, I heard of the Lt. say something about the soldier, Pfc Mucklerath, calling him a nigger at the Bus Station. He was talking direct to Pfc Mucklerath, And he told him that if he ever saw him again he would break him in two. The soldier did not make any reply to the colored Lt., but told the Sergeant of the Guard to be sure and put that in his report that the Lt. had threatened him, and asked the Sgt of the Guard to get the names of all the witnesses present. The Sgt of the Guard sent me after Capt. Wigginton, the camp officer of the day, and when we returned Capt. Wigginton walked in and he naturally asked the trouble, and this colored Lt. and Pfc Mucklerath were both trying to tell the story and the Lt. finally told the white soldier to tell the story first, and while Pfc Mucklerath was then trying to explain everything to Captain Wigginton; that the colored Lt. was cursing and using profane and vulgar language at the Bus Station in the presence of ladies, the colored Lt. butted in, and did not want Pfc Mucklerath to tell about it. Captain Wigginton told the Lt. to be at ease and wait until he had heard the soldier's story. Pfc Mucklerath also told Captain Wigginton about the colored Lt. threatening his life, and the Lt. butted in again, and said that when he threatened the enlisted man he said that if he "ever called me a nigger again, I will break you in two," the Lt. also indicated all us MP's present and said that we were witnesses and asked us if that wasn't what he had said, but that was not what he had said, he had said, "if I ever see you again, I'll break you in two," all the MP's told him that Pfc Mucklerath was telling the truth, that he had told the story correctly

198

and used mostly the words that the Lt. had used when he threatened him. Then the Lt. kept saying that, "Well, I'm glad I have one witness," but I didn't know who he was talking about. The Lt.'s attitude toward Captain Wigginton was very disrespectful, not only to Captain Wigginton, but to the Sgt. of the Guard and the Cpl. of the Guard. After that I left the Guard Room and did not hear any more of the conversation.

Appendix N

Sworn Statement of
Capt. Edward L. Hamilton,
Camp Prison Officer, Camp Hood, Texas,
7 July 1944

$\mathcal{A}$t approximately 0100, 7 July 1944, as Duty Officer, Provost Marshal Branch, I was in the MP Orderly Room, Camp Hood, Texas, along with Captain Peelor L. Wigginton, Camp Duty Officer, and First Lt. George Criberi, MC, Camp Hood, Texas. We were witnessing 2nd Lt. Jack R. Robinson giving his statement to Captain Gerald M. Bear, Assistant Provost Marshal, concerning an incident which occurred a few hours previous to that time at the Central Bus Station. While making his statement Lt. Robinson was very disrespectful and discourteous to Capt. Bear in his attempts to be facetious. During his statement, while referring to a Pfc calling him a "nigger," Lt. Robinson turned to Captain Wigginton and stated the "If you, Captain," and pointed to me and Lt. Criberi, "or you, or you, should call me a nigger, I would break you in two." He went ahead to state that any General or anyone else who called him a nigger, he would break them into. This threat was made in the presence of four officers, one enlisted man, Sgt. Howard C Hyatt, MP, and Miss Wilson, stenographer. This was very unbecoming, and his manner of conversation was very unbecoming to an Officer of the United States Army.

Sworn Statement of
1st Lt. George Cribari,
Station Hospital, Camp Hood, Texas
7 July 1944

I was present in the MP Orderly Room, when the above described statement was taken. I have read the above statement of Captain Edward L. Hamilton, and any statement I could make would be identical in substance.

Appendix P

Sworn Statement of Pvt. Walter H. Plotkin, MP Section, Enl Det, 1848 U, Camp Hood, Texas, 8 July 1944

I was in the MP Guard Room, Camp Hood, Texas, 6 July 1944, when the Sgt. of the Guard received a call from the Central Bus Station. Sgt. Painter, Sgt. of the Guard, then radioed Cpl. Elwood to go to the bus station and investigate the trouble there.

I was in the Guard Room later when Cpl. Elwood reported to the Sgt. of the Guard and brought in a colored Lt. whom I learned to be Lt. Robinson from the 761st Tank Battalion, and a white soldier, Pfc Mucklerath, from the IRTC, Camp Hood. Lt. Robinson seemed to be mad and he said he was in the McCloskey General Hospital, and that he would be back out here tomorrow, and said that if he saw Pfc Mucklerath again he would break him in two. Pfc Mucklerath told Sgt. Painter that he wanted that put down, and wanted the name of all the witnesses who heard the Lt. say that. The Lt's attitude certainly was not becoming to an officer and a gentleman, and he was very disrespectful of the white soldier. Pfc. Mucklerath told Sgt. Painter that at the Bus Station, Lt. Robinson said, "You better quit fuckin' with me," to a white lady. The Lt. admitted saying that, but said he was saying it to the bus driver. The Lt. told Sgt. Painter that the bus driver of the bus he was riding on told him to go to the rear of the bus, and he admitted that he refused to go to the rear, and that the bus driver told him he was going to cause trouble for him, and that he told the bus driver to go ahead and cause all the trouble he wanted to.

When Captain Wigginton, the Camp OD, walked in the Guard Room the colored Lt. started telling him about what happened. He told Captain Wigginton that nobody could call him a nigger and he said to the Captain, "If you yourself, called me a nigger I would tell you the same thing." He said that he would say that to anyone who called him a nigger. The colored Lt. was lay-ing on the Sgt.'s of the Guard desk, he was leaning over with his head toward the Sgt., and when he said that he didn't move his body, but just moved his head and directed his words to Captain Wigginton in an insolent manner, and said, "If you, Captain, called me a nigger I would tell you the same thing." When the Lt. and the Pfc, were both trying to tell their story, the Lt. finally told Pfc. Mucklerath to go ahead and tell his story first, and then he started interrupting him and Captain Wigginton told him to be quiet so Pfc Mucklerath could finish his story. I left shortly after that and went back to the Stockade.

Appendix 2

Sworn Statement of Pvt. Lester G. Phillips, Stu Regt, TDS, Camp Hood, Texas, 7 July 1944

I was at the Central Bus Station last night, 6 July 1944, sometime after 10:00, when the bus drove up and the people unloaded. The first thing I knew of any trouble on the bus was when I heard a colored Second Lieutenant, who got off the bus, cursing and using vulgar language in the presence of the large number of ladies who were there. I heard this colored Second Lieutenant say something about God-damned sons of bitches, and I heard him say, "What the matter with you fuckin' people around here," and said, "You better quit fuckin' me around like this." He said all of this in the presence of the ladies. I left then and came back a few minutes later, and the MP's had arrived when I returned. I did not hear any of his conversation with the MP's. I did not hear anyone call this colored Lieutenant a nigger, and did not hear anyone say anything at all to him. All the people there were trying to quiet him down and there was such a crowd around there that I couldn't see very well.

Appendix R

Final Charge Sheet,
Camp Hood, Texas,
17 July 1944

*N*ame of accused: Robinson, Jack R. 0-1031586 Second Lieutenant, Cavalry Company C 758th
Tank Battalion

Charge I: Violation of the 63rd Article of War
Specification 1: In that Second Lieutenant Jack R. Robinson Cavalry, Company C, 758th Tank Battalion, did, at Camp Hood, Texas, on or about 6 July 1944, behave himself with disrespect toward Captain Gerald M. Bear, Corps Military Police, 1848th Unit, Eighth Service Command, Army Services Forces, his superior officer, by contemptuously bowing to him and giving his several sloppy salutes repeating several times "OK Sir," "OK Sir" or words to that effect, and by acting in an insolent, impertinent, and rude manner toward the said captain Gerald M. Bear.

Charge II: Violation of the 64th Article of War
Specification: In that Second Lieutenant Jack R. Robinson, Cavalry, Company C, 758th Tank Battalion, having received a lawful order from Captain Gerald M. Bear, Corps Military Police, 1848th Unit, Eighth Service Command, Army Service Forces, his superior officer, to remain in a receiving room and be seated in a chair on the far side of the receiving room, did, at Camp Hood, Texas, on or about 6 July 1944 willfully disobey the same.

Appendix S

Summary of Telephone Conversation, 17 July 1944

$\mathcal{H}$EADQUARTERS XXIII CORPS
Office of the Chief of Staff

Summary of Telephone Conversation
From: Col Kimball, 5th Armored Group, Camp Hood, Texas
To: Col Buie, C of S, XXIII Corps
Time: 0930 17 July 1944

K: I have a case here involving a colored officer who got into trouble in connection with a bus. This officer was with the 761st and is in the process of being transferred to one of my battalions.

　　This is a very serious case, and it is full of dynamite. It requires very delicate handling, and it should, in my opinion, be handled by someone off Post. I wonder if you can send an Inspector down here?

B: We would like to send an inspector right away, but have none available. Of course if this is an emergency we can get you an Inspector somehow, even if we must go to higher Headquarters to do so. Can't this investigation be conducted by your Headquarters?

K: Yes it can, but the matter is so delicate that I think it would be better if an outside Inspector handled it. This bus station situation here is not at all good, and I am afraid that any officer in charge of troops at this Post might be prejudiced. However, we will go ahead and handle it if you say so.

B: I believe you had better go ahead and handle it. Keep me informed, and do not hesitate to call me at any time. Do not consider this decision final, we want to stay right with you on it. If the situation should change we will take other action.

K: Could you get an inspector down here in about a week? We could handle the preliminary investigation and have it all ready when he arrives.

B: Yes. I believe we can. In the meantime be sure to keep me advised.

Walter D. Buie
Colonel, G.S.C.
Chief of Staff

Letter to Assistant Secretary of War
Truman K. Gibson,
16 July 1944

Truman K. Gibson   16 July 44
Ass't to Sec of War
Washington, D.C.

Sir:

I am sorry to bother you again but under the circumstances there seems to be no alternative.

On or about the 7th of July I was at Camp Hood, Texas visiting the colored officers club and upon leaving I took a shuttle bus from the club to the central station. As I moved to the rear I noticed one of the officer's wife and sat down beside her. The lady is very fair and to many people looks to be white. It is evident the driver seemed to resent my talking to her and told me to move to the rear. He didn't ask the lady to move so I refused. When I did he threatened to make trouble for me when we reached the bus station. Upon reaching the station a white lady tells me that she is going to proffer charges against me. She said she heard the driver tell me to move to the rear. I told her I didn't care if the proffered charges against me and she went away angry. This is the last that was said to the lady and the next thing I hear is I've cursed one out and I certainly didn't start with her.

I need a little advice. I want to know just how far I should go with the case. What I mean is should I appeal to the NAACP and the Negro Press? I don't want any unfavorable publicity for myself or the Army but I believe in fair play and I feel I have to let someone in on the case. If I write the NAACP I hope to get statements from all the witnesses because a broad minded person can see how the people framed me.

You can see sir that I need your advice. I don't care what the outcome of this trial is because I know I am being framed and the charges aren't too bad. I would like to get your advice about the publicity. I have a lot of good publicity out and I feel I have numerous friends on the press but I first want to hear from you before I do anything I will be sorry for later on.

Sir as I said I don't mind trouble but I do believe in fair play and justice. I feel that I'm being taken in this case and I will tell people about it unless the trial is fair. Let me hear from you so I will know what steps to take.

> Lt. Jack Robinson
> Ward 11 B
> McCloskey Gen. Hosp.
> Temple, TX

(Note: On receipt, Gibson passed the letter up his chain of command after scribbling in the margin, "This man is the well-known athlete. He will write you. Follow this case closely." There is no evidence, however, that Gibson or anyone else in the Office of the Secretary of War responded before Robinson's court-martial.)

Appendix U

Second Sworn Statement of Capt. Gerald M. Bear, Assistant Provost Marshal, Camp Hood, Texas, 19 July, 1944

On the morning of 19 July 1944, Major Daugherty, Investigating Officer, Fifth Armored Group, Camp Hood, Texas, notified me that he was making a pre-trial investigation regarding 2nd Lt. Jack R. Robinson, 0-1031586, 761st Tank Battalion, who caused a disturbance on a bus at Camp Hood, Texas, on the night of 6 July 1944. Major Daugherty gave me the full name and address, Mrs. Virginia Jones, 702 South Pearl St, phone—569-W, Belton, Texas, who was believed to have been the person riding with Lt. Robinson on the bus at the time of the disturbance. Attempts had been made previously to obtain the name of the person in order that we could obtain a statement from her regarding the incident. Shortly after learning her name I proceeded to Belton, Texas, and contacted Mrs. Virginia Jones. I talked with her at approximately 1030, 19 July 1944, and asked her if she wished to make a statement regarding the incident which occurred on the bus the night of 6 July 1944. She informed me that she had received a call from Lt. Robinson, and that she expected him to come along on the bus to Belton to see her. She was expecting him to arrive when I talked with her. She told me that Lt. Robinson had told her that he wanted to talk to her before she went before the investigating officer. Mrs. Jones further stated that she wanted to talk to Lt. Robinson before making a statement to anyone. She refused at that time to make a statement before discussing it with Lt. Robinson.

Appendix V

Statement of Mrs. Virginia Jones, Wife of 1st Lt. Gordon H. Jones, Jr., Camp Hood, Texas, 19 July 1944

I am the wife of 1st Lt. Gordon H. Jones, Jr., 761st Tank Battalion, Camp Hood, Texas, and reside in Belton, Texas. I was with Lt. Jack R. Robinson on the night of 6 July 1944. We left the colored officers club and caught the bus in front of the officers club. I got on the bus first and sat down, and Lt. Robinson got on and came and sat beside me. I sat in the fourth seat from the rear of the bus, which I have always considered the rear of the bus. The bus driver looked back at us, and then asked Lt. Robinson to move. Lt. Robinson told the bus driver to go on and drive the bus. The bus driver stopped the bus, came back and balled his fist and said, "Will you move back?" Lt. Robinson said, "I'm not moving," so the bus driver stood there and glared a minute and said, "Well, just sit there until we get down to the bus station."

We got to the Bus station and Lt., Robinson and I were the last two to leave the bus. The bus driver detained Lt. Robinson and demanded to see his pass. Lt. Robinson said, "My pass?", and the bus driver said, "Yes, I want to see your pass." Lt. Robinson asked him what did he mean wanting to see his pass, and we then got off the bus. A woman walked up to Lt. Robinson and shook her finger in his face and said, "I'm going to report you because you had a right to move when he asked you too." She stood there and argued with Lt. Robinson awhile, and I don't remember what all was said. Lt. Robinson did not say anything at first and then he said, "Go on and leave me alone." So she walked into the bus station, and about that time the crowd around the bus driver and Lt. Robinson thinned out, and the bus driver said something to the Lt. which I did not hear.

Then Lt. Robinson and I walked over to the Temple Bus Stop and we stood there for a few minutes and the MP's arrived. The crowd gathered around the MP's and started to talk. Lt. Robinson said, "Pardon me, I'm going over here to see what's going on." He walked over to the MP's and just about that time this same woman walked up and started to accuse him of something, and when I saw her walk up I walked over there. I did not hear what she said, but I knew she was accusing him of something. I asked Lt. Robinson what did she say and he was busy talking to the MP's and did not answer me. That's all that I heard except I heard the MP say, "I'll have to take you down to the station." There were two or three soldiers around there, they told the MP's that if they needed any help just to let them know and they would be glad to help him. The only thing Lt. Robinson said to this lady was "Go away and leave me alone," and she walked away immediately. I did not hear him say anything vile nor vulgar at any time, nor he did not raise his voice.

Appendix W

Request for Retirement
from Active Service

Headquarters
659th Tank Destroyer Battalion
North Camp Hood, Texas

25 August 1944

Subject: Orders
To: Adjutant General
Washington, D.C.

1. Request information of Adjutant Generals Office upon recommendation of Army Retiring Board of McCloskey General Hospital, Temple, Texas concerning Lt. Jack R. Robinson, 2nd Lt, Cav, 659th Tank Destroyer Battalion, North Camp Hood, Texas.

2. I appeared before the board 21 July 1944 and was recommended for permanent limited duty and am now with the 659th Tank Destroyer Battalion, North Camp Hood, Texas pending orders from your office. In checking with the Special Service Branch I was told there were no openings for Colored Officers in that field. I request to be retired from the services and be placed on reserve as I feel I can be of more service to the government doing defense work rather than being on limited duty with an outfit that is already better than 100% over strength in officers.

3. Would appreciate immediate action in regards to action taken by War Department in regards to recommendation of Army Retiring Board and of my request.

(Signed)

Jack R. Robinson
2nd Lt. Cav.

Follow Up Request for Retirement from Active Service

Antitank Company, 372nd Infantry
Camp Breckinridge, Kentucky

September 1944

Subject: Release From Active Duty

To: Adjutant General, War Department, Washington, D.C.
(THRU CHANNELS)

1. Some time ago, I requested to be placed on the inactive list because of an injury that has placed me on Limited Service. Since that time, I have been transferred to an Infantry unit, and to do duty with this organization would only further aggravate my injury.

2. Since nothing has been done about my first request to be placed on inactive status, I am again requesting some consideration on the subject. Being an Infantry Officer requires a man that is physically fit and since I have been informed that I would be responsible for any future injury, I feel I would not give the government the services that are required of an officer. Therefore, I am requesting my request for inactive status be accepted.

(signed)
Jack R. Robinson
2nd Lt., Cavalry

Appendix Y

Court–Martial Transcript

Proceedings of a General Court Martial
which convened at Camp Hood, Texas
2 August 1944

Organization of the Court
The court met pursuant to foregoing orders at 1:45 o'clock p.m.

Present

Colonel Louis J. Compton	07419	224th FA Gp
Lt. Col. John E. Perman	016419	224th FA Gp
Major John H. Shippey	0910620	Hq XXIII Corps
		(Law Member)
Major Charles O. Mowder	0292834	669th TD Bn
Captain Tom W. Moore	0041527	547th FA Bn
Captain James H. Carr	0358577	614th TD Bn
Captain Thomas M. Campbell	0418737	614th TD Bn
Captain Robert L. Spencer	0391594	549th FA Bn
Captain William G. Kellogg	0339525	293rd FA Obsn Bn

Trial Judge Advocate

2nd Lieutenant Milton Gordon   01824743   665th TD Bn
(Now Hq 23d TD Gp)

Assistant Trial Judge Advocate

2nd Lieutenant Knowles M. Tucker   01825085   669th TD Bn

Defense Counsel

2nd Lieutenant William Cline   01824137   658th TD Bn
(Now Hq 23d TD Gp)

Absent

Captain Charles H. Angell   0350633   529th FA Bn
excused by the appointing authority
1st Lt. Joseph O. Hutcheson   01172922   635th FA Bn
Assistant Defense Counsel, excused by the appointing authority

The court proceeded to the trial of 2nd Lt. Jack R. Robinson, 01031586, Cavalry, Company "C" 758th Tank Battalion, who, on appearing before the court, was asked by the trial judge advocate whom he desired to introduce as counsel. The accused stated he desired to be defended by regularly appointed defense counsel, assisted by 1st Lt. Robert H. Johnson, 679th Tank Destroyer Battalion, as his individual counsel.

Herbert Reed was sworn as reporter.

PROSECUTION TO ACCUSED: Do you want a copy of the record?

ACCUSED: Yes, sir.

The trial judge advocate then announced the names of the accuser, the investigating officer, officers who forwarded the charges and any members of the court who would be called as witnesses for the prosecution as follows: None.

PROSECUTION: If any member of the court is aware of any fact which he believes to be ground of challenge by either side against any member, it is requested he state such facts.

PRESIDENT: There appear to be none.

PROSECUTION: The prosecution has no challenges.

PROSECUTION TO ACCUSED: You now have the right to challenge any member or members of the court for cause, and any one member, other than the law member, peremptorily.

DEFENSE: The accused has no challenges.

The accused was then asked if he objected to any other member present, to which he replied in the negative.

The members of the court and the personnel of the prosecution were then sworn.

ARRAIGNMENT

The accused was then arraigned upon the following charges and specifications:

Charge I: Violation of the 63rd Article of War
Specification: In that Second Lieutenant Jack R. Robinson Cavalry, Company C, 758th Tank Battalion, did, at Camp Hood, Texas, on or about 6 July 1944, behave himself with disrespect toward Captain Gerald M. Bear, Corps Military Police, 1848th Unit, Eighth Service Command, Army Services Forces, his superior officer, by contemptuously bowing to him and giving him several sloppy salutes repeating several times "OK Sir," "OK Sir" or words to that effect, and by acting in an insolent, impertinent, and rude manner toward the said Captain Gerald M. Bear.

Charge II: Violation of the 64th Article of War
Specification: In that Second Lieutenant Jack R. Robinson, Cavalry, Company C, 758th Tank Battalion, having received a lawful order from Captain Gerald M. Bear, Corps Military Police, 1848th Unit, Eighth Service Command, Army Service Forces, his superior officer, to remain in a receiving room and be seated in a chair on the far side of the receiving room, did, at Camp Hood, Texas, on or about 6 July 1944 willfully disobey the same.

/s/ Lawrence F. Becnel
Maj. Inf (and) 758th (L) Tk Bn

AFFIDAVIT

Before me, the undersigned, authorized by law to administer the oaths in the cases of this character, personally appeared the above named accuser, this 19th day of July, 1944, and made oath that he is a person subject to military law and that he personally signed the foregoing charges and specifications, and further that he has investigated the matters set forth in specifications Chg I Spc 1,2; Chg II, Spc 1; Chg III, Spc 1,2; and that the same are true in fact, to the best of his knowledge and belief.

/s/ Henry S. Daugherty
Major 5th Armored Gp
Summary Court

1st IND.

Headquarters XXIII Corps, APO 130, Brownwood, Texas, 25 July, 1944.

Referred to trial to 2nd Lt. Milton Gordon, 665th TD Bn.

Trial Judge Advocate of general court martial appointed by paragraph 6, Special Orders No. 120, Headquarters, XXIII Corps, APO 130, Brownwood, Texas, 10 June 1944.

By command of Major General Craig.

/s/ L. K. Olson
1st Lt. AGD, ASST AG

The accused then pleaded as follows:

Special pleas and motions: None.

To the Specification of Charge I: Not Guilty

To Charge I: Not Guilty

To the Specification of Charge II: Not Guilty

To Charge II: Not Guilty

By direction of the court the following matters were read to the court by the trial judge advocate, to 'wit: None

The prosecution then made no opening statement to the court.

TESTIMONY FOR THE PROSECUTION

2nd Lt. Howard B. Campbell, a witness for the prosecution, was sworn and testified as follows:

DIRECT EXAMINATION

Questions by the Prosecution:

Q–State your full name, organization, and station.

A–Howard B. Campbell, Second Lieutenant, 758th Tank Battalion, Camp Hood, Texas.

Q–Do you know the accused? If so, state his name.

A–I do; Jack R. Robinson

Q–Is he in the military service of the United States?

A–He is.

Q–What is his grade and organization?

A–Second Lieutenant, Company C, 758th Tank Battalion

Q–Is the accused present in the court room? If so, point him out.

A–Yes, sir (pointing out the accused).

(There being no further questioning, the witness is excused.)

CAPTAIN GERALD M. BEAR, a witness for the prosecution, was sworn and testified as follows:

DIRECT EXAMINATION

Questions by the prosecution:

Q—State your name, rank, organization, and station.

A—Gerald M. Bear, Captain, Corps Military Police, 1848th Unit, Camp Hood, Texas.

Q—Do you know the accused? If so, state his name.

A—I do; Lt. Jack R. Robinson.

Q—Is the accused present in the court? If so, point him out.

A—That is the Lieutenant (pointing to the accused).

Q—Captain, what are your duties?

A—My duties, Assistant Provost Marshal, Camp Hood, Texas.

Q—What do your duties consist of?

A—Investigating officer, and I am also commanding officer of the Military Police Detachment.

Q—How long have you been in this position?

A—Since June 1st.

Q—Of this year?

A—That's right, sir.

Q—I believe you mentioned that you were a member of the 1848th Unit; is that correct?

A—Yes, sir.

Q—Is that the Eighth Service Command forces?

A—Yes, sir.

Q—Were you on duty July 6, 1944?

A—Yes, I was on duty that day.

Q—Where?

A—At Camp Hood, Texas.

Q—Did you have occasion to see the accused on July 6, 1944.

A—I did.

Q—Where?

A—I first saw him in the guard room of the Military Police; the M.P. guard room.

Q—When you first saw him was he alone?

A—No, sir.

Q—Who was present at the time?

A—In the guard room was Captain Wigginton, the Camp Officer of the Day; the Sergeant of the Guard, Sgt. Painter; Corporal Elwood; Corporal Feris, Private Plotkin, and Private Mucklerath.

Q–When you came into the guard room, did you address the accused?

A–Not right away.

Q–Will you tell the court what transpired?

A–Yes, I will; as I came in the guard room, Captain Wigginton, the Officer of the Day, was listening to Private Mucklerath relate some incident and Lt. Robinson was interrupting Captain Wigginton. Captain Wigginton said to me, "I am glad you have come, as the Assistant Provost Marshall, I want you to take charge of this investigation and hear this story."

Q–Did Captain Wigginton address that remark to the accused?

A–I believe he did; he said it for the benefit of all that were present.

PRESIDENT: Give your answers to the court; you are talking to us.

A–Yes, sir, I will.

Q–Continue?

A–So I said to Lt. Robinson, "You go outside of the guard room, and wait out in the receiving room, I will call you when I want you"; Captain Wigginton then started to relate to me what he had heard up to the present time of that incident, and while he was doing this, Lt. Robinson continued to come to this half gate door of the guard room, and resting his hands on it in this way—

Q–May I have that indicated for the record?

A–He leaned on the half gate, down in a slouching position with his elbows resting on the gate, and he kept interrupting so I could not get the conversation from Captain Wigginton; and I said to Lt. Robinson, "You wait outside the guard room, away from the door and I will call you when I am ready for you"; this happened on several occasions when I told him to go away, from the door, and as I told him to go away, he bowed in this manner and said, "O.K., Sir, O.K. Sir, O.K. Sir".

Q–May I have that described as you have demonstrated it?

A–He stood in this manner and bowed this way–

Q–Bent his trunk forward to a horizontal position, forming a 75 degree angle at the same time bringing his right hand just above his right eye, hand palm facing toward you, with fingers outstretched and closed together, and then slowly bringing himself to his original position; is that right?

A–That's right and then he kind of smirked or grimaced his face, or grinning like while he was doing that.

Q–How many times did he give you that so-called salute?

A–Each time I told him, "Lieutenant, go away from that door, I will call you later"; I did not do that only two or three times, but it was several times, and each time I told him to go away, he bowed in that same manner with that same form of salute and would say "O.K., Sir. O.K., Sir, O.K., Sir", in the same facetious like manner.

Q–Continue?

A–Finally, after that went on for sometime, I told Sgt. Painter to place a chair on the far side of the room, and then I said, "Lieutenant, you go over and sit down in that chair on the far side of the room and you remain sitting there until I call you, do you understand that"; and he said "O.K., Sir, O.K., Sir, O.K., Sir."

Q–Was that an order direct to him?

A–Yes, sir, it was a direct order; I ordered him to go over and sit there until I called him.

Q–What transpired after you gave him that order?

A–I made a telephone call to the O.D. of the 761st Tank Battalion–

Q–Well, any conversation you may have had not in the presence of the accused do not relate that.

A–The next thing that transpired, I had gone out of the building over to the orderly room to make arrangements to take those statements, to get the legal stenographer there, and I came back by way of the Guard Room; the orderly room is in the M.P. Detachment, the next building over. When I came back I found Lt. Robinson outside the building talking to the driver of a jeep; this jeep belonged to the O.D. of the 761st Tank Battalion. I said to Lt. Robinson, "Lieutenant, go back in that room and remain in that room, remain sitting, do you understand that"; and he reluctantly went back inside.

Q–Just show us how he did?

A–He walked kind of this way.

Q–With his hands in his pockets, swaying. Lt. Cline, do you have any objection to my description of the way the witness is demonstrating?

DEFENSE: Go ahead.

A–He walked like this.

Q–Will you describe how you are walking?

A–Shifting his weight from one foot to the other, and went on inside in that manner. When we got ready for him to make his statement, we brought him into the orderly room, and from the time we started out, I asked him to relate his statement, and everything he said seemed to be facetious to him, and he seemed to be trying to make fun of it.

Q–What was the tone of his voice?

A–He would raise and lower his words, and he would say, "Oh yeah" when I would ask him a question, and several times I asked him not to go so fast and tone his language down, he said, "Well, you want me to tell the truth and nothing but the truth, that's enough isn't it"; and he continued to raise and lower his voice, and continued to act in a contemptuous and disrespectful manner; in fact I had lost control of this lieutenant.

DEFENSE: We think a little less about what this witness thought or thinks would enlighten the court more; this witness is stating a great many conclusions to the court, and I would ask that the TJA ask for the statements, and not what this witness thought about it.

LAW MEMBER: The conclusions are to be drawn by the court; it is difficult, however, for certain descriptions to be made without some conclusions. In so far as you can, we want statements of facts to aid the court in arriving at the conclusions as to what is or is not contemptuous or disrespectful.

Q—You have mentioned the fact, in what way was he disrespectful, either by speech or mannerisms; would you describe that to the court?

A—Well, the way he would answer me when I was taking his statement; he was at the desk and I had the legal stenographer there and he would lay his arms over on the desk and say, "Well, all right" or "Well, yeah"; and he did not seem helpful, yet it was his own statement that I was asking him for.

Q—In what way did you lose control of him, Captain; describe that to the court?

A—He seemed to be argumentative, he would ask me questions and say, well, he would say "Well, do I have to answer that" and I would say, "No, this is your statement, and all I want is the material facts and circumstances surrounding this incident, and it is your voluntary statement".

Q—How did he talk, did you have occasion to stop him?

A—Yes, I did, he talked very rapidly; he would talk so fast sometimes that this legal stenographer could not take it down; and I said, "Lieutenant, take it slower"; I told him that several times and he continued to go fast. I said to him, now, Lieutenant, she cannot take this statement that fast, she is not an expert, will you slow down in your speech so she can get it down" and then he started baby talk.

Q—How did he talk?

A—I will tell you how he talked, he said, for example, "I-tell-you-I-went-over"; he was relating an incident. I said, "Lieutenant, there will be no more of this; I want you to slow your speech, but to talk in an ordinary manner and tone."

LAW MEMBER: Let the record show the response of this witness in which he stated the words, "I tell you I went over" was related in an exaggerated slow pause between the words.

Q—Continue your story from there?

A—After we had taken his statement, I arranged for transportation for Lt. Robinson to Temple, and explained that to him, that I had arranged transportation to take him on back, and he wanted to argue with me, saying that he did not want to go back, that he did not have to go back, and said he had a pass until eight o'clock in the morning. I had other things to do, and I told him that we had this arrangement made and I wanted him to go; and he still continued to argue, saying he had a pass until the next morning and that he had some other things he wanted to do, and continued to argue in this manner, and questioning my authority to send him on in the transportation I had arranged. He said, "I don't see why I have to go with the MPs." I tried to explain to him and he continued to argue and didn't want to go, and then Captain Wigginton interrupted and said, "Lieutenant, I have heard enough of this argument and your conversation, and your manner, and if you do not go, I am going to lock you up for insubordination and disrespect to your superior officers."

Q—Captain, while you were in the orderly room, did you have occasion to see Lieutenant—the medical officer—I don't remember his name?

A—Yes, Lt. Cribari.

Q—When did he come in the orderly room?

A—When we started to take Lt. Robinson's statement.

Q—Who came in with Lt. Cribari?

A—Captain Hamilton.

Q—During the time you had this conversation with the accused, were there any civilians present?

A—Yes, Miss Wilson, the legal stenographer.

Q—Any other than her?

A—No.

Q—And you have given the court the names of the military personnel present?

A—That is correct.

CROSS-EXAMINATION

Questions by the defense:

Q—Captain, what do you mean when you say you lost control of Lt. Robinson?

A—During the questioning of him and asking him to give the statement, he gave me such a superior attitude that was entirely unnecessary, and everything I asked him, he would grimace his face and sort of laugh and say, "Well, O.K., that's O.K. Sir" and he did not put any serious thought on the matter; it seem to him a trivial matter.

Q—In your opinion that was the way he acted?

A—Yes.

Q—You stated that he asked you questions; what was the nature of those questions?

PROSECUTION: I object to that unless it is in relation to the specifications; we are trying the accused for purely military offenses.

LAW MEMBER: This witness stated on direct examination that the Lieutenant asked him questions during the time he has referred to; the objection is overruled.

Q—You may answer the question, Captain; do you want it read?

A—No, I believe I know the question. That was as we went along getting the statement, he would say, "Well, do I have to relate that" or "Is that necessary"; that is what I meant when I said he would ask me questions.

Q—Did you consider that improper for an accused to make such inquiry as that?

A—Yes, I did.

Q—Your answer is that you did consider that improper for the accused to ask such questions?

A—Yes, in the way he did it.

Q—In what way?

A—Well, we were trying to take his statement, and trying to take it in a manner of sequence, and when he would say, "Well, do I have to relate that" or "Is that necessary"; and if it followed in sequence I thought it was necessary.

Q—And you thought it was improper for him to ask you if it was necessary?

A—I would not say that, but the way he asked it.

Q—When he asked you if it was necessary, you thought that was out of order?

A—At certain times, I did.

Q—Did he ask at any time, "Do I have to answer that question?"

A—I don't know if those were his exact words; he would say, "Do I have to relate that" when what he meant was "Do I have to go with the facts", that is the facts of the story.

Q—And that interrupted the sequence?

A—Yes, sir.

Q—But you did want the whole story?

A—Yes, I did.

Q—How long had you been investigating officer?

A—Since June 1st of this year.

Q—Have you done a good deal since that time?

A—Yes, sir.

Q—Had you done any since that time—or before that time?

A—Yes, sir.

Q—In what capacity had you acted before June 1st.

A—I had done the same work for ten months in the Alexandria area.

Q—Had you on occasion before to run into witnesses that talked too fast for the stenographer?

A–Yes, I have.

Q–How many times did you ask the Lieutenant to slow down?

A–At least on two occasions.

Q–Do you know what baby talk is, Captain?

A–Yes, I do.

Q–And you considered that example you gave the court baby talk?

A–Yes, when he talked the slow drawl and mentioned each word slowly and use one syllable words, I do.

Q–Captain, was it the next morning when you were arranging to send this officer back to McCloskey Hospital?

A–No, it was right at the same time.

Q–In the evening?

A–As soon as he came in, I arranged within an hour or two for transportation.

Q–Did you have occasion to see this officer the next morning?

LT. COL. PERMAN (of the court): I object; the offense charged in this case was on July 6th and now you are speaking of July 7th.

DEFENSE: I am trying to clarify the testimony about the accused being unruly and unwilling to obey the order to go back to the hospital.

LAW MEMBER: The question directed to that is proper.

A–Right at that time it was in the early morning hours of July 7th.

Q–It was after midnight before this was over?

A–Yes, sir.

Q–Before this matter closed, that evening, did you have occasion to talk to this man's commanding officer?

A–Yes, sir, I did.

Q–Did the accused return to McCloskey Hospital that morning?

A–Yes, sir, he did.

Q–Did he go under guard?

LT. COL. PERMAN: I object to that, it was not brought out in direct examination.

DEFENSE: May I make one statement; the record of the testimony will show that the accused was arguing and wrangling about whether he had to go back to the hospital that night; now; I can restate the question-

LT. COL. PERMAN: There was nothing mentioned on direct about the accused going to the hospital; he was to go to some place, but nothing was said about a hospital.

Q–Let me ask you in another way, Captain, what was the nature— stating if you can the exact objection this accused had—what was the nature of his objection in regard to his leaving the investigation you were conducting?

A—Well, he stated that he had a pass until eight o'clock in the morning and that he had some other things to do and he did not want to go back then.

Q—Do you recall what questions if any he asked you at that time, when he objected specifically to going?

A—Well, sir, he asked if I denied him the privilege of talking to his Commanding Officer, and I said "no"; and he said that in such a manner, he said, "Then you are not going to let me talk to him"; that was his attitude about everything I said, in that attitude that I was not trying to help him out, whereas, I was trying to help him out.

Q—Do you recall, Captain, if he asked you whether he was under arrest at that time?

A—Yes, I do recall.

Q—Did you give him an answer, Captain?

A—Yes, I gave him an answer, with an explanation at the same time.

Q—What was your answer?

A—I told him that he could consider that he was going, that we had arranged for transportation and he was going.

Q—Excuse me, sir; would you just answer my question; what was your answer to him, to his question?

A—I mentioned that I gave him an answer and explanation.

Q—I did not want the answer too long, but what did you say?

A—I said, "We have arranged the transportation, and you are to go back over there, and we will consider that you will be in arrest in quarters and taken over there."

Q—How many times did he ask if he was under arrest before you gave him that answer?

A—I believe he asked me a couple of times; two times, I believe.

PROSECUTION: I object to this line of cross-examination on the ground that it is immaterial to the issue here.

DEFENSE: If the court please, before I continue further, if the Trial Judge Advocate does not object, I will go back and ask some questions concerning the events in the guard room.

Q—Going back, Captain, I believe you testified that you requested the accused to go back to the anteroom or receiving room of the guard room?

A—Do you mean while on the outside of the building?

Q—Maybe we should go over that scene again; where was he when you first came in to the guard room?

A—He was on the inside of the guard room.

Q—And you requested him to go to the outside, or to the outer room?

A—Yes, and to remain there until I called him.

Q–I would like to show you a statement purported to have been made by you and ask if you recall making that statement?

A–Yes, that is my statement.

Q–In this particular statement, certified as a true copy, which I have in my hand, you stated, I believe—

LT. COL. PERMAN: I object; I would like to determine the purpose of the introduction of the statement? It was not brought out on direct, and I would like to inquire of the purpose, since the witness has not proven hostile to questions by the Defense or the Trial Judge Advocate.

DEFENSE: Sir, I would like to show the court the language the witness used in his direct testimony is not the same as appears in the statement.

LAW MEMBER: Your purpose is to establish a contrary statement to the testimony given on direct examination?

DEFENSE: Yes, sir.

LAW MEMBER: Then you should ask the witness if he made such a statement.

Q–Let me ask you, Captain, did you or not state in writing, "I cautioned and requested Lt. Robinson on several occasions to remain at ease and remain in the receiving room and I would talk to him later"; and did you or did you not make that statement?

A–I made that statement.

Q–While the stenographer was taking Lt. Robinson's statement, Captain, did anything occur that brought her to anger or caused her to leave the room, that you recall?

A–No, I do not recall her leaving the room; she took the statement in its entirety.

Q–After the statement was completed, she typed the statement, did she not?

A–Yes.

Q–Do you recall the stenographer leaving the room in more or less a huff, because the accused pointed out several inconsistencies in the statement?

A–No, I do not recall that.

Q–Do you recall her leaving before the business at hand was completed?

A–No, she typed the statement in the outer room.

Q–Do you recall whether the accused signed that statement that she had typed?

A–Yes, I do.

Q–Without correction?

A–No, he made some corrections; I believe he drew a line and initialed the correction.

Q–Do you recall having words with the accused, or reprimanding him, for not signing that statement as it came back from her typewriter?

A–No, sir, I do not, except that he wanted it corrected and I told her what he wanted corrected and told her to cross it out, or told him to cross it out and initial it.

Q–Was there anything at that time occurred, after the statement had been typed, that made you angry and caused you to reprimand the accused?

LT. COL. PERMAN: I object, since all this transpired after the incident covered by the specifications and was not brought out on direct examination, it is not proper cross-examination; the defense can introduce the witness at a later time.

LAW MEMBER: What time do you have reference to in your questions?

DEFENSE: At the end of the incident, sir, before it was closed up; the statement was taken and I am attempting to bring out whether or not there was an atmosphere there, the background of this whole case should be before the court, and I do not understand that I am limited to what was brought out on direct examination.

LAW MEMBER: You are not entirely, but the time your question was directed to with reference to this interpretation you make would control; you may inquire what action this witness took by way of admonition to the accused in connection with the accused's conduct towards him; is that what you have in mind?

DEFENSE: Yes, sir.

LAW MEMBER: The witness may answer.

DEFENSE: Is it proper on cross-examination to interrogate the witness as to his bias and prejudice? This is the purpose of my examination at this time.

PROSECTION: No bias or prejudice has been shown.

LAW MEMBER: Let the witness answer the question.

A–I do not recall reprimanding him about his statement, or talking to him about it at all after it had been typed.

RE DIRECT EXAMINATION

Questions by the prosecution:

Q–You were asked a question by Lt. Johnson on cross-examination if you had made a statement to the effect that you stated to the accused to remain at ease and remain in the receiving room and you would talk to him later; you answered him that you did make that statement; is that correct?

A–Yes, in the statement I signed.

Q–Will you explain what you meant and what was done subsequent there to? What was that in connection with?

A–They asked me to give a kind of brief and concise statement, without too much detail, and without relating specific conversation; so, in accordance with that request, I drew up as short and compact statement as I could on the matter.

Q–Will you tell the court what was your direct order to the accused in connection to his remaining outside in the receiving room; your exact words?

A–I said, "Go out and remain at ease"; about three times I told him that.

Q–Repeat the order again, please?

A–I said, "You go out and remain at ease and when we get ready, we will call you"; and then I said, "You take a seat in the far side of the room and remain seated until I call for you"; that was after he would not pay attention to what I had told him.

Q–Did you ask him if he understood your order?

A–Yes, each time, and he would say "O.K., Sir".

RE CROSS-EXAMINATION
Questions by the defense:

Q–Captain, the purpose of that direction was to get the accused beyond your hearing, was it not?

A–The purpose was to stop him from interrupting until Captain Wigginton could relate the matters to me, as he had heard them up to that moment.

Q–As a matter of fact, you wanted him beyond your hearing?

A–Well, yes, we wanted him away for he was interrupting when I first came in.

Q–How long after that was it before he was called in; how much time elapsed?

A–Until such time as he was called to the orderly room?

Q–That is correct, sir?

A–Well it was not very long; Captain Wigginton told me the statements very briefly that he had taken, and we got the O.D. of the 761st—

Q–What did you mean by "not very long"?

A–Well, I don't recall exactly how much time had elapsed, and I mean it was not very long.

Q–Was it an hour?

A–No, it was not an hour.

Q–Half-hour?

A–No, I would judge it was a matter of fifteen or twenty minutes; not very long.

EXAMINATION BY THE COURT
Questions by Captain Moore:

Q–With reference to that transportation, how compulsory was it that he use the transportation you stated you had provided?

A–Well, we had arranged this transportation, and at that hour of the morning the busses were not running on regular schedule.

Q–Was it necessary for him to take the transportation you had provided?

A–I don't believe any other was available and we wanted him to go then.

Q–Was he under arrest?

A–Yes, sir.

Q–When was he under arrest and what did you say to him?

A–I finally told him, "You can consider yourself under arrest", or "in arrest".

Q–When did you make that statement to him?

A–At the time we decided to place him in arrest.

Q–You wanted to make sure to send him where you wanted him to go, so you arrested him?

A–Yes, we call it arrest in quarters.

Questions by Major Mowder:

Q–Did you say you used your transportation because no busses were available?

A–There were no busses running at that hour and I had called some other places and they told me it would be an hour and a half before they could get a driver, and so the arrangement was made that we would take him over.

Q–If buses had been available, would you have let him go back by himself?

A–No, sir, Major, I would not.

Q–I wish you would state definitely whether you did order him back, or did you just think this was the best type of transportation he should have?

A–No, sir; I ordered him to go back.

DEFENSE: I would like to ask this through the court: What was the transportation and who, if anyone, went with the accused?

PROSECUTION: I think that is immaterial.

LAW MEMBER: Do you want the court to adopt your question?

DEFENSE: I am not familiar with whether or not it should be asked through the court; I would prefer to ask him direct.

Questions by Captain Carr:

Q–Did you say the accused was in the inner room of the guard house and you told him to remain at ease?

A–He was at the gate, or half door.

Q–While he was at the gate, was that when you told him to be at ease?

A–Yes, sir.

Q–When he was in the position like this, would you consider that at ease?

A–He was doing that and interrupting me, and I told him to be at ease.

Q–I want the question answered; was he at ease while he was leaning on the gate in this manner, or whatever manner you have described; was he at ease then?

A–If he was not talking and interrupting, he would be; well not at ease either.

Q–My point is: I do not see that this manner in which he leaned on the gate had anything to do with you, if you had not given him an order commanding him at attention, even if it was a sloppy position, if you had not told him to remain at attention?

A–I told him "at ease and to remain quiet".

Q–I am talking now of the sloppy manner; that part of the charges?

A–I did not call him to attention, Captain.

Q–But you have given the court an example of the sloppy manner in which he leaned on the gate?

A–Yes, and he interrupted while leaning on the gate and when he was ordered to get away, he grimaced and saluted in the manner I have described.

RE CROSS-EXAMINATION

Questions by the defense:

Q–Captain will you state for the record what form of transportation you sent the Lieutenant back in, and who, if anyone, you sent with him?

PROSECUTION: I object to that as irrelevant to this case.

DEFENSE: It is material as to whether this man was under arrest; and I want to say to the court, there is more in this case than meets the eye in reading the specifications.

PROSECUTION: I object to the speech by the defense counsel.

LAW MEMBER: Your question with reference to the mode of transportation can be answered by the witness.

A–It was a pick-up truck.

Q–Excuse me, but will you please speak louder?

DEFENSE: By your ruling, do you mean that I cannot ask who went with the accused?

LAW MEMBER: You may ask who went with this officer back to Mc-Closkey Hospital.

PROSECUTION: I object to that because it has nothing to do with this case.

LAW MEMBER: The objection is overruled.

A–The M.P.'s went with him.

Q–How many, Captain?

A–I can not recall, but I think it was two or three.

Q–Two or three?

A–I would say so.

Q–In a regular M.P. truck?

A–Yes.

RE EXAMINATION BY THE COURT

Questions by Lt. Col. Perman:

Q–Was the sole purpose of using the transportation you have mentioned in the furtherance of some duty on the part of the Provost Marshall's office to see that Lt. Robinson was returned to his destination?

A–Yes, sir, it was.

Questions by Captain Campbell:

Q–I have a question that I would like to ask the Captain; a few minutes ago you stated that when Lt. Robinson was on the outside, and you told him to go back inside of the guard house, and that was when he went back in, as you demonstrated in a sort of rolling walk?

A–Yes, sir.

Q–I was wondering if the court has ever seen Lt. Robinson walking, and if not, if it would be possible to have him walk normally up and down the court room and let the court observe his walk?

LAW MEMBER: The defense can present that, however, if it is desired by the court and is the desire of the accused, he may do so; that is subject to the same limitations as his testimony; it must be at his request. In any event, we should proceed with the examination of this witness.

RE CROSS-EXAMINATION

Questions by the defense:

Q–Captain, you sent the M.P.'s with this man, with the direct instructions to them that he was under arrest, did you not?

A–Not specifically under arrest; we call it "in arrest in quarters"; but I told him to go to his destination.

Q–And you sent those M.P.'s to take him there?

A–Yes, sir.

RE EXAMINATION BY THE COURT

Questions by Captain Carr:

Q–Do you know the difference between confinement and in arrest in quarters?

A–Yes, I do.

Q–In arrest in quarters can carry no bodily restrictions?

A–I considered him in arrest in quarters.

Q–In arrest in quarters, yet you admit that you sent three M.P.'s to see that he got back to where you decided to send him?

A–Yes, I did.

DEFENSE: Captain, is it true the Hospital called you the next day and asked if Lt. Robinson was supposed to be in arrest in quarters, and you answered "no"?

PROSECUTION: I object to that as immaterial.

LAW MEMBER: The objection is sustained; that would be something transpiring after the offense is alleged.

(There being no further questions, the witness was excused.)

CAPTAIN PEELOR L. WIGGINTON, a witness for the prosecution, was sworn and testified as follows:

DIRECT EXAMINATION

Questions by the prosecution:

Q–State your name, rank, organization and station.

A–Peelor L. Wigginton, Captain, Quartermaster Corps, Laundry Officer for the Camp, Camp Hood, Texas.

Q–Do you know the accused? If so, state his name.

A–I know him by sight and know his name.

Q–What is his name?

A–Lt. Robinson

Q–Is he present in the court room?

A–Yes, sir (Pointing to the accused).

Q–What were your duties on July 6, 1944?

A–I was the Camp Officer of the Day.

Q–Did you have occasion to see the accused on July 6th?

A–Yes, sir.

Q–Where and under what circumstances?

A–At the Military Police guard room, South Camp Hood.

Q–Who was present?

A–Lt. Robinson, Captain Bear, Private Mucklerath, and three or four members of the Military Police.

Q–Were you present when Captain Bear was questioning the accused?

A–Yes, sir.

Q–Can you tell the court what transpired in your own words?

A–When I was called in, or when Captain Bear came in?

Q–When Captain Bear came into the guard room, start from there?

A–As Camp Office of the day, I called on Captain Bear to come to the M.P. Guard room, and when he came into the room, I was making an attempt to relate something of the incident that had occurred that evening and Lt. Robinson continued to interrupt us and I asked him to remain in an outside room until I had discussed this incident. During the conversation, Lt. Robinson kept coming up to the swinging door or half door that divided the two rooms; he would come up to that door and interrupt us. So, I had turned the situation over to Captain Bear and he told the Lieutenant to remain in the outer room until we finished the discussion and we would call him when we were ready for him. Lt. Robinson kept coming to this gate and leaning over on it and saying something and interrupting me so that I could not continue, and Captain Bear gave him a direct order to go and sit down in the outer room, and the Lieutenant seemed to think it was quite funny and he bowed and said "O.K., Sir, O.K., Sir," repeated it several times and went back and I suppose sat down, but I did not see him sit down. Later Captain Bear made arrangements to take some statements, and at that time the Lieutenant was outside, pitching rocks and talking to the driver of his Battalion's jeep. Later we moved into another room to take the statements and during this questioning, Lt. Robinson, in my opinion, was very disrespectful and seemed to think it was a joke, and many questions asked him, he answered in a disrespectful manner, for example, he was talking very rapidly and the legal stenographer was not able to take down the testimony and Captain Bear asked him to slow down and not talk so fast, so the stenographer could take it down, and them mockingly started out slowly, with a pause between his words of several minutes—no seconds, not minutes, but seconds elapsed between each word. Then after his statement was taken, he spent some twenty or thirty minutes arguing with Captain Bear about going back, and the Lieutenant didn't want to do this or that and I was the first to tell him that I would place him under arrest for insubordination, in fact I told him this, "Lieutenant, if this continues, I am going to place you in arrest in the Stockade." Captain Bear had asked him to return to McCloskey Hospital, which he did not want to do. I did not think he acted at all like an officer should to—

DEFENSE: I object to the conclusion of the witness.

LAW OFFICER: Let's skip the opinion, rather give your observations of the act and conduct of the accused and it will be for the court to determine.

A–Well, during the time he was being questioned by Captain Bear, instead of sitting in an upright manner, he would lean over on the desk in this manner and in a rapid speech—

LAW OFFICER: You are now leaning on the desk next to your chair, with your elbows on the desk, with your right hand at the top of your head, is that right?

A–Yes, sir. And in coming back from outside the guard room, after Captain Bear ordered him back to the guard room he walked like this—

LAW OFFICER: You are now on your feet, with your hand in your pocket?

A–Yes, sir.

Q–You take a few steps in front of the court; can you describe what you are doing?

A–The impression I am trying to convey is the idea or my impression of the way he returned after he was told to return to the guard room, which was in this manner—

LAW MEMBER: You are now taking steps and swaying from side to side, with your hands in your pockets?

A—Yes, sir; that is correct, that is the manner in which he went swaying back to the guard room.

Q—Captain, can you tell the court the order that was given to the accused by Captain Bear, and what, if anything, happened after the issuance of that order?

A—Yes, sir, Captain Bear said, "Lieutenant, you go to the outer room and remain in that chair until you are called; do you understand that"; then later the Lieutenant was outside the building; I saw him out there tilting rocks in the air on the outside of the guard room, near this jeep, which I think belonged to the O.D. of some battalion.

CROSS-EXAMINATION

Questions by the defense:

Q—Captain, can you tell us why it was that everybody's story in connection with that case was taken in that investigation before the accused's story was taken?

LT. COL. PERMAN: I object; I don't think this witness could tell what the investigator had in mind.

LAW MEMBER: It is not a matter shown to be within the personal knowledge of the witness; the objection is sustained.

DEFENSE: I thought he started the investigation and took the other statements and in turn related to Captain Bear what the other testimony was.

LAW MEMBER: To the extent this witness might know the order in which he might have interviewed persons, he may state.

Q—In connection with your investigation of this case, or if you know of Captain Bear's investigation in your presence, do you know why the testimony was taken of all other witnesses before the accused was requested to give his statement?

A—No, sir.

Q—Do you suppose that might have had something to do with his comments and—

PROSECTION: I object to that as improper cross-examination.

LAW MEMBER: The objection is sustained.

Q—Captain, is it true that you told Major Daugherty that you did not see the accused make any of these motions?

A—No, sir.

Q—That is not true?

A—No, sir; you mean that I saw him make no motions?

Q—That you saw him make no salutes or bows?

A–I did not see him make any salutes at that time, I do not call that saluting; I was trying to demonstrate what he did.

Q–And you did see him leaning on the desk?

A–Yes.

Q–And walk with his hands in his pockets?

A–Yes.

Q–And you also saw him stoop, as you told the court; was that in the guard house?

A–The guard room where the M.P.'s forces are located.

Q–That was the time he was told to leave the room?

A–That is true.

Q–And you saw him outside throwing stones after that?

A–That was after he told him to remain in the outer room that I saw him out in the yard.

Q–Captain, is it true that the purpose in asking the accused to leave the room was so that Captain Bear could find out what happened in the case you were investigating?

LT. COL. PERMAN: I object, this witness is not competent to know what Captain Bear wanted.

DEFENSE: In all my questions I assume the witness will only answer if he knows.

LAW MEMBER: If the witness has knowledge, he may answer.

Q–If you don't know the answer, Captain, say so; but do you know if that was the purpose?

A–I didn't know Captain Bear's purpose, but I had been conducting the investigation, and I was turning it over to him and the Lieutenant kept interrupting and would not let me tell Captain Bear what had been related to me up to the time he was taking over.

Q–Do you recall how many times the accused was asked to slow down his testimony when he was giving his statement, so the legal stenographer could take it? Was it more than once?

A–Not to my knowledge; I recall just the one time.

Q–Did you, at any time, place the accused under arrest?

A–No, sir.

Q–In your presence or hearing, did Captain Bear ever place him under arrest?

A–No, sir.

Q–At any time during the investigation, was the accused told to sit at attention or to stand at attention?

A–No, the only time he was told to sit in a chair the word "attention" was not used.

Q–Captain, were you present when the stenographer left the room?

A–I believe she left the room two or three times.

Q–I refer, of course, to the last time she left the room, were you present when she left after completing the typing of Lt. Robinson's statement?

A–Do you mean when everyone left; I was about the first to leave, as I had other duties; but she left the room two or three times during the evening.

Q–Did she leave the room, Captain, to make her final exit before you did?

A–No, I left before she left to go home; if that is what you mean.

Q–Were you there when she typed Lt. Robinson's statement?

A–Yes.

Q–Do you recall Captain Bear becoming angry, and the stenographer becoming angry because Lt. Robinson asked the statement be corrected?

PROSECUTION: I object to that question; the witness can tell what he heard.

LAW MEMBER: The witness is on cross-examination, however, the objection is good to the question asking for a conclusion. You may restate the question.

Q–Did you see the stenographer become angry during the evening while taking down the statement?

A–Well, I don't know the word "angry"–no, I did not see the stenographer became what I would term angry, I thought she became impatient, but anger has a different meaning; I would say that she did become impatient.

Q–Let me clear it up; were you present when she brought the statement back after having typed it?

A–Yes.

Q–In your opinion did she become angry when the accused asked for certain corrections to be made? Did she get very excited and refuse to make the corrections?

A–No, sir.

Q–Is it true that she picked up her purse and walked out and left the statement without making the corrections? If you remember?

A–I do not remember that; there was some discussion, but I do not think it was about corrections in the statement; but she became impatient with Lt. Robinson over something that he stated or asked.

Q–Do you remember that Captain Bear became angry?

A–No.

Q–Do you recall if you became angry?

A–I don't think so at that time, I became angry later on, but not during the taking of his statement.

Q–In what connection did you become angry?

A–The discussion and argument between Lt. Robinson and Captain Bear at the time Lt. Robinson did not want to return as Captain Bear had directed him to.

Q–Did you hear the accused ask Captain Bear whether he was under arrest?

A–Yes.

Q–Do you recall if he was given an answer?

A–No.

Q–Do you say that he would not give the accused an answer?

A–No, sir.

Q–What did Captain Bear answer?

PROSECTION: I object to that as immaterial and improper cross examination.

LAW MEMBER: This witness has testified on direct examination that to his knowledge the accused was not in arrest, and for that reason, the matter was not brought out on direct; the objection is sustained.

Q–Captain Wigginton, in regard to this incident, the words that passed between Miss Wilson, the legal stenographer, and Lt. Robinson, that you testified about a moment ago, you got pretty incensed over that conversation, didn't you?

LAW MEMBER: Miss Wilson had not been identified here before; is it correct that she is the legal stenographer referred to?

DEFENSE: That is my understanding, but I would have to confirm that.

Q–Captain, you became incensed over the conversation between the legal stenographer and the accused, didn't you?

A–No, sir; I really don't remember the conversation.

Q–As a matter of fact did you and she step outside and discuss the matter beyond the hearing of the accused?

A–No, sir.

LAW MEMBER: If there was any discussion outside and not in the presence of the accused and not concerning this incident, it is not material to the specifications here and I do not see the purpose of the cross-examination.

DEFENSE: I am trying to determine the bias and prejudices of the witnesses on this basis.

PROSECUTOR: I object to bringing any foreign matter into this case on any such basis.

LAW MEMBER: What transpired as between this witness and the legal stenographer and in the absence of the accused, is not material and is not proper examination.

DEFENSE: Very well, I withdraw the question.

RE DIRECT EXAMINATION

Questions by the prosecution:

Q–On direct examination you demonstrated to the court how the accused acted, the manner he bowed or walked, and on cross-examination you told the defense counsel that he did not give any salute, will you describe to the court what the accused was doing when he was bowing and what he did with his right hand; will you demonstrate that action by the accused?

A–The reason I answered that it was not a salute was because it was not a salute; he would lean over the gate in this manner and do this with his hand; that is not a salute at all in my opinion.

EXAMINATION BY THE COURT

Questions by Captain Carr:

Q–Captain, you were relating to Captain Bear about some incident that had been related to you?

A–Yes, sir.

Q–Did you have any personal knowledge of the incident itself?

A–No, sir.

Q–Why did you object to the accused making corrections to the hearsay matters you were relating to the investigating officer?

A–When I came in the guard room, I asked for Lt. Robinson's version of the incident first, and many others, and when I called Captain Bear, I wanted him to try and clear up the case, and naturally I wanted him to know why I had called him and I was telling him the stories that had been told to me.

Q–In other words, you were telling him what Lt. Robinson had said and what others had said to make the story?

A–Yes, that was for the purpose of letting him determine whether to take statements or not; in other words, I was turning the case over to him.

(There were no further questions, the witness was excused.)

PROSECUTON: The prosecution rests.

DEFENSE: The accused had been apprised of his rights with reference to becoming a witness and he elects to become a sworn witness.

LAW MEMBER: With the permission of the court I will advise him further. Lt. Robinson, as the accused in this case, you cannot become a witness and testify unless you request to do so yourself. You cannot be required to testify or to say anything. If you desire to become a sworn witness you can do so at your own request, and if you do, you will be subject to cross examination by the Trial Judge Advocate and to questioning by members of the court in the same manner as any other witness. Now, in the event you do not desire to become a sworn witness, you may make a statement to the court without taking an oath; in that event you would not be subject to cross examination, either by the prosecution or by members of the court; but you would only say whatever you wanted to say and when you finish you would return to your seat. However, an unsworn statement is not evidence in the same sense as sworn testimony is, but the court can give it such consideration as they feel it is entitled to receive, and to the extent they see fit to consider it. In testifying under oath or making an unsworn statement should you make any admissions, the court can consider them against you. Now, you do not have to either testify under oath or make an unsworn statement; you can remain silent and make no statement at all. In that case the court will attach no significance whatever to your remaining silent with reference to whether you are guilty or innocent. Do you understand what your rights are?

ACCUSED: Yes, sir.

LAW MEMBER: And do you still desire to become a sworn witness?

ACCUSED: Yes, sir.

2nd LT. JACK R. ROBINSON, a witness for his defense, was sworn and testified as follows.

TRIAL JUDGE ADVOCATE: State your name, rank, organization, and station.

A—Jack R. Robinson, Second Lieutenant, Cavalry, Company C, 758th Tank Battalion, Camp Hood, Texas.

TRIAL JUDGE ADVOCATE: Are you the accused in this case?

A—Yes, sir.

DIRECT EXAMINATION

Questions by the defense:

Q—In responding to questions, I wish you would speak out so every member of the court can hear you. How old are you?

A—Twenty-five years old.

Q—Where is your home?

A—Pasadena, California.

Q—How long have you been in the army?

A—Since April 3, 1942.

Q—Now, you have heard what the various witnesses appearing against you have had to say; I want you to relate in your own words what transpired there at the Guard Room of Provost Marshall's office on the night you were taken there?

A—Just at the Guard Room?

Q—That's right; what transpired there?

A—I was brought in there by one of the M.P.'s; he suggested that we go see the Provost Marshall on some matters. I agreed to go with him, for I had no reason to object. I got there and it took some time before they found any officer to question me.

Q–Direct your remarks to the court and go a little slower so the court can understand you.

A–We waited there some little while before they found any officers; and I believe the first officer was Captain Wigginton and he asked me some questions, first he wanted to know what happened at the bus station and I told him; well, he got together between Private Mucklerath and myself, Mucklerath gave his statement and I gave mine and there was not much that came between Captain Wigginton and myself. Mucklerath explained the situation as he understood it and I told my story. Captain Wigginton said I was interrupting him, but to my mind it was not interrupting him at all; Private Mucklerath stated something that I did not think was quite right and I interrupted him to see if I could refresh his memory and to get him to correct his statement. Now, they say I did interrupt them, the officers, but I don't believe I did. Captain Wigginton said he was Camp O.D. and that he would get Captain Bear down there if possible and for me to wait outside until Captain Bear came—

Q–Talk a little slower, Lieutenant, the court wants to understand you and the reporter is taking your testimony.

A–Well, I stayed outside of the room and waited for Captain Bear to come, and I was outside when he came and I started to follow him through the guard room or into the guard room, and he turned around and wanted to know why I was following him in there. I told him that I had been there and had been told to come in when he came; and he said, "Nobody comes in the room until I tell him" and he looked and saw Mucklerath in there and I inquired what he was doing in there and Captain Bear said he was a witness. Captain Bear sat down and Captain Wigginton started to tell him the story, and he started in with the story that Private Mucklerath had told him that I had said if I ever saw him again I would break him in two, and I told them that what I had actually said was that if he ever called me a nigger again I would break him in two; that I was in the M.P. truck and Private Mucklerath came up and said, "Did you get that nigger lieutenant" and that was when I made that remark—

Q–Let me interrupt you, Lieutenant—do you know what a nigger is?

A–I looked it up once, but my Grandmother gave me a good definition, she was a slave, and she said the definition of the word was a low, uncouth person, and pertains to no one in particular; but I don't consider that I am low and uncouth. I looked it up in the dictionary afterwards and it says the word nigger pertains to negroid or negro, but it is also a machine used in a saw mill for pushing logs into the saws. I objected to being called a nigger by this private or by anybody else. When I made this statement that I did not like to be called nigger, I told the Captain, I said, "If you call me a nigger, I might have to say something to you, I don't mean to incriminate anybody, but I just don't like it." I do not consider myself a nigger at all, I am a Negro, but not a nigger. Captain Bear said I was insolent, and—

Q–Now wait a minute, I just want you to relate exactly what did transpire on that occasion; you heard what Captain Bear said, that you leaned on the door and saluted him in a sloppy manner?

A–Yes, sir, but I do not recall that and Captain Wigginton did not recall it, that I was bowing and saluting like that when Major Daugherty was asking him about it and I asked the Major to put that down; he stated that I did not make any kind of salute and I asked the major to put that in his statement, and he read it back as he had written it, and that was sent in, but we do not see it; so, I asked the Lieutenant to subpoena Major Daugherty, because the Major asked Captain Wigginton if he saw me bow from the waist and come up and give such a salute, and Captain Wigginton told him that he did not see me do any of those things, and I don't know why he has now changed his story. If we could get the notes that Major Daugherty had, they would show what he said about bowing and saluting. I certainly do not recall saluting Captain Bear or leaning on the door as he described; while I was right at the door, I did not lean. Captain Wigginton was relating the incident to Captain Bear, and Captain Bear had an idea that what was happened was at Killeen, and he wanted to know where it happened—

Q–Just a minute, now, I want to direct your attention to the order that has been referred to; how was the directive given to you at that time with reference to going into the other room?

A–I was already in the room at the time I interrupted, and Captain Bear told me to get away from the door and said he would call me; but he never did give me any order to sit in a chair; all he did was to tell me to get away from the door, and I stepped outside.

Q–How long did you stay outside?

A–I believe it took Captain Bear twenty or thirty minutes to finish his conversation with Captain Wigginton in that room, for I was outside there tossing rocks some twenty or thirty minutes, and Captain Bear and Captain Wigginton came out and passed by me and went into the mess hall and they were in there for about fifteen minutes, and in the meantime this 761st Tank Battalion soldier came up and asked—he asked what the trouble was, and wanted to know where Captain Bear was; and I told him that he was in the mess hall. So he stayed in the mess hall some fifteen minutes and when he came back, I was talking to the driver of that jeep; I happened to know the soldier, he was the driver for Lt. Lightfoot.

Q–When Captains Wigginton and Bear came out of the Provost Marshall's office and went into the mess hall, did they say anything to you?

A–No, sir, they never said a word.

Q–Did they say anything when they came back?

A–Captain Bear told me that he had ordered me to stay inside the room; he said, "You get back in that room" and I went back inside.

Q–Did you go in the room he told you to go in?

A–Yes, sir, and if I stuck my hands in my pockets I don't recall doing it; I don't believe I did. Captain Wigginton said that I did. Lt. Lightfoot was standing there and if I had known this was coming up I would have had him here or asked him about it, but before this nothing had come up about it in the investigation.

Q–All right, now, this interruption that you mentioned; what was the purpose of your making that interruption?

A–My only purpose was to clarify Captain Bear's mind as to where it happened; I didn't know anything was coming up of the matter.

Q–Did you intend at that time to be impudent?

A–No, sir, I did not intend to be impudent in any way at all; all that I wanted was for Captain Bear to get a true story of where I was and when I heard what I knew was not true, that was when I interrupted and he jumped up and said, "You get away from that door: and then said he would call me when he wanted me, and that was when I went outside and was waiting for him to get ready for me.

Q–Do you remember how many times you interrupted him?

A–One time exactly, and when he ordered me away from the door, I went outside.

Q–Did you construe that direction to mean—just how did you construe that directive when he told you to get away from the door?

A–I figured he meant for me to go away so I would not interrupt him; and I figured that if I heard the statement or any other that was not correct, I would interrupt again, and that was why I did go outside to wait for him to call me.

Q–During all of this time were your relations with those officers pleasant?

A–No, sir; when Captain Bear first walked in the office, for no reason at all I was told to come back in when Captain Bear came, and I started to walk in and he was not polite at all; that is simply my opinion. When he called me back in the office at the time he was taking my statement, in his questions, he was, in my opinion, very uncivil toward me; and he did not seem to recognize me as an officer at all; but I did consider myself an officer and felt that I should be addressed as one; and they asked that private to sit down—

Q–Well, just a minute, when he directed you to get away from the door, did you protest that directive in any way?

A–No, I did not.

Q–All right, now, what happened when you were summoned back into their presence?

A–I was not summoned back in until they went back to the orderly room to take my statement, I don't know, I might have been talking fast, but I thought I slowed down when he told me to, and he told me again to talk slow, and I believe he did that three times; and when he did that the third time I did slow down to where I knew the stenographer would be sure and get it; but when he then told me to go ahead and speak up, I did.

Q–Did you slow down to the gross exaggeration as has been demonstrated here?

A–No, I did not.

Q–During the time you were giving your statement to the stenographer, was there any incident that happened there that created a bad feeling or an unpleasant atmosphere between the parties present there?

A–Not until she had typed the statement, everything went smoothly until she had typed the statement. Captain Bear, in some way had asked me if he had seen me some place before; I don't know just how he put it, but he asked me if I had played football, and I told him, I thought it was off the record; and he asked me where I played football, and I told him in California; he asked if I had played in the East and I told him I had played in Chicago; and all of that was in the record and I did not see why that should belong in the record, and I crossed it off, and there was some statement to the effect, "I don't know whether he was or not" that did not sound right and I crossed that off; and the Secretary said, "If you had completed your statement it would have made sense" and I told her if she had put down Captain Bear's question, it would have made sense; and she then picked up her purse and said, "I don't have to make excuses to him" and went out, and Captain Bear went outside with her and talked awhile and came back. After I had finished with the statement, he stated about his arrangement for me to go back and I asked him if I was in arrest, and I told him if I was not, I had a pass and that I could get back on the bus the next morning. I also asked permission to talk to Major Wingo; but Captain Bear thought it best that I go back.

Q–Who is Major Wingo?

A–He is the executive officer of the Battalion and he was acting commander in the absence of the colonel. I explained to Major Wingo and he said the reason Captain Bear want me to go back was that he figured I would get in trouble with the busses, and I told him I would not, that I abided by the Texas Law, but that I knew there was no Jim Crow rule on the Post and the bus driver had tried to make me move to the rear, and I told him that I would not move back.

Q—Just where were you sitting at that time with reference to the front and rear of the bus.

A—I imagine about four seats from the rear, I believe it was, and I imagine it was a little better than half way.

PROSECUTION: I object to this line of testimony, for it has nothing to do with this specification; what happened on the bus, or this testimony about what happened has no place in this case.

LAW MEMBER: I do not see the materiality of it; the objection is sustained.

CROSS EXAMINATION

Questions by the prosecution:

Q—When you came to the orderly room, what time was it?

A—Approximately 2245 hours.

Q—Was Private Mucklerath with you?

A—He was in the rear of the truck.

Q—When you arrived at the orderly room at that time, who was present in the room?

A—I believe it was the Sergeant of the Guard.

Q—Sgt. Painter?

A—I did not know his name.

Q—Would you recognize him if you saw him?

A—I don't know whether I would or not; I don't know.

Q—Was Corporal Elwood there?

A—Corporal Elwood, I believe he is the M.P. that came down and I went in his truck back to the station.

Q—Did anyone in the orderly room call you an abusive name?

A—When and where?

Q—In the Guard House?

A—No.

Q—Did private Mucklerath call you a nigger?

A—He did.

Q—In the presence of Captain Bear?

A—In the presence of Corporal Elwood.

Q—In the orderly room?

A—No, sir.

Q—I am talking about there, in the orderly room?

A—No, sir.

Q—Did anyone insult you there in anyway?

A–Captain Bear did.

Q–Did he call you any abusive name?

A–No, sir.

Q–Did he call you a nigger?

A–No, sir.

Q–Did he provoke you in any manner?

A–Yes, he did.

Q–In what way?

A–I had instruction that I was to wait until Captain Bear came and to follow him in when he came, and I started to go in following him and Captain Bear turned to me and said very angrily that I was not to come in there until he called me; and I thought I was supposed to be in there, since Private Mucklerath was in there.

Q–How long have you been in the service?

A–Since April 3, 1942.

Q–You know that was an investigation in connection with an incident, and that it had to be conducted in an orderly manner, didn't you?

A–Yes, but I felt that I was involved and I had been told to come in when Captain Bear arrived.

Q–Did you ever conduct an investigation as an officer?

A–No, sir.

Q–Was Captain Bear anxious to get the testimony of each one on that occasion?

A–Yes, I am sure of it.

Q–Was it necessary to call each one in and take their statements?

A–The only ones there—

Q–Just answer my questions; was it necessary to call individuals in?

A–Yes, it was.

Q–When you injected certain remarks, were you interrupting?

A–I thought that it was in order that some important thing get in; I did not do it in a disorderly manner; I have visited court rooms in civilian life and have seen the same thing done in an orderly manner and I did not know of any objection to it.

Q–But when Captain Bear told you to desist, you kept on?

A–I did not, I went outside on his first order, for I felt he wanted me out and I did not go back and he did not say anymore to me until he came back from the mess hall,

Q–Do you think Captain Wigginton was lying about what he told on the witness stand?

A–Do you think I should answer that?

Q–Yes?

A–Yes, he was. I talked with Captain Wigginton at the investigation, and he did not testify that way at the time.

Q–Did Captain Wigginton insult you in anyway?

A–He has never insulted me.

Q–He treated you like a gentleman, didn't he?

A–He did.

Q–And so did Captain Bear?

A–I don't believe Captain Bear did.

Q–Did you see Captain Hamilton?

A–At the time of my statement, I saw him.

Q–He was not abusive, was he?

A–He did not say anything to me until I asked him why Captain Bear would not tell me whether I was under arrest?

Q–Did you know him?

A–Only on sight.

Q–Would you believe him if he told the same story?

A–If he told me the right story, I would.

Q–He had no bias against you, has he?

A–I assumed that he was not up there, he was very nice and then he made a statement that I was facetious and disrespectful, and I don't know why he thought I was facetious unless it was because of what I told the lady about my statement, where the sentence was not complete, and when she got up and walked out and said she did not have to make excuses to me; and I just figured it was typical down here; and I suppose that was why Captain Hamilton said I was facetious.

Q–Coming down to the time that you were in the guard room; you don't remember leaning on the gate or anything about that?

A–Did I say that?

Q–Didn't you?

A–It is possible, but I don't remember.

Q–And is it possible that you had your hands in your pockets too, isn't it?

A–Yes, it is possible.

Q–And is it possible that you bowed, isn't it?

A–No, that is not possible.

Q–Do you remember it?

A–I do remember; I was commissioned as an officer nineteen months ago.

Q–And you know what a proper salute is?

A–Yes, and I know when I should get one.

Q–You never saluted Captain Bear that entire evening?

A–Not to my knowledge.

Q–You had not been drinking, had you?

A–That's what I want to know.

Q–Did you drink anything that evening?

A–Evidently they figured I had.

Q–Well, did you?

A–No.

Q–You knew what you were doing that evening?

A–That's right.

Q–And I will ask you if you had control of your mental faculties, full control?

A–I certainly did.

Q–Having full control of your mental faculties, I ask you now whether you remember saluting at any time, whether it was Captain Bear, Captain Wigginton, or any others?

A–To the best of my knowledge, I don't remember saluting.

Q–Do you remember bowing?

A–I did not bow, and Captain Wigginton testified to that at the investigation, and Major Daugherty had it in a statement and he brought that question up; Private Mucklerath and all the M.P.'s testified that I was bowing, and I asked Wigginton if he could see me at all times, and he said he could.

Q–Were Corporal Elwood and Sgt. Painter in the room while this was taking place?

A–At different times they were, they kept going and coming.

Q–They were with the M.P. personnel in there?

A–That's right.

Q–Other than the sergeant and corporal, and Mucklerath, the others were commissioned officers?

A–That's right; they were the enlisted men.

Q–They know what happened in there, do they not?

A–That's right.

Q–Coming back to the time that you were told to stay out of the room; did Captain Bear give you any order after you were constantly interrupting him?

A–I did not constantly interrupt; the only time that he gave me any semblance of an order was when he told me to get away from the door and stay until I was called, and that was not disobeyed, not willfully.

Q–I did not ask if you willfully disobeyed; I asked you if Captain Bear gave you any order; and I will ask you to the best of your recollection, what did Captain Bear tell you?

A–Best of my recollection, he told me to get away from the door and not interrupt and he would call me when he wanted me.

Q–Did he direct you to any place?

A–No, he did not.

Q–What did you do?

A–Well, I went outside and started to tossing rocks across the street.

Q–What happened then?

A–I was out there fifteen or twenty minutes before Captain Wigginton and Captain Bear came out, and they walked right passed me and went to the mess hall. Lt. Lightfoot was there, and when they came back that was when Captain Bear told me that he gave me an order to stay in the room and he told me then to go back in there.

Q–Coming back to the time when you were speaking rapidly to the stenographer, were you told to slow down?

A–I was.

Q–Did you slow down?

A–I did.

Q–How did you slow down your speech?

A–I merely slowed down my speech.

Q–Do you remember how you slowed it down?

A–I think I do.

Q–Will you read the first paragraph here in this pamphlet and show the court how you slowed down?

A–"Regulations governing Court-Martial proceedings are contained in the—"

Q–The second time you slowed down; how did you do it?

A–Something like this, "Regulations governing Court-Martial" and then he interrupted me and I slowed down a little more.

Q–Did you pause between words?

A–Not to my knowledge.

Q–Did you pause then between words?

A–Not to my knowledge.

Q–With a sneer on your face?

A–I don't recall anything like that.

Q–And grimacing?

A–I was not, I had no reason for grimacing.

Q–As a matter of fact, Lieutenant, this argument between you and Captain Bear—withdrawn. Was it necessary for Captain Wigginton to tell you to behave toward the end of the investigation, or he would have to do something.

A–He did and the reason he told me that was because I wanted to know whether I was under arrest, and I asked him a half dozen times; I was being sent back to McCloskey Hospital under guard, and an armed guard, and if I was not supposed to be under arrest I could not understand that proceeding.

Q–After you asked him, did you get an answer?

A–I did not.

Q–Then you were pretty persistent about it?

A–Yes, sir.

Q–You became very argumentative, didn't you?

A–I merely asked.

Q–Did he tell you that you were arrest in quarters?

A–He said, "If that is the way you want it, we will let it go."

Q–And you still persisted in your argument, didn't you?

A–When he told me that, that was after Captain Wigginton came back from talking on the telephone, and I left then, and one of the sergeants came out and said, "Lieutenant, I would not worry about this, these people don't know what they are doing" and he told another sergeant the same thing and we had a very nice discussion—

Q–You just answer my question in connection with this incident; what did Captain Wigginton tell you?

A–He threatened to put me under arrest.

Q–For what reason?

A–If I did not take what Captain Bear told me about going back in the patrol wagon and quit talking.

Q–Did he tell you that you were insubordinate?

A–No, he did not; he said if I didn't quit talking to Captain Bear about being under arrest, he would place me under arrest.

EXAMINATION BY THE COURT

Questions by Captain Spencer:

Q–Was there any chair in the receiving room?

A–Yes, sir.

Q–Did Captain Bear point out any chair to you?

A–I don't believe he could see any chair from where he was sitting; the chair was approximately in the position where Lt. Cline is sitting, and the door here; I don't believe he could have seen the chair, sir.

Q–He did not point out a chair to you?

A–Not to my knowledge; he did not tell me anything about a chair; all that he told me to do was to get away from the door and he would call me.

(There being no further questions, the accused returned to his seat by the defense counsel.)

LT. COL. R. L. Bates, a witness for the defense, was sworn and testified as follows:

TRIAL JUDGE ADVOCATE: State your name, rank, organization, and station.

A–R. L. Bates, Lieutenant Colonel, Cavalry, 761st Tank Battalion, Camp Hood, Texas.

TJA: Do you know the accused?

A–I do.

TJA: What is his name?

A–Lt. Jack Robinson

TJA: Is he present in the court room?

A–He is, here on my left.

DIRECT EXAMINATION

Questions by the defense:

Q–Colonel, will you state your official duties?

A–I command the 761st Tank Battalion.

Q–Is the accused, or has the accused been a member of your command?

A–He was from April 3, 1944, to July 6, 1944.

Q–Do you know his reputation in the community in which he lived? By that I mean his camp, post, and station?

A–Particularly with the enlisted men, he is held in very high regard; he is a well-known athlete—

PROSECUTION: I object, the answer is not responsive.

LAW MEMBER: The objection is sustained.

Q–Would you just answer the question yes or no, Colonel, do you know his general reputation in the community in which he lived? By that I mean his post, camp, and station.

A–It is excellent.

Q–Would you mind responding as to whether you know it?

A–Yes, I do know it and it is excellent.

Q–You anticipated my next question, Colonel; is that reputation good or bad?

A–Good.

Q–How do you regard him as to his ability as a soldier?

A–Excellent.

Q–Would you like to have him as a member of your organization, Colonel?

A–Yes, I tried to have him assigned to the Battalion, and was unable—

PROSECUTION: I object to this voluntary statement.

LAW MEMBER: Overruled.

Q–Continue, sir?

A–I was unable to have him assigned to the Battalion, he was attached unassigned, and I tried to have him assigned to the Battalion because of his excellent work.

Q–Sir are you familiar with what is known as 66-1?

A–Yes, I am.

Q–What rating would you give to this officer on his 66-1?

A–Excellent.

(There being no further questions, the witness was excused.)

CAPTAIN JAMES R. LAWSON, a witness for the defense, was sworn and testified as follows:

TJA: State your name, rank, organization, and station.

A–James R. Lawson, Captain, Company B, 761st Tank Battalion, Camp Hood, Texas.

TJA: Do you know the accused? If so, state his name.

A–I do; Second Lt. Jack R. Robinson.

DIRECT EXAMINATION

Questions by the defense:

Q–Will you just state to the court your official duty assignment, Captain Lawson?

A–I am commander of Company B, 761st Tank Battalion.

Q–Has the accused been a member of your command?

A–He was.

Q–How long?

A–From about April 20th to July 6th.

Q–From your association with him, do you know his general reputation in the community, in which he lived? By that I mean his post, camp, and station?

A–I do.

Q–Is that reputation good or bad?

A–Good.

Q–How do you regard the accused as to his ability as a soldier?

A–Excellent.

Q–Would you like to have him as a member of your command?

A–I would.

(There being no more questions, the witness was excused.)

2d Lt. HAROLD KINGSLEY, a witness for the defense, was sworn and testified as follows:

TJA: State your name, organization, and station.

A–Harold Kingsley, Second Lieutenant, 761st Tank Battalion, Camp Hood, Texas.

TJA: Do you know the accused? If so, state his name.

A–I do, Jack Robinson.

DIRECT EXAMINATION

Questions by the defense:

Q–Lt. Kingsley, how long have you known Lt. Robinson?

A–I have known him since April 8, 1944.

Q–As a result of his acquaintance, do you know his general reputation in the community in which he lived? By that I mean his post, camp, and station.

A–Yes, sir.

Q–Is his reputation good or bad?

A–Good.

Q–How do you regard him as to his ability as a soldier?

A–Excellent.

(There being no further questions, the witness was excused.)

2nd Lt. HOWARD B. CAMPBELL, a witness for the defense, was sworn and testified as follows:

TJA: State your name.

A–Howard B. Campbell, 2nd Lieutenant.

TJA–You are the same witness that testified previously?

A–Yes, sir.

TJA: This is to remind you that you are still under oath.

DIRECT EXAMINATION

Questions by the defense:

Q–How long have you known the accused, Lt. Campbell?

A–About a year and four months.

Q–As a result of your acquaintance, do you know his general reputation in the community in which he lived? By that I mean his post, camp, and station.

A–Yes I do.

Q–Is that reputation good or bad?

A–Good.

Q–How do you regard him as to his ability as a soldier?

A–Very good.

(There being no further questions, the witness was excused.)

DEFENSE: The defense rests.

1st GEORGE PAUL CRIBARI, a witness for the prosecution, was sworn and testified as follows:

DIRECT EXAMINATION

Questions by the prosecution:

Q–State your name, rank, organization, and station.

A–George Paul Cribari, First Lieutenant, Medical Corps, Dispensary N, Camp Hood, Texas.

Q–Lieutenant, do you remember anything occurring on July 6, 1944, in connection—withdrawn. Do you know the accused?

A–Yes, sir.

Q–Is he present in the court room?

A–Yes, sir.

Q–Did you see him on July 6, 1944?

A—I did.

Q—Where did you see him?

A—In the guard room of South Camp Hood, Texas.

Q—How did you happen to be there, Lieutenant?

A—I was returning from the Club about that time from having been to a club session that evening, and was coming from the club to my area and happened to be with Captain Hamilton and Captain Wigginton at the time.

Q—When you went to the guard room, who was present?

A—Lt. Robinson, Captain Hamilton, Captain Bear, Captain Wigginton, and two enlisted men, and a Miss Watson.

Q—Lieutenant, will you tell the court what transpired in that orderly room while you were present?

A—The main thing that took place, was the statement that Lt. Robinson made to Captain Bear.

Q—Did you come in at the time the statement was being taken?

A—I came in prior to the time the statement was begun.

Q—What was Captain Bear's attitude toward Lt. Robinson?

A—I don't know what you mean.

Q—How did he conduct himself toward Lt. Robinson during the entire time you were present?

A—Well, it seemed perfectly orderly and proper for the Provost Marshall to question him; his general statements were "Lt. Robinson did you or did you not do this or that"; but I don't remember the exact questions he put to the Lieutenant, but I presumed he was getting a statement.

Q—I am not interested in that, but what was Captain Bear's general attitude? Did he show any animosity or antagonism toward Lt. Robinson?

A—None whatsoever that I could see.

Q—What was Lt. Robinson's attitude toward Captain Bear while you were present? Will you describe his actions?

A—Do you mean specific incidents?

Q—That is correct.

A—On various occasions I saw Lt. Robinson—I believe that is his name—was what I would say very rude toward Captain Bear.

LAW MEMBER: Will you explain that?

A—By being rude—my interpretation might be somewhat different—on several occasions the Lieutenant, after having been asked a question, he would sit there and put his hands on his knees and shake his head and say, "I ain't got a chance" and kind of smirking or smiling and on one occasion he got up and put his hands in his pockets and walked toward the door and came back—

LAW MEMBER: Now, will you put your hands in your pockets and show us. (Witness demonstrates) You shook you head from side to side?

A–Yes, sir.

Q–Were you there when Captain Bear told the accused not to talk so rapidly?

A–Yes, sir.

Q–What happened?

A–The first that he did was to smile and show his teeth, sort of a grimace or grin more than anything else; I forgot what his statement was at the time he began, but it was something like this, "Well—I—was—on—the—bus" and he would nod his head each time he would say a word, and "from—there—I–took—two—more—steps;" nodding his head each time.

LAW MEMBER: You have recited those words in a slow speech, with an exaggerated pause between each word; is that correct?

A–Yes, sir.

CROSS EXAMINATION

Questions by the defense:

Q–Did you become indignant over what you witnessed there?

A–Did I?

Q–Yes, sir.

A–I don't believe I did, I had no interest in the case at all, Lieutenant; I was merely an innocent by-stander, merely witnessing the disrespect of one officer to his superior.

DEFENSE: I object to the voluntary conclusion of the witness.

PROSECUTION: He asked for it.

LAW MEMBER: The answer was given in part voluntary, and the objection is proper.

Q–How many times was Lt. Robinson requested to slow down his pace of speech?

A–Only on one occasion as I recall it.

Q–Were you there during the entire time?

A–Not the entire time; I think I was there approximately an hour.

Q–And you heard it just one time; is that your answer?

A–Yes, sir.

EXAMINATION BY THE COURT

Questions by Law Member:

Q–Did you know Captain Bear?

A–You mean personally? He is an acquaintance; I just know him from having met him at the Stockade when I was called there professionally.

Q–Was Captain Bear present on this occasion?

A–Yes, sir.

Q–What was his rank at that time?

A–Captain, sir.

Questions by Captain Spencer:

Q–Did you hear Captain Bear give Lt. Robinson any order while you were present relative to his being quiet?

A–I don't recall anything of that sort, sir.

LAW MEMBER: This is something this witness does not appear to have knowledge of.

Questions by Captain Carr:

Q–You said something or demonstrated something about Lt. Robinson putting his head between his hands; would you consider that as being rude to you?

A–Yes, sir.

Q–Will you tell me why?

A–When an enlisted man comes to his superior, he is at attention or at ease and he is not permitted to be slouching around and bowing, and I find that inferior officers should not do so in the presence of superior officers; they should conduct themselves in the same manner they expect enlisted men to do in their presence.

Q–Is that the custom of the service?

A–I believe so, sir.

Q–You think so?

A–I do it myself.

Q–Was the accused permitted to sit down?

A–Yes, sir.

Q–He could lower his hands or rest them on his knees, could he not?

A–It was not that, sir; I think that would be permissible; but it was the expression on his face and features; in my opinion any man may put his hands down, or rest his head on his hands, for he might be feeling pain; but that does not mean that he could grimace and smirk at the same time.

Q–What do you mean by grimace?

A–Grimace is assuming a contemptuous position of your facial muscles; assuming a contemptuous attitude toward another person.

Q–I do not quite understand you, Doctor?

A–Grimacing is done by the muscles of the face.

Q–Am I grimacing now? (demonstrating)

A–I think so, if your attitude toward me was that of resentment, and the tone of your voice was such that would go with it.

Questions by Major Mowder:

Q–If a man was at ease, and had been given "at ease" by his superior officer, would you consider that conduct rude?

A–I think a man is always at ease when sitting down.

Q–You brought out that he was supposed to be at attention?

A–I was merely using that as an analysis between an enlisted man and his superior officer.

DEFENSE COUNSEL: I wonder if the record shows that this accused had his head between his legs when he made the answer to a question and said, "I haven't not a chance" or substantially that statement?

WITNESS: He had his head between his hands and he was bent over, sort of, you might say between his legs.

DEFENSE COUNSEL: Did you mention that he said "I haven't got a chance"?

WITNESS: Yes, sir.

(There being no further questions, the witness was excused.)

CORPORAL GEORGE A. ELWOOD, a witness for the prosecution was sworn and testified as follows:

DIRECT EXAMINATION

Questions by the prosecution:

Q–State your name, grade, organization, and station.

A–George A. Elwood, acting corporal, Military Police Section, Enlisted Detachment, 1848th Unit, Camp Hood, Texas.

Q–Do you know the accused?

A–Yes, sir.

Q–What are your duties, Corporal?

A–I am on motor patrol; I patrol the Camp area.

Q–Were you on duty July 6, 1944?

A–Yes, sir.

Q–Did you on occasion to see the accused at the Guard Room that evening?

A–Yes, sir.

Q–When you arrived there, who was present?

A–The sergeant of the guard—

Q–What is his name?

A–Painter; and Corporal Feris, and Private—

Q–Was Captain Bear there?

A–Not right at that time, sir.

Q–Was Captain Wigginton there?

A–Not at that time.

Q–When did Captains Bear and Wigginton arrive?

A–Captain Wigginton arrived there about twenty minutes later, and Captain Bear about twenty-five minutes later.

Q–When Captain Bear arrived, will you tell what transpired from that time until Lt. Robinson left?

A–Captain Bear came into the guard room and Lt. Robinson started to follow him in there and Captain Bear told Lt. Robinson to wait outside, that he would tell him or see him later; Captain Bear then started talking to Captain Wigginton, who was the O.D., and Lt. Robinson came in and interrupted him and Captain Bear told Lt. Robinson to be quiet and he would call him in later; and Captain Bear continued his discussion with Captain Wigginton of what had happened, and Lt. Robinson insisted on saying something and Captain Bear told Sgt. Painter to put a chair in the outer office and told Lt. Robinson to be seated in that chair.

DEFENSE: I object unless the accused was present.

Q–Was the accused present when Captain Bear gave him the order you just stated?

A–Yes, sir.

Q–What was the order that Captain Bear gave Lt. Robinson?

A–He told him, "Lieutenant, you be seated in the outer office in that chair until I call you" or words to that effect.

Q–What happened?

A–Well, sir, Lt. Robinson went out and sat down in the chair and stayed there for a while and then got up and went outside.

Q–Did you see him outside?

A–Yes, sir.

Q–What was he doing outside?

A–Talking to a jeep driver, the driver for the O.D. of the 761st Tank Battalion.

Q–Did Captain Bear see him out there?

A–Yes, sir.

Q–What did he say to him?

A–I did not hear it, sir.

Q–What was the attitude of Lt. Robinson, when Captain Bear gave him the order to go sit in the chair?

A–May I stand up, sir?

Q–Stand up and show the court?

A–Captain Bear gave him the order to go to the outer office and the Lieutenant said, "Yes, sir, yes sir" mockingly and with a smile on his face, and as he did that, he turned around and put his hands in his pockets and sauntered off.

LAW MEMBER: Could you put in words what he did, how you have demonstrated it? Did he bend forward as he said the words you have repeated?

A—Yes, sir, I would say he bent about a 70 degree angle, and had a smile or grin on his face, just like he was making fun of the Captain, and did this way; I would not call it a salute.

Q—Was his right hand touching his right eye?

A—Yes, sir.

Q—Describe that action?

A—He just seemed to bow from his waist on up. When he came in from the outer room to interrupt Captain Bear, he was leaning over this half door on his elbows and he was addressing Captain Bear in that manner.

Q—Continue, what else happened from the time that Captain Bear arrived?

A—Well, after Captain Bear gave him the order and he bowed and gave that half salute and went in the outer office and sat down, and as he did so, he had his hands in his pockets and sort of sauntered towards the chair.

CROSS-EXAMINATION

Questions by the defense:

Q—Corporal, how big a desk is that?

A—It was not a desk, sir, it comes to about here on me.

Q—About three feet and a half?

A—Just about, sir; it's just a door cut in half.

Q—I am asking about the desk and you are telling about a door?

A—It is not a desk, sir; but a half door.

Q—Is it a half door between the two offices and not a desk?

A—That's right, sir.

Q—Were his elbows on the door?

A—That's right, sir.

Q—At the time—at no time did you see him lean on a desk?

A—No, sir.

Q—Did you hear Captain Bear say to the accused when he first came in, "What are you doing following me in?"

A—No, sir.

Q—What did you hear Captain Bear say; the first thing he said in your presence?

A—The first thing in my presence, when he came in told the Lieutenant to wait in the outer room and he would call him later.

Q—Was there any other witnesses in that room?

A—Yes, sir, Sgt. Painter was in there.

Q—Was Private Mucklerath in there?

A—Yes, sir.

Q—Were they told to leave the room?

A—No, sir.

Q—They were in the room or on the outside?

A—Inside, sir.

Q—How could you see the accused sitting in the chair from where you were inside the room?

A—I did not see him sitting in the chair, but he was told to sit in it.

Q—Do you remember testifying that he went back and sat down in the chair and then went outside?

A—Yes, sir.

Q—Why did you say that?

A—Because I left the guard room and he was in the chair when I went through going to the orderly room to see if Miss Wilson was ready.

Q—He was not outside tossing stones when you went out?

A—No, sir, but when I came back from the orderly room, he was outside.

Q—Was Sgt. Painter sitting in there guarding the Lieutenant?

A—No, sir.

Q—So far as you knew he was not sitting out there?

A—No, sir.

Q—Then he did not do what he was ordered to do?

A—He was not ordered to sit there, he was ordered to get a chair for Lt. Robinson to sit in.

Q—There was no chair in that room and Captain Bear ordered the Sergeant to get one for the Lieutenant to sit in?

A—That's right, sir.

Q—Is Captain Bear over you?

A—Yes, sir.

Q—How many times have you gone over this with him?

A—I have not gone over it, sir.

Q—You have not talked to Captain Bear about it?

A—No, sir.

RE DIRECT EXAMINATION

Questions by the prosecution:

Q—Did you hear any abusive language used by either Captain Bear or Captain Wigginton toward Lt. Robinson?

A—No, sir.

Q—Did you hear Private Mucklerath use the word "nigger?"

A—No, sir.

(There being no further questions, the witness was excused.)

PRIVATE FIRST CLASS BEN W. MUCKLERATH, a witness for the prosecution, was sworn and testified as follows:

DIRECT EXAMINATION

Questions by the prosecution:

Q–State your name, grade, organization, and station.

A–Ben W. Mucklerath, Private First Class, Company D, 149th Training Battalion, Camp Hood, Texas.

Q–Do you know Lt. Robinson?

A–Yes, sir.

Q–Do you remember seeing him on July 6, 1944?

A–Yes, sir.

Q–Did you ever call him a nigger?

A–No, sir.

CROSS EXAMINATION

Questions by the defense:

Q–Private Mucklerath, do you recall Lt. Robinson telling you that if you ever called him a nigger he would break you in two?

A–Yes, sir.

Q–Why do you suppose he said that to you?

A–I don't have any idea what he was thinking; I was repeating something that I had heard, of an incident that had happened at the Military Police Station at Camp Hood.

Q–Do you deny that you went to the M.P. on the truck at the bus station and said "Do you have that nigger lieutenant in the car"; do you deny you made that statement?

A–At no time did I use the word "nigger."

Q–You deny you made that statement?

A–I never used the word "nigger" at any time, sir.

(There being no further questions, the witness was excused.)

PROSECUTION: The prosecution rests.

CORPORAL GEORGE A. ELWOOD, recalled by the defense, testified as follows:

TJA: What is your name?

A–George A. Elwood, sir.

TJA: You are the same witness who testified previously?

A–Yes, sir.

TJA: This is to remind you that you are still under oath.

DIRECT EXAMINATION

Questions by the defense:

Q–Corporal, do you know Private Mucklerath?

A–Not personally, sir.

Q–Would you know him if you saw him?

A–Yes, sir.

Q–Did he ever ask you at any time if you had a nigger lieutenant in your car?

A–Yes, sir, he did at the bus station.

CROSS EXAMINATION

Questions by the prosecution:

Q–Where was Lt. Robinson at the time?

A–I had him sitting in my vehicle.

Q–To your knowledge, could Lt. Robinson have heard him ask that question?

A–Yes, sir, I guess he could.

(There being no further questions, the witness was excused.)

PROSECUTION: The prosecution has no further evidence, does the court desire any witnesses called or recalled?

PRESIDENT: The court does not.

Closing arguments were made by the defense and prosecution.

PRESIDENT: The court will be closed.

FINDINGS

Neither the prosecution or defense having anything further to offer, court was closed and voted in the manner prescribed in Articles of War 31 and 43. Upon secret written ballot, two-thirds of the members present at the time the vote was taken the court finds the accused: of all specifications and charges: Not guilty; and therefore acquits the accused.

The court was opened and the president announced the findings.

The court then, at 6:00 o'clock P.M., 2 August, 1944, adjourned until the next call of the President.

AUTHENTICATON OF RECORD

(signed)

JOHN E. PERMAN, Lt. Col. F.A.

a member in lieu of the president

because of his absence.

(signed)
MILTON GORDON
2nd Lt., A.U.S.
Trial Judge Advocate

I examined the record before it was authenticated.
(signed)
WILLIAM A. CLINE
2Lt., A.U.S.

Defense Council

Sources/Bibliography

$\mathcal{N}$o American athlete has received more media coverage than Jackie Robinson. A simple Internet search of his name reveals nearly 400,000 citations while Amazon has more than 1,000 entries. Journalists, sports reporters, baseball fans, and family members have all produced books in various forms including traditional, coffee table, youth, and even comic. Jackie contributed two autobiographies. Television and motion picture producers have released more than a half dozen films about the life of Jackie Robinson. Some of these stories detail Jackie's entire life while others focus on his first year with the Brooklyn Dodgers when he broke the color barrier. Others detail his entire Major League Baseball career.

Most of these mediums gloss over Jackie's time in the U.S. Army in a few pages. His court-martial receives but a paragraph or two. The lengthy, best, and most detailed account of Jackie's life, *Jackie Robinson: A Biography,* by Arnold Rampersad, allots fewer than ten pages, including some inaccuracies, to his court-martial. The most complete record of interviews of Jackie's teammates, opponents, news writers, friends, and family are in Maury Allen's *Jackie Robinson: A Life Remembered,* but it contains a scant dozen paragraphs about Jackie's court-martial. A television movie, *The Court-Martial of Jackie Robinson,* featuring major Hollywood actors and actresses, attempted to bring the story to the small screen on TNT in 1990. The overdramatized, and somewhat novelized film was little watched or reviewed and is available today only in the antiquated VHS format. Most, if not all, of the many presentations in print and other media of Jackie's life, particularly his time in the U.S. Army, are at best incomplete, and at worse filled with inaccuracies, misunderstandings, and out-and-out fiction. Several of these errors are repeated in account after account.

The greatest problem of writers with the inclusion, analysis, and conclusions about Robinson's time in military uniform and his court-martial is that none thus far have had previous military experience of their own. This has greatly limited their understanding of Jackie's service in the U.S. Army, the "move to the back of the bus incident," and the military court-martial system and procedures.

The primary source for Robinson's military service and his court-martial are the more than 450 pages of his service and medical records and his court-martial Record of Trial, including witness sworn statements that are found in his Department of the Army official file. However, there are many things in Jackie's army file (as with those of all veterans) that are difficult to understand or are confusing because of gaps caused by records that are missing or never filed. For the researcher who has not served, the military terms, abbreviations, and acronyms are difficult to decipher and at times misinterpreted.

Three of these record groups provide the most information on Jackie's time in the military. The first is his enlisted record, War Department Adjutant Generals Office Form No. 24 (March 1, 1941 edition) titled simply Service Record, contains pre-printed entries to be checked or added to, and rubber-stamped dates, places, and approving authorities. The cover page notes the soldier's name, serial number, and period of service. In the middle of the form is an entry for race. Included in the following records are enlistment records, military qualifications, financial affairs, and organizations to which assigned.

The second are his records after receiving his commission as a second lieutenant. His War Department Adjutant Generals Office Form 66-1 (February 1, 1942) contains much the same type of information as his Enlisted Service Record except in a more abbreviated form.

His enlisted and officer service are also contained on IBM punch cards that record his various training, assignments, and attachments. These forty-fives punch cards are helpful in following the "who," "where," and "when" of his military career, but offers none in the way of "why."

(Yes, World War II was the first, albeit extremely archaic, computer-assisted military conflict. The IBM card format, introduced in 1928, has rectangular holes, eighty columns, and twelve rows on cards measuring $7 \frac{3}{8}$ by $3 \frac{1}{4}$ inches. Often called Hollerith Cards after their originator Herman Hollerith, they were originally used for collecting census data. At the outbreak of World War II, the army sought an efficient, flexible, and fast system to manage the staggering numbers of enlistees. The IBM punch cards met much of these requirements and with its Machine Record Units recorded and controlled the army's manpower, payroll, and supplies. As a part of their undistinguished history, IBM punch cards were employed to manage the internment of Japanese citizens in the United States. Also, unfortunately, before the war IBM sold the technology to Germany who later used the system to manage their concentration and death camps.)

The third group is Jackie's medical records that include details on the evaluation of his ankle injury that restricted him to limited duty and to his ultimate discharge. The file also includes other routine medical matters.

The sworn witness statements to Jackie being told to move to the back of the bus and the aftermath at the bus and MP stations are the best sources of information about the incident that led to his court-martial. The eighty-seven-page Record of Trial contains the complete transcript of Robinson's General Court-Martial trial organization, testimony, and verdict.

There are no redactions of any information in the documents in Jackie's military files. In fact, the argument could be made that certain personal medical information should have been redacted rather than have been made available to the public.

More than 160 pages of documents released by the Federal Bureau of Investigation, many only recently declassified, provide extensive information on Robinson's post-court-martial career in baseball and afterward. Unlike his military records, Jackie's FBI files are heavily redacted—some with half or more of pages blacked out. In the margin of each redaction is a reference to the paragraph of Title 5 of the United State Code, Section 552 that authorizes the restriction of information. The most frequent cited paragraphs are b-7 (c) "unwarranted invasion of personal privacy" and b-7 (d) "disclosure of the identity of a confidential source."

It is also noteworthy that unlike Jackie's military file that is neat and nearly entirely legible, several of the FBI non-redacted documents are not readable and are labeled "Best Copy Available." Most of the margin notes, other than the redaction authorization paragraph references, cannot be deciphered. Page content is faded or blurred in several others.

Major Adam Kama, an officer in the U.S. Army Judge Advocate General's Corps, made significant contributions to this work through his extensive collections of sources on Robinson and his court-martial. Kama's experience as a military attorney and his analysis was extremely helpful in determining many of the "hows" and "whys."

Finally, the author's personal service in the U.S. Army for more than twenty years, including three years at Fort Hood, Texas, and sitting on numerous court-martial boards was extremely helpful in understanding Robinson's military service and his trial.

The following sources supplemented the information found in Robinson's U.S. Army and FBI files.

BOOKS

Allen, Maury. *Jackie Robinson: A Life Remembered*. New York: Franklin Watts, 1987.

Barber, Red. *1947: When All Hell Broke Loose in Baseball*. New York: DaCapo Press, 1982.

Chalberg, Charles C. *Rickey and Robinson: The Preacher, the Player, and America's Game*. Wheeling, IL: Harlan Davidson, 2000.

Cohen, Barbara. *Thank You, Jackie Robinson*. New York: Lothrop, Lee and Shepard, 1974.

Denenberg, Barry. *Stealing Home: The Story of Jackie Robinson*. New York: Scholastic, Ind., 1997.

Dorinson, Joseph, and Joram Warmund, eds. *Jackie Robinson: Race, Sports, and the American Dream*. Armonk, NY: Sharpe, 1998.

Dorocher, Leo. *The Dodgers and Me*. Chicago: Ziff-Davis, 1948.

Falker, David. *Great Time Coming: The Life of Jackie Robinson from Baseball to Birmingham*. New York: Simon and Schuster, 1995.

Foley, Nick. *The White Scourge: Mexicans, Blacks, and Poor Whites in Texas Cotton Culture*. Berkeley: University of California Press, 1997.

Frommer, Harvey. *Rickey and Robinson: The Men Who Broke Baseball's Color Barrier*. Lanham, MD: Taylor Trade Publishing, 1982.

Gibson, Truman. *Knocking Down Barriers: My Fight for Black America*. Evanston, IL: Northwestern University Press, 2005.

Holway, John B. *Blackball Stars: Negro League Pioneers*. Westport, CT: Meckler Books, 1988.

Lamb, Chris. *Blackout: The Untold Story of Jackie Robinson's First Spring Training*. Lincoln: University of Nebraska Press, 2004.

Lanning, Michael Lee. *The African American Soldier: From Crispus Attucks to Colin Powell*. New York: Birch Lane Press, 1997.

Lester, Larry. *Black Baseball's National Showcase, the East-West All Star Game: 1933–1953*. Lincoln: University of Nebraska Press, 2002.

Lipman, David. *Mr. Baseball: The Story of Branch Rickey*. New York: Putnam, 1995.

Long, Michael G. and Chris Lamb. *Jackie Robinson: A Spiritual Biography: The Faith of a Boundary-Breaking Hero*. Louisville, KY: Westminster John Knox Press, 2017.

Lowenfish, Lee. *Branch Rickey: Baseball's Ferocious Gentlemen*. Lincoln: University of Nebraska Press, 2007.

Mann, Arthur William. *Rickey*. Boston: Houghton Mifflin, 1957.

———. *The Jackie Robinson Story*. New York: Grosset and Dunlap, 1956.

Marshall, William. *Baseball's Pivotal Era, 1945–1951*. Lexington: University of Kentucky Press, 1999.

Mead, Chris. *Champion Joe Louis: A Biography*. London: Robson Books, 1993.

Peterson, Robert. *Only the Ball Was White: A History of the Black Players and All-Black Professional Teams*. New York: Oxford University Press, 1970.

Polner, Murray. *Branch Rickey: A Biography*. New York: Atheneum, 1982.

Powell, Colin. *My American Journey*. New York: Ballantine, 2003.

Rampersad, Arnold. *Jackie Robinson: A Biography*. New York: Ballantine Books, 1997.

Robinson, Jackie and Alfred Duckett. *I Never Had It Made.* New York: G. P. Putnam's Sons, 1972.

Robinson, Jackie and Wendell Smith. *Jackie Robinson: My Own Story.* New York: Greenberg, 1948.

Robinson, Rachel and Lee Daniels. *Jackie Robinson: An Intimate Portrait.* New York: Abrams, 2014.

Robinson, Sharon. *Promises to Keep How Jackie Robinson Changed America.* New York: Scholastic Press, 2004.

Rowan, Carl, with Jackie Robinson. *Wait Till Next Year: The Life Story of Jackie Robinson.* New York: Random House, 1960.

Sasser, Charles W. *Patton's Panthers: The African American 761st Tank Battalion in World War II.* New York: Pocket Books, 2004.

Schutz, J. Christopher. *Jackie Robinson: An Integrated Life.* Lanham, MD: Rowman & Littlefield, 2016.

Tygiel, Jules. *Baseball's Great Experiment: Jackie Robinson and His Legacy.* New York: Oxford University Press, 1997.

Wilson, Joe, Jr. *The 758th Tank Battalion in World War II: The U.S. Army's First All African American Tank Unit.* Jefferson, NC: McFarland, 2018.

Zeiler, Thomas W. *Jackie Robinson and Race in America: A Brief History with Documents.* Boston: Bedford/St. Martin's, 2014.

PERIODICALS

Biemiller, Carl L. "Florida's Baseball Riviera." *Holiday,* March 1955.

Burley, Dan. Negroes in the Major Leagues." *Inter-Racial Review,* July 1944.

Chamberlin, John. "Brains, Baseball, and Branch Rickey." *Harpers,* April 1948.

Cohane, Tim. "A Branch Grows in Brooklyn." *Look,* March 19, 1946.

Downs, Carl E. "Timid Negro Students!" *The Crisis,* June 1936.

Fox, Stephen. "The Education of Branch Rickey." *Civilization,* September/October 1995.

Harris, Mark. "Branch Rickey Keeps His 40 Year Promise." *Negro Digest,* September 1947.

Loy, John W. and Joseph McElvogue. "Racial Segregation in American Sport." *International Review of Sport Sociology,* 1970.

Oursler, Fulton. "Rookie of the Year." *Reader's Digest,* February 1948.

Rickey, Branch. "Goodbye to Old Ideas." *Life,* August 2, 1954.

Smith, Ron A. "The Paul Robeson—Jackie Robinson Saga and a Political Collision." *Journal of Sport History,* Summer, 1979.

Tygiel, Jules. "The Court-Martial of Jackie Robinson." *American Heritage,* August–September 1984.

Vernon, John. "Jim Crow, Meet Lieutenant Robinson." *Prologue.* Spring, 2008.

———. "The Search for Jackie Robinson." *Federal Records and African American History.* Summer, 1997.

FILMS

Burns, Ken, (Director) (2016). *Jackie Robinson*. [Television Documentary]. United States: PBS.

Green, Alfred E., (Director) (1950) *The Jackie Robinson Story*. [Motion Picture]. United States: Eaglehorn Films.

Helgeland, Brian, (Director) (2013). *42* [Motion Picture]. United States: Warner Brothers.

Peersan, Larry, (Director). (1998). *The Court-Martial of Jackie Robinson*. [Television Movie]. United States: Turner Home Entertainment.

BLOGS

Crow, Carla. "Cline's Narrative on Jackie Robinson's Court-Martial Trial." Posted February 12, 2012.

———. "My Visit With Jackie Robinson's Court-Martial Defense Attorney." Posted June 18, 2012.

Index

witnesses: on Charge Sheet, 65; racism
by, 59. *See also specific witnesses*
Woodruff (captain), 174
World Series, 116–17, 123, 126, 135,
153
World War I: African Americans in, 8,
23, 159; athletes in, 95; United States
in, 4
World War II, 4; Camp Hood during,
171; cavalry in, 163; desegregation
after, 97; Double V campaign in,
33; drafts in, 32; equal rights after,

95; Europe in, 64, 84, 141; history
of, 69; in Japan, 98; North Africa
in, 42, 66; Olympics and, 21; Pearl
Harbor attack in, 30; Philippines in,
49; training in, 46; Tuskegee airmen
in, 40, 163; for United States, 29, 54,
92, 141, 147, 158–59
Wright, John Richard, 103, 105, 108,
148

Younger, Bevlia B., 59, 184, 187–88,
192

About the Author

Michael Lee Lanning is the author of twenty-six nonfiction books on military history, sports, and health. More than 1.1 million copies of his books are in print in fifteen countries, and editions have been translated into twelve languages. He has appeared on major television networks and the History Channel as an expert on the individual soldier on both sides of the Vietnam War.

The New York Times Book Review declared Lanning's *Vietnam 1969–1970: A Company Commander's Journal* to be "one of the most honest and horrifying accounts of a combat soldier's life to come out of the Vietnam War." The *London Sunday Times* devoted an entire page to review his *The Military 100: A Ranking of the Most Influential Military Leaders of All Time*. According to the *San Francisco Journal*, Lanning's *Inside the VC and NVA* is, "A well-researched, groundbreaking work that fills a huge gap in the historiography of the Vietnam War."

A veteran of more than twenty years in the U.S. Army, Lanning is a retired lieutenant colonel. During the Vietnam War he served as an infantry platoon leader, reconnaissance platoon leader, and an infantry company commander. In addition to having earned the Combat Infantryman's Badge and Bronze Star with "V" device with two oak leaf clusters, Lanning is Ranger-qualified and a senior parachutist.

Lanning was born in Sweetwater, Texas, and has a BS from Texas A&M University and an MS from East Texas State University. He currently resides in Lampasas, Texas.